Designing Adaptive Organizations

The ability to organize is our most valuable social technology, and the successful organizational design of an enterprise can increase its efficiency, effectiveness, and ability to adapt. Modern organizations operate in increasingly complex, dynamic, and global environments, which puts a premium on rapid adaptation. Compared with traditional organizations, modern organizations are flatter and more open to their environments. Their processes are more generative and interactive – actors themselves generate and coordinate solutions rather than follow hierarchically devised plans and directives. They also search outside their boundaries for resources wherever they may exist and coproduce products and services with suppliers, customers, and partners, collaborating – both internally and externally – to learn and become more capable. In this volume, leading voices in the field of organization design demonstrate how a combination of agile processes, artificial intelligence, and digital platforms can power adaptive, sustainable, and healthy organizations.

CHARLES C. SNOW is Professor Emeritus of Strategy and Organization at Pennsylvania State University. He has long been associated with the field of organization design and is the coauthor of the classic book *Organizational Strategy, Structure, and Process* (1978). He is a founding member of Organization Design Community and the cofounder of the *Journal of Organization Design*.

ØYSTEIN D. FJELDSTAD is a professor in the Department of Strategy and Entrepreneurship at BI Norwegian Business School. He is a former manager in the technology practice of Andersen Consulting (now Accenture). His research on value creation and actor-oriented organizing has been extensively applied by leading organizations in consulting, technology, healthcare, and education, and he has taught strategy and organization design to students and executives in many industries and countries.

Cambridge Companions to Management provide an essential resource for academics, graduate students and reflective business practitioners seeking cutting-edge perspectives on managing people in organizations. Each *Companion* integrates the latest academic thinking with contemporary business practice, dealing with real-world issues facing organizations and individuals in the workplace, and demonstrating how and why practice has changed over time. World-class editors and contributors write with unrivalled depth on managing people and organizations in today's global business environment, making the series a truly international resource.

Designing Adaptive Organizations

Edited by

CHARLES C. SNOW
Pennsylvania State University

ØYSTEIN D. FJELDSTAD
BI Norwegian Business School

Shaftesbury Road, Cambridge CB2 8EA, United Kingdom

One Liberty Plaza, 20th Floor, New York, NY 10006, USA

477 Williamstown Road, Port Melbourne, VIC 3207, Australia

314–321, 3rd Floor, Plot 3, Splendor Forum, Jasola District Centre, New Delhi – 110025, India

103 Penang Road, #05–06/07, Visioncrest Commercial, Singapore 238467

Cambridge University Press is part of Cambridge University Press & Assessment, a department of the University of Cambridge.

We share the University's mission to contribute to society through the pursuit of education, learning and research at the highest international levels of excellence.

www.cambridge.org
Information on this title: www.cambridge.org/9781108486750

DOI: 10.1017/9781108762441

© Cambridge University Press & Assessment 2024

First published 2024

A catalogue record for this publication is available from the British Library

Library of Congress Cataloging-in-Publication Data
Names: Snow, Charles C. (Charles Curtis), 1945– editor. | Fjeldstad, Øystein D., editor.
Title: Designing adaptive organizations / edited by Charles C. Snow, Pennsylvania State University, Øystein D. Fjeldstad, BI Norwegian Business School.
Description: New York : Cambridge University Press, [2024] | Series: Cambridge companions to management | Includes bibliographical references and index.
Identifiers: LCCN 2023016409 | ISBN 9781108486750 (hardback) | ISBN 9781108762441 (ebook)
Subjects: LCSH: Organizational change. | Organization.
Classification: LCC HD58.8 .D4696 2024 | DDC 658.4/06–dc23/eng/20230720
LC record available at https://lccn.loc.gov/2023016409

ISBN 978-1-108-48675-0 Hardback

We dedicate this book to

Raymond E. Miles,

whose extraordinary understanding of how organizations work – and should work – has benefited each of us in countless ways throughout our careers

Contents

Figures

Tables

Contributors

KENNETH J. CARRIG is President of KJC Advisory Services, a firm providing advice on issues related to strategy execution, acquisition integration, and executive succession planning. He is also Executive Director of the Center for Executive Succession at the Darla Moore School of Business, University of South Carolina. He was previously the corporate executive vice president and chief human resources officer at SunTrust Banks, Inc. and the vice president and chief administrative officer at Sysco Corporation. Carrig is the coauthor of *Building Profit through Building People* (2006) and *Strategic Execution* (2019), which won gold in the business intelligence/innovation category of the Axiom Business Book Awards.

CARY L. COOPER is 50th Anniversary Professor of Organizational Psychology and Health at Alliance Manchester Business School, University of Manchester, and President of the Institute of Welfare. He is a founding president of the British Academy of Management, the immediate past president of the Chartered Institute of Personnel and Development, and a former president of RELATE. Cooper is the founding editor of the *Journal of Organizational Behaviour*, a former editor of *Stress and Health*, and the editor-in-chief of the *Wiley-Blackwell Encyclopedia of Management*. He is the author/editor of more than 250 books in the field of occupational health psychology, workplace well-being, women at work, and occupational stress. He is the chair of the National Forum for Health and Wellbeing at Work, which is comprised of forty global companies.

MICHAEL A. CUSUMANO is Sloan Management Review Distinguished Professor of Management and Deputy Dean of the MIT Sloan School of Management, Massachusetts Institute of Technology. He specializes in strategy, product development, and entrepreneurship in computer software as well as automobiles and consumer electronics. He has published 14 books and more than 120 articles and columns. His most recent coauthored book is *The Business of Platforms: Strategy in the Age of Digital Competition, Innovation, and Power* (2019). Cusumano has been a visiting professor at several international universities and has consulted and lectured at more than one hundred technology companies.

ØYSTEIN D. FJELDSTAD is a professor in the Department of Strategy and Entrepreneurship at BI Norwegian Business School. He is a former consulting manager in the technology practice of Andersen Consulting (now Accenture). His research on value creation and actor-oriented organizing has been extensively applied by leading organizations in consulting, technology, healthcare, and education. He has taught strategy, organization design, and digital transformation to students and executives in many industries and countries.

ANNABELLE GAWER is Chaired Professor of Digital Economy and Director of the Centre of Digital Economy at Surrey Business School, University of Surrey, UK. She is also Visiting Professor of Strategy and Innovation at Saïd Business School, University of Oxford. For over twenty years, she has been a leading scholar and thought leader on the business of digital platforms and innovation ecosystems, which constitute the dominant business model of our times. She has extensive public policy and private consultancy experience, having served as an expert for the EU Commission and Parliament, UK House of Lords, the Organisation for Economic Co-operation and Development, and UK government departments. Gawer was recently appointed as the digital expert for the UK Competition and Markets Authority and is currently consulting with the World Bank on the regulation of digital platforms in developing countries.

STÉPHANE J. G. GIROD is Professor of Strategy and Organizational Innovation at International Institute for Management Development (IMD), Switzerland. His research, teaching, and consulting interests are in strategic transformation of large established businesses, including digital, sustainability, and agility transformations. At IMD, he codirects the Leading Digital Execution program. His research has been published in leading academic journals, and his most recent coauthored book, *Resetting Management* (2021), focuses on agility transformation. In 2017, Girod launched IMD's Reinventing

Luxury Lab, open to professionals across luxury sectors. He writes a column for Forbes.com that covers sustainability, innovation, and transformation in luxury sectors.

VIVIANNA FANG HE is an associate professor at the School of Management, University of St. Gallen, Switzerland. She is the founding director of the Institute of Responsible Innovation, an interdisciplinary research center focusing on innovative technologies and organizational forms for the social good. She studies collaboration in innovation-related contexts, including self-managing R&D teams, online communities, and decentralized autonomous organizations. Her research has won competitive grants from organizations such as the Swiss National Science Foundation, and she has published her research in leading academic journals such as *Natural Reviews Drug Discovery*, *Strategic Management Journal*, *Organization Science*, and *Information Systems Review*.

IAN HESKETH is an organizational psychologist on the National Forum for Health and Wellbeing at Work at Manchester Business School, University of Manchester. He is also the lead for Police Wellbeing at the UK College of Policing and the senior responsible owner for the National Police Wellbeing Service in the United Kingdom. He is an honorary fellow of Durham University Business School and a visiting fellow at the Open University. He is a chartered manager, fellow of the Chartered Management Institute, and a member of the Society for Education and Training.

AMY KATES is a senior managing director in Accenture's Operating Model & Organization Design global practice. In 2020, Accenture acquired Kates Kesler Organization Consulting, a boutique firm that Greg Kesler and Amy Kates built over the previous fifteen years. The Kates Kesler organization design methodology is the standard in the field, built on the pioneering work of Jay Galbraith. Kates is a key contributor to the field of organization design, having published several books on the topic with Galbraith and Kesler. Her most recent book is *Networked, Scaled, and Agile: A Design Strategy for Complex Organizations* (2021).

GREG KESLER is a senior managing director at Accenture. He consults with CEOs and other senior leaders on global organization design and activation. He has led enterprise-level, global redesign projects for many leading multinational companies in the consumer goods, capital equipment, healthcare, and life sciences sectors. He provides counsel to CEOs to align their teams around transformational priorities, often featuring new business models, helping them to design and activate changes in their operating models. Kesler is the coauthor of *Networked, Scaled, and Agile* (2021), *Bridging Organization Design and Performance* (2016), and *Leading Organization Design* (2011), as well as numerous articles and book chapters. He teaches and speaks on the subject of organization design to executive groups in public and in-house programs. He cofounded Kates Kesler Organization Consulting with Amy Kates, which was acquired by Accenture in 2020.

VEGARD KOLBJØRNSRUD is an associate professor in the Department of Strategy and Entrepreneurship at BI Norwegian Business School and a senior research fellow at Accenture. He researches, teaches, and speaks on strategy, new organizational forms, problem-solving, and the impact of artificial intelligence on managing and organizing. Prior to becoming a full-time academic, he was a strategy consultant with Accenture for sixteen years.

CHRISTOPHER LETTL is Professor of Entrepreneurship and Innovation at the Department of Strategy and Innovation, Vienna University of Economics and Business. He is Director of the Institute for Strategy, Technology and Organization at the same institution and Academic Director of the Vienna Innovation Program. He is a founding member of the Open and User Innovation Society and has consulted with numerous companies and policymakers in their efforts to leverage open and user innovation. Lettl researches and teaches entrepreneurship, innovation, and organization design.

JEANNE LIEDTKA is United Technologies Corporation Professor of Business at University of Virginia's Darden Graduate School of Business. She is a thought leader in Design Thinking and innovation. She has published numerous books and articles on Design Thinking and has taught the subject to thousands of students and executives and to hundreds of thousands in her popular online Design Thinking courses on the Coursera platform.

CARSTEN LUND PEDERSEN is an associate professor at IT University of Copenhagen. His research interests revolve around business transformation – how businesses adapt to change and renew themselves. His research has been published in leading academic journals, and he has published digital articles in Harvard Business Review (HBR.org), Sloanreview.mit.edu, CMR Insights, and Nature.com, among others. He is the coeditor of *Big Data in Small Business: Data-Driven Growth in Small and Medium-Sized Enterprises* (2021).

JOHN A. MATHEWS is a professor emeritus in the Macquarie Business School at Macquarie University, Australia. A teacher of strategy and organization, he is the cofounder of the *Journal of Industry Studies* (now *Industry and Innovation*). For the past decade, he has focused his research and writing on the greening of industry, industrial dynamics of energy transition to renewables, resources transition to a circular economy, and the greening of finance. In 2018, he was a corecipient of the Schumpeter Prize.

PHANISH PURANAM is Professor of Strategy at INSEAD, Singapore. His research in organization science focuses on how organizations work and how they can work better. He has served in advisory/ training roles with global corporations as well as public sector agencies and as an organization design advisor on a pro bono basis for several nongovernmental organizations and the United Nations High Commissioner for Refugees. His books include *The Microstructure of Organizations* and *Corporate Strategy: Tools for Analysis and Decisions* (coauthored with Bart Vanneste, 2016).

THOMAS RITTER is Professor of Market Strategy and Business Development in the Department of Strategy and Innovation, Copenhagen Business School. His research on business-to-business relationship management, strategy, and business models has been published widely and applied in many organizations across various industries. He is a regular contributor in executive education programs (especially Copenhagen Business School Board Education programs) and in customized strategy development programs.

SCOTT A. SNELL is Frank Sands, Sr. Chair in Business Administration and a former senior associate dean for Executive Education at the University of Virginia's Darden Graduate School of Business. He teaches courses in strategic management and works internationally with senior executives to help their companies align strategy, organizational capability, and investments in talent. His research has been published in leading academic journals, and he has coauthored several books, notably *Strategic Execution: Driving Breakthrough Performance in Business* (2019), *Management: Leading and Collaborating in a Competitive World* (2016), and *Managing Human Resources* (2018).

CHARLES C. SNOW is Professor Emeritus of Strategy and Organization at Pennsylvania State University. He has published highly influential books and articles on strategy and organization, including as the coauthor of the seminal book *Organizational Strategy, Structure, and Process* (1978). He is a fellow of the Academy of Management and was awarded an honorary doctorate by BI Norwegian Business School. He is a founding member of Organization Design Community and the cofounder of the *Journal of Organization Design*. Snow has taught management subjects to students and executives in more than thirty-five countries.

DAVID B. YOFFIE is Max and Doris Starr Professor of International Business Administration at Harvard Business School (HBS). A member of the HBS faculty since 1981, he has chaired the HBS Strategy Department (1997–2002), Advanced Management Program (1999–2002), Harvard's Young Presidents' Organization program (2003–2012), Harvard's YPO Gold program (2012–2022), and Competing in the Age of Digital Platforms program(2020–present). From 2006 to 2012, he served as the senior associate dean and the chair of HBS Executive Education programs. Yoffie is the author or coauthor of ten books as well as more than fifty scholarly and business articles on international trade, firm strategy, and global competition in technology. He has published more than 200 case studies and teaching notes on technology, business strategy, and international management, which have sold more than four million copies.

Preface

An organization is a goal-directed activity system. Organizations are born from creative acts – conceived and put in place in order to achieve desired outcomes. In his classic book *The Sciences of the Artificial*, Herbert Simon distinguished between the natural and the artificial sciences: "The natural sciences are concerned with how things are [...] Design, on the other hand, is concerned with how things ought to be, with devising artifacts to attain goals" (1969: 132–133). Organizational designs reflect the opportunities and challenges of their time. During the past few decades, organizations have increasingly been "opening up." Modern organizations search outside their boundaries for resources wherever they may exist. They coproduce products and services with suppliers, customers, and partners. They collaborate, both internally and externally, to learn and become more capable. And they use digital technologies extensively in order to adapt rapidly to today's complex, dynamic, and highly interconnected environments.

We believe that organization design is in the midst of a paradigm shift. The established organization design paradigm focuses on structures and complementary processes by which collective activities can be controlled and coordinated. Control and coordination are accomplished by the use of hierarchy – higher-level units control the goals, resources, and actions of subordinate units. The new paradigm focuses on *means* that enable goal-directed self-organizing – control and coordination by the actors themselves. This paradigm shift is allowing novel organizational designs to flourish; modern organizations are more agile, and they can adapt quicker and more effectively to their environments.

This book is about adaptive organizing. If you are an executive or manager with responsibility for organizational design and development, a management consultant, a scholar in the organization sciences, or a student wanting to understand how modern organizations work, we invite you to explore the chapters in this book. It is intended to be a resource for anyone seeking cutting-edge knowledge about designing organizations. The book examines important real-world issues facing organizations, placing particular emphasis on the effects of design on organizational adaptability and performance, employee engagement and well-being, collaboration between human and digital actors, and resource usage and sustainability. As you read the book, we hope you will come to see the value in viewing organizing as an ongoing process and design as the creation of means that enable actors to self-organize resources and activities.

To create the book, we invited noted scholars and professionals who, by researching, writing about, and practicing organization design, are advancing the field. These individuals are experts in their subject matter, and they carefully crafted their chapters to show how organizations can be designed for adaptability. We are grateful for their contributions to the book.

1 | *Design Thinking in Organization Design*

JEANNE LIEDTKA

One might expect Design Thinking and Organization Design to be closely related fields, yet there is little published research showing how the two areas intertwine. Of nearly 100,000 organization design articles in a recent Google Scholar search, less than 1 percent mention "design thinking." There are notable exceptions. In one, Romme (2003: 558) distinguished between "science" and "design" modes of research and argued that organization studies should include design as a primary mode of scholarly engagement. He exhorted scholars in the organization sciences to "guide human beings in the process of designing and developing their organizations toward more humane, participative, and productive futures." In another, Yoo, Boland, and Lyytinen (2006) took the perspective of organization design in its verb form to argue that organizations should develop a "design gestalt" – a "holistic, organizing pattern" of elements. They asserted that developing such a gestalt would become increasingly important in the burgeoning knowledge and experience-based economy. Most recently, Gruber et al. (2015) renewed calls for attention to Design Thinking among management scholars, particularly around the topic of new workplace experiences.

For evidence that Design Thinking *should* be capable of informing studies of organizations, one need only consider the meaning of the term "organizing." Organizing is a problem-solving process that involves dividing and integrating resources in structures and processes that allow for the control and coordination of organizational activities (Fjeldstad et al., 2012; Lawrence & Lorsch, 1967; Puranam, Alexy, & Reitzig, 2014). The process of organizing, therefore, lends itself to the application of Design Thinking methods, which we argue represents a distinctive approach to problem-solving. The "users" of an organization design are members of the resulting organization.

Though Design Thinking is often viewed through the lens of new product development, emerging research suggests that it impacts the design and conduct of organizations beyond producing innovative products and services. Elsbach and Stigliani (2018), in a comprehensive literature review, note that Design Thinking profoundly affects culture, promoting a culture of experimentation and collaboration while producing positive emotional experiences for organization members. Hölzle and Rhinow (2019) describe Design Thinking as a "meta-professional" way of working in teams. Beckman and Barry (2007) discuss its use as a generic form of experience-based learning. Stephens and Boland (2015) argue that Design Thinking promotes "aesthetic knowing" and creates deep emotional carrying capacity in organizations. Design Thinking appears especially promising as a potential offset to challenges related to hierarchical organizational structures in uncertain and complex environments that call for collaborative problem-solving (Adler, 2001; Fjeldstad et al., 2012).

In line with Romme's (2003) proposal, some organizations apply Design Thinking methods and principles to their own operations. For example, IDEO, a design consulting firm, has an organization design practice based on three guiding principles: (1) Mobilize: Get people inspired and on board with the notion of change. (2) Pioneer: Create manifestations of change that show what it could look like inside the company or organization. (3) Scale: Grow capabilities, tools, and systems to transform the organization and its culture (IDEO, Organization Design, www.ideo.com/jobs/organizational-design). IDEO has applied Design Thinking to organization design for companies such as HBO and Kaiser Permanente as well as to the design of its own organization. The design steps IDEO advocates are similar to those applied in product design, but rather than prototyping a minimal viable product (MVP), a minimal viable organization (MVO) is created instead (Brown, 2019). Other organizations that have used organizational prototyping in an iterative process relying heavily on input from organizational actors include the National Aeronautics and Space Administration (NASA) (Carroll et al., 2006) and SAP (Liedtka, King, & Bennett, 2013).

Our research over the past decade suggests that Design Thinking's transformational impact may lie less with improved products and more with psychological and social benefits to the innovators themselves and to organizing activities in the organizations in which they work. In addition to contributing to improved product quality, as well as the psychological safety and creative confidence of practitioners, we observe significant improvements in organizational performance by providing the processes and infrastructure for greater collaboration, accelerating the successful implementation of new ideas, and encouraging resource sharing (Liedtka & Bahr, 2019). Seen through this lens, Design Thinking is a *social technology*, deserving of both managerial and scholarly attention (Liedtka, 2020).

Design Thinking's ability to achieve organizational benefits should not surprise us – the reasons why Design Thinking works are already evident in the broader social sciences literature, in areas such as positive psychology, cognition and decision-making, complex adaptive systems, and business strategy. In this chapter, we build the case for *why* connecting Design Thinking to organization design matters for organizational health and performance. We trace the roots and nature of Design Thinking's impact on the journeys of practitioners as they experience the design process, learn about design tools, and adopt a design mindset. In doing so, we focus on the possibilities inherent in Design Thinking done well. Certainly, this is not always – or perhaps even usually – the case in practice. There are many barriers to Design Thinking's implementation in organizations (Carlgren, Elmquist, & Rauth, 2016). Design Thinking implemented superficially – taught in one-day hackathons and sprints to people who spend 95 percent of their time in business-as-usual mode – will not achieve desired outcomes. A few ethnographic interviews do not empathy make. Design Thinking's impact rests on its ability to transform the experience of those who use it. How it accomplishes that and the implications for organization design are the focus of this chapter.

What Is Design Thinking?

Historically within the organization sciences, there has been a general misperception about design as a mode of engagement. Michlewski (2008: 385) points out:

The meaning of the word "design" in the organization studies literature tends to concentrate on the notion of careful planning, upfront decision-making and alignment with pre-defined criteria.... Within the culture of professional product designers, "design attitude" signifies quite the opposite. It underlines the freedom to explore and to follow unexpected but promising leads, while keeping the overall vision as a subliminal yardstick for the project's success.

Michlewski's "design attitude" includes five attributes: (1) consolidating multidimensional meanings and reconciling diverse perspectives; (2) creatively manifesting ideas; (3) embracing discontinuity and open-endedness; (4) engaging polysensorial aesthetics; and (5) engaging personal and commercial empathy.

Design Thinking is not only an attitude or mindset but also a user-centric set of processes and tools (Liedtka & Ogilvie, 2011; Liedtka, Ogilvie, & Brozenske, 2014; Liedtka, Salzman, & Azer, 2017). There is broad consensus that the process is comprised of three discrete sets of activities: need finding, ideation, and testing (Seidel & Fixson, 2013). Each Design Thinking stage makes use of a recognized set of tools: ethnographic tools such as job-to-be-done and journey mapping in the need-finding phase, concept generation tools such as visualization and brainstorming in the ideation phase, and prototyping and in-market experimentation in the testing phase. In my own work with managers, I emphasize Design Thinking as a problem-solving approach that has distinguishing properties: (1) It begins as human-centered (rather than driven by new technology or organizational needs and capabilities) and seeks empathy for those we design for and with; (2) it is driven by possibilities rather than constraints; and (3) it relies on visualization and iteration, coupled with experimentation for testing, rather than traditional analytics. My research and experience reveal five core design practices: the development of a deep understanding of user needs, the use of diverse teams, the development of multiple solutions winnowed through experimentation, the use of dialogue-based processes, and the presence of a supporting infrastructure of mindsets, tools, and processes (Liedtka, 2017).

One question consistently raised by skeptics is whether Design Thinking constitutes "old wine in new bottles." Though key elements of Design Thinking, like ethnography and prototyping, have long been in use, preliminary research suggests a gestalt is created in their combination. For example, Seidel and O'Mahony (2014) found that desired outcomes around a shared and coherent concept did not occur in new product development teams when prototyping was used alone; it was only in combination with experimentation that the potential was realized. Micheli et al. (2019), in their recent literature review, conclude that Design Thinking has both common and unique elements that combine in a distinctive way and yield differentiated results from other approaches such as lean innovation management and agile organizing.

Echoing similar themes, Stephens and Boland (2015) concur, concluding that Design Thinking's differentiating attributes include its level of attention to emotions and meaning, direct sensory experience of immersion in a specific context, and iterative recombination of products or organizational features.

In practice, we find that Design Thinking's scalable process methodology that moves its practitioners from exploration through testing, its teachable tools, and its human-centered mindset combine to offer an approach to decision-making that the MBAs and managers we work with – hundreds of them in classrooms and over 60,000 in online experiences – say constructively challenges their current ways of thinking and behaving. In that uniqueness, there lies significant value for the innovators themselves and for the design of their organizations.

Importance of Design Thinking

Design Thinking offers managers and their organizations (as well as individual professionals) a social technology for navigating some of today's most urgent problems, as leaders face the challenge of building resilient and motivated organizations amid accelerating uncertainty and change (Liedtka, 2020).

Design Thinking and Uncertainty

Regardless of the specific aspects of Design Thinking one might examine – design mindsets, tools, or processes – a strong theme is Design Thinking's ability to engage uncertainty more intelligently than traditional predictive approaches. Encouraging managers, particularly those raised in large bureaucratic organizations with risk-averse cultures, to actively engage with uncertainty rather than avoid it is a challenging yet critical task in a world of accelerating change. Schultz (2010) chronicles a litany of reasons why humans love being right and fear being wrong. She points out the emotional costs of the choice to acknowledge and live in the uncertainty of doubt rather than succumb to the allure of certainty. However, the negatives associated with craving certainty, she asserts, go far beyond just missing opportunities. They also result in the loss of imagination and empathy. Without the humility of doubt, none of Design Thinking's key stages – need finding, ideation, testing – can thrive. Cultivating curiosity and positive or *investigative* doubt, aimed at moving possibilities forward, lies at the core of Design Thinking.

Design Thinking's attention to deep exploration of the problem's setting before acting (Dorst, 2015), its use of data-driven methods to create a portfolio of different ideas, and then treating those ideas as testable hypotheses in an iterative process of "small bets" using tangible prototypes allow design practitioners to actively manage their doubt and the irreducible risks of innovation without forfeiting the ability to act. In doing so, it helps them iterate their way to better solutions. These processes also aid decision makers in avoiding well-documented cognitive biases, like egocentric empathy and hypothesis confirmation bias, that impede their ability to be effective at hypothesis generation and testing (Liedtka, 2015). To aid strategists and decision makers, design has been tied in the strategic management literature to the creation of organizational capabilities for innovation and change (Dong, Garbuio, & Lovallo, 2016; Liedtka, 2020).

Design Thinking's ability to foster learning helps to increase an organization's adaptive capacity (Beckman & Barry, 2007). Contemporary views on knowledge treat it as emergent, social in nature, and always changing, rather than as processed information that produces an accumulated stock of knowledge (Ewenstein & Whyte, 2007). Knowledge emerges through interaction with other people and with tangible objects. Scharmer (2001) argues that moving beyond existing knowledge to "self-transcending knowledge" is essential to identifying new possibilities. Self-transcending knowledge occurs in the space between the self and the other, and only a learning infrastructure that fosters generative dialogue with the "requisite conversational complexity" can achieve it. Design Thinking is optimized for producing such a space – its collaborative, dialogue-based conversations and hypothesis-driven approach make room for higher-order concepts to emerge in a collaborative setting while leveraging the diversity participants bring to the conversation.

Design Thinking and Diversity

Research shows that diverse groups are more creative (Sawyer, 2012). This is because a focus on *efficiency* leads to convergent thinking that reduces variation through standardization, while *creativity* relies on divergent thinking that amplifies variation, allowing multiple potential paths to be envisioned. In a complex world, diversity is not a problem to be resolved; it is the path to successful adaptation. Yet, while diverse perspectives contribute to higher decision quality in theory, they often lead to lower quality outcomes in practice (Brown & Eisenhardt, 1995; Lovelace, Shapiro, & Weingart, 2001).

Leveraging differences to produce higher-order solutions takes time and requires both perspective *taking* – making one's own perspective visible and reconcilable to others – and perspective *making* – the creation of a coherent shared belief system (Boland & Tenkasi, 1995). If meaning is not accomplished before solutions are generated, conversations across differences can deteriorate quickly into divisive debates. The boundaries that successful diverse groups must cross are complicated. They are both personal (we attach personal meaning to information and events) and political (different organizational interests clash and interfere with knowledge sharing). So diverse groups have a complex task: They must *transfer* information, *translate* across personal interpretations, and *transform* to rise above their political differences (Boland & Tenkasi, 1995). One effective path for navigating this process is through the creation of shared meaning, based on a common understanding of the needs of critical stakeholders, especially those that groups seek to serve (Majchrzak, More, & Faraj, 2012). When successful, a shifting from self to other moves organization members away from parochial individual blinders based on background and expertise toward a common and more meaningful shared focus on users. Design Thinking's need-finding phase, with its extensive set of accessible and teachable ethnographic tools, like journey mapping and job-to-be-done, offers innovators low- risk, reliable methods for focusing groups on stakeholders' actual needs rather than imposing their own preferences.

Conversations are the building blocks of collaborative creativity. Dialogue's focus on inquiry, on listening to understand others, and on surfacing one's own unexamined beliefs reconciles the paradox of difference. Since the differences that underlie diversity are often deeply rooted and value-related, making them threatening to surface and difficult to change, mindsets must shift before behaviors can change. Successfully cocreating across differences relies on fostering safe conditions that allow for the emergence of new problem definitions and solutions during the process. This is how self-transcending knowledge emerges. Design Thinking's emphasis on dialogue is critical

here – it provides conversational tools capable of managing the interactions needed for stakeholders to work together to find higher-order
solutions.

Without Design Thinking's emphasis on inquiry, diverse groups typically resort to debate, with advocates for competing ideas marshaling
selective evidence in support of individual points of view while doing
negligible listening. Design conversations have clear "rules" to generate
a portfolio of solutions: Focus on the needs of those you are designing
for, listen actively to understand, and ask the question "what if anything
were possible?" Those solutions are based on stakeholder-focused criteria rather than personal preferences and beliefs. The possibility-driven
nature of Design Thinking's idea generation is essential here. Holding
practitioners in the question "what if anything were possible?" to brain-
storm ideas based on jointly held design criteria invites the emergence
of novel, value-creating concepts. Setting aside existing constraints
encourages the kinds of breakthrough ideas that generate real energy
for change while stimulating creativity focused on how to surmount
constraints to make exciting new visions a reality. The upfront investment in holding groups in the problem space and giving team members
tools for discovery that foster shared sensemaking is critical to successful organizing in diverse groups (Weick, 1995).

Design Thinking, Motivation, and Mood

Another important contribution of Design Thinking lies with its ability
to improve the creativity of solutions by fostering positive affect that,
in turn, encourages open-mindedness and the willingness to collaborate. The relationship between positive affect and creativity is well recognized (Amabile et al., 2005). Mood is one of the most widely studied
and least disputed predictors of creativity (Baas, De Dreu, & Nijstad,
2008). Ewald et al. (2019) have completed preliminary research findings on the emotions generated during the Design Thinking process.
They found that positive affect on teams using Design Thinking was
significantly higher than on other teams, due to positive emotions like
happiness that the process produced. The teams' negative emotions
were not significantly different from other teams.

Design Thinking's ability to encourage positive affect and to instill
confidence that uncertainty can be managed is especially important for
people with particular types of mindsets (Dweck, 2008) or regulatory

focus (Higgins, 1998). Individuals with a rigid mindset and a preventive or reactive regulatory focus (as opposed to a growth mindset and a promotion/proactive regulatory focus) fear failure and experience heightened anxiety in the face of uncertainty and change. This creates a reluctance to act. Since learning requires action, rigid mindsets struggle and can become paralyzed in the face of change. Fostering creativity requires encouraging a promotion focus and discouraging a prevention one. The use of what Healey and Hodgkinson (2017) call "cold" cognitive tools like scenario planning can actually heighten anxiety and reduce willingness to act. Anxiety reduction, they argue, requires "hot" tools that acknowledge and use emotion. Design Thinking's tools and process reduce anxiety and increase engagement. This engenders both psychological safety (Edmondson, 1999) and increased confidence in one's own ability to innovate (Kelly & Kelly, 2013), encouraging would-be innovators to step into ambiguous situations where the threat of failure is real and adopt an action-oriented, investigative approach. Albeit in a small sample, Kröper et al. (2011) studied the regulatory focus of design team members and found that different phases significantly affected motivation and emotions during the Design Thinking process. Though individuals had a preference for promotion or prevention, circumstances also stimulated one approach or the other. A promotion focus, for instance, was triggered by novel tasks and was positively associated with creativity in the Design Thinking process. Design Thinking's front-end tasks increased both promotional focus and emotions like cheerfulness. At the same time, the more analytically oriented testing activities did not promote a prevention focus, suggesting an overall positive impact.

Design Thinking as an Embodied Practice

Design Thinking's emphasis on sensory activities creates an embodied practice (Ewenstein & Whyte, 2007) that encourages "aesthetic knowing," a combination of feelings and thoughts (Stephens et al., 2013). Rather than attending only to the traditional instrumental concerns and rational intellectual discourse characteristic of organizations, it attends to organization members' "felt sense of something." This helps to overcome what Taylor (2002) calls the "aesthetic muteness" of organizations. Aesthetic knowing is needed to deepen the emotional carrying capacity of both individuals and teams, which in turn develops heightened resilience in the face of adversity and change (Stephens & Boland, 2015). The kind of aesthetic knowing that Design Thinking encourages promotes a deeper form of meaning making that makes generative learning possible. Researchers have shown how an aesthetic approach that attends to emotions and bodily senses, and incorporates material artifacts, accelerates collaborative sensemaking (Boxenbaum et al., 2018; Stigliani & Ravasi, 2012). Thus, as organizations and their individual members struggle to build capabilities for resilience and ongoing adaptation in the face of heightened uncertainty and change, Design Thinking's attention to emotions, social cognition, dialogue, positivity, and aesthetic knowing are differentiating and valuable.

How Design Thinking Impacts the Personal Journey of Its Users

The various aspects of Design Thinking work together to change the experiences of organization members in profound ways. Tangible outputs of the need-finding, ideation, and testing phases carry corresponding psychological and sociopsychological impacts that affect members individually and set the stage for more productive collaboration. The sequence of need finding–ideation–testing not only creates a flow that helps practitioners perform individual activities successfully, it explicitly links the pieces in a larger end-to-end process. Design Thinking's careful layering of the cognitive complexity of tasks increases practitioners' comfort with uncertainty and keeps them from becoming overwhelmed by the "messiness" and divergence of dealing with ill-structured problems and by the demands of good hypothesis testing in the later phase. Using physical props like the ubiquitous Post-It note, and structured tools like journey mapping, the design process moves practitioners through orchestrated steps with tangible deliverables in the form of user data and stories, insights, design criteria, ideas, assumptions, prototypes, and experiments.

At the front-end of the process, Design Thinking helps its practitioners escape the blinders of egocentric empathy biases, productively holds them in the question, assists with translating qualitative data into insights and design criteria, and aligns diverse teams around a common definition of what matters. At the back-end of the process, the structure leads them carefully through the challenging elements of designing and executing good experiments: articulating their assumptions, specifying their solutions clearly, and inviting and utilizing feedback. Behind each activity and its tangible deliverable lies a corresponding aspect of Design Thinking's social technology that shapes the experience of the innovator and allows him or her to complete important jobs. Let us look in depth at how these influences impact the journey of an individual and his or her team as they navigate the Design Thinking process and read some short stories from practitioners experiencing it.

Need Finding

During need finding, Design Thinking practitioners immerse themselves in the lives of those they are designing for. The goal is to shift their mindsets from "expert" to "inquirer" and to develop empathy. As the leader of a team dedicated to rethinking the medical-centered treatment approach in a large children's hospital explained as she guided the movement of the medical staff from a "place of judgment to a place of possibilities":

Rather than "this is how the system works and how they should be using it," we want to help them shift their lens – get them out of their expert hat and into a beginner's mindset that is willing to look at the problem differently. When you create conditions where people can listen and dialogue, then you set things up for success. (Liedtka, Salzman, & Azer, 2017: 228)

Increased engagement is one of the most often reported outcomes of the use of Design Thinking (Liedtka & Bahr, 2019). It is the experience of immersion that sets this up. Using ethnographic tools to immerse practitioners in the day-to-day lives of those they are designing for provides a direct sensory experience. Walking with a patient to the X-ray room is a very different experience than examining a process map, as Stephens and Boland (2015) explain. This has important benefits, not only for how new data are gathered and deeper insights obtained but also for the emotional connection and the development of empathy that is part of the Design Thinking process.

One particularly memorable story from our research takes place in an institute serving adults with Asperger's Syndrome. A young designer visited one of Kingwood's residents, Pete, at home. She observed him doing destructive things – picking at a leather sofa, ripping a magazine, and creating scuff marks on a wall by rubbing against it. She wondered how she could design solutions that would prevent such behavior in the future. On her second visit to Pete's house, she took a more empathetic approach and decided to mirror Pete's behavior. She discovered, to her surprise, the sensory enjoyment that came from ripping paper, flipping a magazine, picking at the leather on a couch, or holding an ear against a wall. Unable to ask Pete directly what he liked about doing these things, she experienced them for herself. On her first visit to his home, she had used her own frame of reference and labeled Pete's acts as negative. On her second visit, she began to empathize with Pete – the sofa, wall, and magazine sound revealed vital clues that helped her understand Pete. She explained: "I thought empathy was innate but now realize that it can grow and evolve. For this to happen ... requires a perceptual shift in thinking that is open to different ways of being in the world."

One of the attractions of human-centered design is that most of us are naturally curious about the lives of others. According to Silva (2008: 58), curiosity plays a critical role to approach/avoidance behaviors by driving interest that provides a "counterweight to feelings of uncertainty and anxiety." Interest creates a virtuous cycle of learning – motivating learning that, in turn, motivates interest. His research suggests that what we find to be particularly interesting is something that is both complex and understandable. Enhancing complexity (which Silva equates with novelty, vividness, and surprise) while simultaneously increasing comprehension (defined as coherence, concreteness, and ease of processing) is the sweet spot. Design Thinking's novel tasks (like journey mapping that traces both the functional and the emotional journey of users as they experience the product or service) combine with its structured process to create simultaneously novel and reassuringly comprehensible experiences of knowing another.

Immersive experiences produce emotional engagement that motivates decision makers to loosen parochial perspectives that stand in the way of seeing new solutions as well as providing the raw material for collective sensemaking. Another case from a large medical center illustrates this. Staff at this emergency mental health service knew their system was ineffective (intervals between the visits of patients arriving in crisis were shortening rather than lengthening) but were unable to agree on what to do about it, despite attempts by multiple committees to redesign the system. Frustrated, they turned to Design

Thinking to attempt to break the gridlock and began creating patient journey maps. The story of one particular patient, Tom, became the catalyst that finally allowed the group to set aside their differences and imagine a better approach together. Following a suicide attempt, Tom was referred to the mental health service for outpatient treatment. Just two months later, after treatment, Tom was readmitted to the hospital after another overdose. During that period, the journey map revealed, Tom experienced significant activity as a patient, seeing thirteen different case managers with seventy touch-points and eighteen handoffs.

But despite this large number of interventions, Tom hadn't experienced treatment that made a difference in the longer term. "There was no *care* there," one doctor observed. Clinicians realized their present system was providing an experience for patients entirely unlike the one they wanted to deliver. "We can think all kinds of things about how we believe the system is working, but then seeing the reality of how it was really working, it was shocking to see how far from our intentions reality had come," one observed. "Patients needed someone to be present for them. Despite a flurry of activity, nothing was changing for them. We needed to *feel* their blockages and struggles." Inspired to change, the group created a new model that led to dramatic improvement in patient experiences and in lengthening the interval between patient visits.

Such inspiration comes from new insights. But getting insights is often the single most challenging aspect of the Design Thinking process for many teams – and it is often seen as a black box. Kolko (2010) notes that this stage is treated as "magical" with "no visible connection between the input and the output." It requires a leap of judgment that goes beyond what *is* to what *might be*. One of the great contributions design makes at this stage is to use visualization tools – walls, flip charts, sticky notes – to tame the mass of messy data and take what is in the heads of individuals and shape it into collective intent. Kolko (2010: 18, 19) asserts:

One of the most basic principles of making meaning out of data is to externalize the entire meaning-making process. By taking data out of the cognitive realm (the head), removing it from the digital realm (the computer), and making it tangible in the physical realm in one cohesive visual structure (the wall), the designer is freed of the natural memory limitations of the brain and the artificial organizational limitations of technology.... Implicit and hidden meanings are uncovered.

Making ideas tangible is critical in the move from individual to collective sensemaking. As teams struggle to find convergence around a common interpretation, physical manipulation helps them organize data into patterns. Such sensemaking encourages collective reflection that builds team resilience, Campbell (2019) argues. She rejects sensemaking as an individual cognitive activity, arguing that it should be seen as a "conversational accomplishment" rather than a "cognitive epiphany." Sensemaking is "not an invisible process inside the brain of an individual" but is, instead, the result of interactions in situated conversations. Heedfulness – paying respectful and open-minded attention to each other – is critical for accomplishing this. Lee and Sukoco (2011) focus on team reflexivity – the extent to which team members collectively reflect on, plan, act, and adapt – asserting that it is essential to the kind of "unlearning" necessary to give up old beliefs and take on new ones.

Alignment happens as shared design criteria emerge. The output of a group's collective sensemaking is the explicit identification of those criteria, a concise list of attributes that any ideal design should contain. This is the culmination of the need-finding process. In this stage, individuals' immersive experiences prepare them to think in less egocentric ways and produce shareable data to create a common platform. Such criteria form the basis for idea generation in the next phase, and for testing and selection in the one following that.

Ideation

We think of idea generation as simply the process of brainstorming. But the key to success – in this case the generation of higher-order solutions that leverage the diversity of the group – happens well before idea generation starts. Design criteria provide the "priming" goals that Litchfield (2008) demonstrated are important facilitators of brainstorming success. Each team member's experience of immersion and shared insight generation lays the groundwork for new and better ideas to appear, offering a shared space in which those latent possibilities can emerge and be combined to reach higher-order solutions. Heidegger's (1962) concept of "the withheld" argues that the most powerful futures are discovered when conversations make room for the latent to make itself manifest. The withheld cannot be commanded to appear; it can only be invited. It emerges when the present conditions – psychological safety, empathy, shared meaning, and intention – allow individuals to bring their authentic selves into the conversation.

Design Thinking operates to shape system-level conversations as well. When a group of community organizations in Dallas who had not previously worked together gathered to use Design Thinking to develop a prototype for what a community-centered, rather than medical-centered, care model for children might look like, they decided to begin with asthma, one of the most prevalent and utilization-intensive childhood diseases. Their aim was to define a common agenda and goals. Until then, few of these leaders knew each other. One of them described their coming together:

We had no clue how we related to each other. So, we put together the asthma equation, a visual model for asthma, and the factors that were affecting these families and kids. When we put this together, people were stunned. We were all working on the same thing – but from different parts of the elephant. But none of us had ever looked at the whole elephant ... I had never pursued an ongoing collaboration before with such a range of uncommon partners, one with such a sense of purpose that was pulled together in that very structured and focused way – a group of people who had all been working hard to improve health for kids, but not working together. Doing God's work but with negligible impact and sustainability. Now we have a common agenda, shared measurements, and new funding opportunities. That is very different than anything I have ever experienced previously in the world of health care.

It is collective sensemaking that sets the stage for collaborative cocreation of new solutions.

Testing

Fundamental to the Design Thinking philosophy is the concept of moving multiple ideas into testing, with the winners selected by those being designed *for*. In this final stage, Design Thinking's visualization tools allow the translation of abstract ideas into things that feel real, often in the form of prototypes. Luigi Ferrara, Dean of Toronto's Institute without Boundaries, explains why pushing people out of the discussion of abstract ideas and into action in the form of prototypes is so essential to accomplishing actual innovation and change:

It is easy to stay safely in the debate space and never have your hypothesis interact with reality to get feedback about whether or not it is true. This is what makes everything slow down. It's what paralyzes bureaucracies. You can debate forever. This is where design gets interesting. You have to translate your sentiment into an embodiment that others can see. A fundamental part of design is making things shareable in the world. That forces collaboration because you have to agree on an output. And that changes thinking. You can say, "We want to be the world's best city," but that is really empty until you confront the design challenge: operationalizing the value.

The role of prototypes is to act as provocations to elicit better feedback to test hypotheses as well as ensure team alignment on the specifics of what any given idea looks like in practice. As prototypes move into "learning launches" in the real world, another benefit occurs: Not only does the process allow for iterations that improve the solution, the testing process itself creates an experience for those who are involved in its implementation. As another interviewee in our research described it:

I am more and more convinced that the value of prototypes and learning launches is that they make concepts tangible and create a conversation space for engagement. Language is about the creation of shared meaning. This is achieved through conversations that establish trust and that lead to commitment.... Design tools work on the conversation, and embody the nature of the commitments that bind us.

As those charged with implementation participate in the testing process, it builds the kind of personal experience of "situated novelty" (Janssen, Stoopendaal, & Putters, 2015) that makes innovation feel real and personally significant to them.

Implications of Design Thinking for Modern Organization Design

We have reviewed evidence for how Design Thinking's mindset, processes, and tools combine to help firms organize and problem solve in ways that enhance their ongoing adaptability, focusing on multiple interconnected levels. At the individual level, human-centered design draws on our natural curiosity to build empathy and emotional engagement that help overcome risk aversion in the face of uncertainty, build the creative confidence to act, and foster the kind of psychological safety that invites actors to bring their authentic selves into the organizational conversation. At the team level, design works to resolve the paradox of difference and allow collaborative cocreation of higher-order solutions as it sets the conditions for emergence by making thinking tangible and shaping a shared assessment of needs and a possibility-driven intention. At the organizational level, design builds adaptability and improves the quality of problem-solving and the likelihood that the solutions identified will be successfully implemented. At the systems level, user-centered design builds trust among stakeholders and encourages resource sharing.

Application of Design Thinking accomplishes these outcomes by providing a set of core drivers, identified in the organization design literature, that are essential for an "actor-oriented" rather than hierarchical organizational architecture (Fjeldstad et al., 2012). In articulating a response to the challenges presented to organizations by increasing environmental complexity and uncertainty, Fjeldstad et al. (2012) identify three core elements of a scheme that reduces the negative effects of hierarchy and enables multiactor collaboration: (1) *actors* with the capabilities and values to self-organize; (2) *commons* where knowledge and resources accumulate and are shared by the actors; and (3) *protocols, processes, and infrastructures* that enable multiactor collaboration by allowing the actors to largely control and coordinate themselves.

Design Thinking has the ability to make important contributions to each of these actor-oriented elements. A final story from our research illustrates this. Headquartered in Washington, DC, the Community Transportation Association of America (CTAA) invites local communities throughout the United States to join in achieving its mission of "creating mobility for all Americans regardless of where they live or work." Rather than defining transportation problems centrally and recommending implementation of broad transportation initiatives, CTAA builds the capabilities of the local actors involved by using Design Thinking to empower carefully composed teams of local partners to frame problems and cocreate solutions for their communities' unique circumstances. Design Thinking provides the infrastructure of a common language and protocols across teams for how projects are executed. It creates a commons of shared knowledge and situation awareness within each local team and across the teams working together at a national level via webinars, Skype calls, and face-to-face summit meetings. Galvanizing networks that are both local and global, it builds long-term capabilities for ongoing problem-solving. CTAA's use of Design Thinking represents a model of organizing that addresses the classic tension between centralization and decentralization in ways especially relevant to organizational success in rapidly changing and increasingly complex environments.

The resulting effect is an organization able to act more quickly and effectively in the face of environmental change. Cumulatively, Design Thinking's contribution to organizational speed becomes evident: Organizations whose staff are apathetic, working at cross-purposes from each other, and confused about priorities are likely to be slow to respond. Conversely, organization members who are engaged, both emotionally and cognitively, aligned as to purpose, and clear about what really matters are likely to be more adaptable and quicker to respond. Design Thinking's ability to build engagement, alignment, and clarity on user needs creates the path for organizations to develop the capacity to act.

Conclusion

Our goal in this chapter has been to lay out the case for how Design Thinking can help managers build new kinds of organizations and why it deserves attention from scholars. Effective use of Design Thinking calls for managerial and organizational behaviors that recognize the value of problem setting as well as solving, build a culture of learning from failure rather than punishing it, and provide the resources and autonomy to experiment. We hope we have made the case that, for modern organizations, investments in building Design Thinking capabilities will provide large returns.

References

Adler, P. S. 2001. Market, hierarchy, and trust: the knowledge economy and the future of capitalism. *Organization Science* 12(2): 215–234.

Amabile, T. M., Barsade, S. G., Mueller, J. S., & Staw, B. M. 2005. Affect and creativity at work. *Administrative Science Quarterly* 50(3): 367–403.

Baas, M., De Dreu, C. K., & Nijstad, B. A. 2008. A meta-analysis of 25 years of mood-creativity research: hedonic tone, activation, or regulatory focus? *Psychological Bulletin* 134(6): 779–806.

Beckman, S. L. & Barry, M. 2007. Innovation as a learning process: embedding design thinking. *California Management Review* 50(1): 25–56.

Boland, R. & Tenkasi, R. 1995. Perspective making and perspective taking in communities of knowing. *Organization Science* 6(4): 350–372.

Boxenbaum, E., Jones, C., Meyer, R. E., & Svejenova, S. 2018. Towards an articulation of the material and visual turn in organization studies. *Organization Studies* 39(5–6): 597–616.

Brown, T. 2019. *Change by Design*. HarperCollins, New York, NY.

Brown, S. & Eisenhardt, K. 1995. Product development: past research, present findings, and future directions. *Academy of Management Review* 20(2): 343–378.

Campbell, B. 2019. *Practice Theory in Action*. Routledge, New York, NY.

Carlgren, L., Elmquist, M., & Rauth, I. 2016. The challenges of using design thinking in industry – experiences from five large firms. *Creativity and Innovation Management* 25(3): 344–362.

Carroll, T. N., Gormley, T. J., Bilardo, V. J., Burton, R. M., & Woodman, K. L. 2006. Designing a new organization at NASA: an organization design process using simulation. *Organization Science* 17(2): 202–214.

Dong, A., Garbuio, M., & Lovallo, D. 2016. Generative sensing: a design perspective on the microfoundations of sensing capabilities. *California Management Review* 58(4): 97–117.

Dorst, K. 2015. Frame creation and design in the expanded field. *She Ji: The Journal of Design, Economics, and Innovation* 1(1): 22–33.

Dweck, C. S. 2008. *Mindset: The New Psychology of Success*. Random House Digital, New York, NY.

Edmondson, A. 1999. Psychological safety and learning behavior in work teams. *Administrative Science Quarterly* 44(2): 350–383.

Elsbach, K. D. & Stigliani, I. 2018. Design thinking and organizational culture: a review and framework for future research. *Journal of Management* 44(6): 2274–2306.

Ewald, B., Menning, A., Nicolai, C., & Weinberg, U. 2019. Emotions along the design thinking process. In C. Meinel and L. Leifer (eds.), *Design Thinking Research: Looking Further: Design Thinking Beyond Solution-Fixation*: 41–60. Springer International Publishing AG, New York, NY.

Ewenstein, B. & Whyte, J. 2007. Beyond words: aesthetic knowledge and knowing in organizations. *Organization Studies* 28(5): 689–708.

Fjeldstad, Ø. D., Snow, C. C., Miles, R. E., & Lettl, C. 2012. The architecture of collaboration. *Strategic Management Journal* 33(6): 734–750.

Gruber, M., De Leon, N., George, G., & Thompson, P. 2015. Managing by design. *Academy of Management Journal* 58(1): 1–7.

Healey, M. P. & Hodgkinson, G. P. 2017. Making strategy hot. *California Management Review* 59(3): 109–134.

Heidegger, M. 1962. *Being and Time*. Harper & Row, New York, NY.

Higgins, E. T. 1998. Promotion and prevention: regulatory focus as a motivational principle. *Advances in Experimental Social Psychology* 30: 1–46. Academic Press, Cambridge, MA.

Hölzle, K. & Rhinow, H. 2019. The dilemmas of design thinking in innovation projects. *Project Management Journal* 50(4): 1–13.

IDEO, Organization Design. www.ideo.com/jobs/organizational-design

Janssen, M., Stoopendaal, A. M. V., & Putters, K. 2015. Situated novelty: introducing a process perspective on the study of innovation. *Research Policy* 44(10): 1974–1984.

Jaskyte, K., and Liedtka, J. 2022. Design thinking for innovation: Practices and intermediate outcomes. *Nonprofit Management & Leadership* 32(4): 555–575.

Kelley, T. & Kelley, D. 2013. *Creative Confidence: Unleashing the Creative Potential within Us All.* Currency Publishing (Crown), New York, NY.

Kolko, J. 2010. Abductive thinking and sensemaking: the drivers of design synthesis. *Design Issues* 26(1): 15–28.

Kröper, M., Fay, D., Lindberg, T., & Meinel, C. 2011. Interrelations between motivation, creativity and emotions in design thinking processes – an empirical study based on regulatory focus theory. In T. Taura and Y. Nagai (eds.), *Design Creativity*: 97–104. Springer, London, UK.

Lawrence, P. R. & Lorsch, J. W. 1967. *Organization and Environment.* Harvard Business School, Division of Research, Boston, MA. (Reissued as a Harvard Business School Classic, Harvard Business School Press, 1986.)

Lee, L. & Sukoco, B. 2011. Reflexivity, stress, and unlearning in the new product development team: the moderating effect of procedural justice. *R&D Management* 41(4): 410–423.

Liedtka, J. 2015. Perspective: linking design thinking with innovation outcomes through cognitive bias reduction. *Journal of Product Innovation Management* 32(6): 925–938.

Liedtka, J. 2017. Evaluating the impact of design thinking in action. In S. Taneja (ed.), *Academy of Management Proceedings 2017*, No. 1: 10264–10270. Academy of Management, Briarcliff Manor, NY.

Liedtka, J. 2020. Putting technology in its place: the social technology of design thinking. *California Management Review* 62(2): 53–83.

Liedtka, J. & Bahr, K. 2019. *Measuring the ROI of Design Thinking, Darden School Working Paper 19–13.* University of Virginia Press, Charlottesville, VA.

Liedtka, J. & Ogilvie, T. 2011. *Designing for Growth: A Design Thinking Tool Kit for Managers.* Columbia University Press, New York, NY.

Liedtka, J., King, A., & Bennett, K. 2013. *Solving Problems with Design Thinking: Ten Stories of What Works.* Columbia University Press, New York, NY.

Liedtka, J., Ogilvie, T., & Brozenske, R. 2014. *The Designing for Growth Field Book: A Step-by-Step Project Guide.* Columbia University Press, New York, NY.

Liedtka, J., Salzman, R., & Azer, D. 2017. *Designing for the Greater Good: Innovation in the Social Sector.* Columbia University Press, New York, NY.

Liedtka, J., Sheikh, A., Gilmer, C., Kupetz, M., & Wilcox, L. 2020. The use of design thinking in the US federal government. *Public Performance & Management Review* 43(1): 157–179.

Litchfield, R. C. 2008. Brainstorming reconsidered: a goal-based view. *Academy of Management Review* 33(3): 649–668.

Lovelace, K., Shapiro, D., & Weingart, L. 2001. Maximizing cross-functional new product teams' innovativeness and constraint adherence: a conflict communications perspective. *Academy of Management Journal* 44(4): 779–793.

Majchrzak, A., More, P., & Faraj, S. 2012. Transcending knowledge differences in cross-functional teams. *Organization Science* 23(4): 951–970.

Micheli, P., Wilner, S. J., Bhatti, S. H., Mura, M., & Beverland, M. B. 2019. Doing design thinking: conceptual review, synthesis, and research agenda. *Journal of Product Innovation Management* 36(2): 124–148.

Michlewski, K. 2008. Uncovering design attitude: inside the culture of designers. *Organization Studies* 29(3): 373–392.

Puranam, P., Alexy, O., & Reitzig, M. 2014. What's "new" about new forms of organizing? *Academy of Management Review* 39(2): 162–180.

Romme, A. G. L. 2003. Making a difference: organization as design. *Organization Science* 14(5): 558–573.

Sawyer, R. 2012. *Explaining Creativity: The Science of Human Innovation.* Oxford University Press, Oxford, UK.

Scharmer, O. 2001. Self-transcending knowledge: sensing and organizing around emerging opportunities. *Journal of Knowledge Management* 5(2): 137–151.

Schultz, K. 2010. *Being Wrong: Adventures in the Margin of Error.* HarperCollins Books, New York, NY.

Seidel, V. P. & Fixson, S. K. 2013. Adopting design thinking in novice multidisciplinary teams: the application and limits of design methods and reflexive practices. *Journal of Product Innovation Management* 30(S1): 19–33.

Seidel, V. P. & O'Mahony, S. 2014. Managing the repertoire: stories, metaphors, prototypes, and concept coherence in product innovation. *Organization Science* 25(3): 691–712.

Silvia, P. J. 2008. Interest – the curious emotion. *Current Directions in Psychological Science* 17(1): 57–60.

Stephens, J. P. & Boland, B. J. 2015. The aesthetic knowledge problem of problem-solving with design thinking. *Journal of Management Inquiry* 24(3): 219–232.

Stephens, J. P., Heaphy, E. D., Carmeli, A., Spreitzer, G. M., & Dutton, J. E. 2013. Relationship quality and virtuousness: emotional carrying capacity as a source of individual and team resilience. *Journal of Applied Behavioral Science* 49(1): 13–41.

Stigliani, I. & Ravasi, D. 2012. Organizing thoughts and connecting brains: material practices and the transition from individual to group-level prospective sensemaking. *Academy of Management Journal* 55(5): 1232–1259.

Taylor, S. S. 2002. Overcoming aesthetic muteness: researching organizational members' aesthetic experience. *Human Relations* 55(7): 821–840.

Weick, K. E. 1995. *Sensemaking in Organizations,* vol. 3. SAGE Publishers, Thousand Oaks, CA.

Yoo, Y., Boland Jr., R. J., & Lyytinen, K. 2006. From organization design to organization designing. *Organization Science* 17(2): 215–229.

2 | *The Open Organization*

CHRISTOPHER LETTL, THOMAS RITTER,
AND CARSTEN LUND PEDERSEN

The traditional manufacturing or service organization is characterized by well-defined boundaries at which it contractually exchanges goods and services with other organizations and whose activities are coordinated by hierarchies (Williamson, 1985). Increasingly, organizations are "opening up" the way many of their activities are performed. Openness means that organizational actors and resources are mobilized for the performance of activities irrespective of formal organizational boundaries. In part, this growing phenomenon is enabled by the Internet, which connects employees, independent workers, suppliers, and customers, allowing them to collaborate widely across organizational boundaries and geographies. The organization designs that are emerging to support actors in the performance of their activities are called "actor-oriented" because they allow actors to control and coordinate activities themselves, with only minimal reliance on hierarchical mechanisms (Fjeldstad et al., 2012).

Some observers have argued that open organizations are ushering in a new organizational paradigm (Greer, Lusch, & Vargo, 2016; Lusch & Vargo, 2014). The emerging paradigm is characterized by the cocreation and coproduction of goods and services (Normann & Ramirez, 1993), collaborative knowledge development and sharing, worker autonomy and mobility, relational leadership (Uhl-Bien, 2006), and relational competitive advantages (Dyer & Singh, 1998). The new paradigm also embodies a new mindset regarding the nature of organizations. In contrast to the traditional view that organizations are atomistic entities engaged in transactions with other organizations, the new mindset views organizations as dynamic resource configurations in which joint value creation occurs as collaborating actors cocreate and coproduce products and services (Greer et al., 2016).

In this chapter, we discuss the open organization, devoting particular attention to how the concept is being used and the capabilities required to make it work. We seek to answer three main questions: (1) Why and how are organizations opening up? (2) What are the capabilities needed to collaborate with actors beyond a firm's formal organizational boundaries? (3) What are the organizing processes and mechanisms that support goal-directed openness? In the first section, we discuss the three main ways organizations open up: an outside-in process, an inside-out process, and processes where firms collaborate with external actors. Next, we discuss the capabilities that enable open organizations to collaborate with external actors in a dynamic manner. Such capabilities are relational in the sense that they enable internal and external actors to combine and leverage their resources. Lastly, we discuss the organizing processes and mechanisms used by firms to transform a closed organization into an open organization.

How Organizations Open Up

There is increasing consensus among academics and practitioners alike that we are in the midst of a shift from producer-centered organizational processes toward user-driven, open, and coproducing processes (Chesbrough, 2003; Keinz, Heinerth, & Lettl, 2012; von Hippel, 2005). In the industrial era, firms achieved competitive advantages by configuring and controlling activities and resources, which they guarded closely (Barney, 1991; Caves & Porter, 1977). There was a clear boundary between the firm and its customers – the firm created value and customers consumed it. Companies offered their customers affordable products and services that met essential needs for food, clothing, housing, heating, refrigeration, and transportation. Efficiency in the production of such standard goods was key to value creation.

Over the past few decades, value has come to be seen as being coproduced by a variety of actors such as customers, suppliers, and complementors (Fuchs, 1968; Lusch & Vargo, 2014; Norman & Ramirez, 1993; Ramirez, 1999). To take advantage of the benefits of coproduction, a traditional or closed organization must open up. According to Gassmann and Enkel (2004), this can occur in three ways: (1) an outside-in process whereby firms enrich their knowledge base by integrating the resources of customers, suppliers, and other organizations; (2) an inside-out process that exploits internal ideas and knowledge by channeling those resources to new markets through licensing, selling intellectual property, and so on; and (3) a "coupled" process in which firms collaborate with complementary companies to coproduce products and services. Such open processes make more resources available for value creation by engaging a broad set of actors in the development and production of products and services. An early example of coproduction is found in the Swedish furniture company IKEA, which in 1956 started flat packaging furniture in order to have it fit into a car and avoid damage during transit. This practice led to customer assembly of products becoming part of IKEA's highly successful business model. Customer involvement is taken further in kitchen design. Using IKEA's 3D Kitchen Planner, customers design custom kitchens and, if they wish, consult with an IKEA designer. Today, coproduction of products and services is the norm across a wide variety of sectors, and firms have many sources of coproduction opportunities: the crowd; customers; universities and research laboratories; technology-based start-ups; suppliers; and regionally based clusters of competitive firms (Vanhaverbeke, 2006).

Open innovation is a particular form of coproduction directed at innovation. It entails managing knowledge flows across organizational boundaries (Chesbrough & Bogers, 2014). Historically, many product and service innovations have originated from or with users and customers (von Hippel, 1988, 2005, 2016). As managers and entrepreneurs recognized the importance of users and other stakeholders in the innovation process, they developed practices, tools, and platforms that facilitate open innovation. Additional factors that affected the growth of open innovation include: (1) the increasing availability and mobility of skilled workers, (2) growth of the venture capital market, (3) external options for ideas and technologies sitting on the shelf, and (4) expanding capabilities of external suppliers (Chesbrough, 2003). Essentially, such factors allowed organizations to tap into resources not previously available as they pursued innovation opportunities and projects.

Organizational boundaries become permeable with the implementation of open approaches (Santos & Eisenhardt, 2005; Zobel & Hagedoorn, 2020). The challenge for executives is to determine the extent to which an organization *should* be open. There is no generic answer to this question. The optimal degree of openness depends on external conditions, such as the pace of technological change and the institutional environment, as well as internal conditions, such as a firm's strategies and capabilities. Inevitably, tensions arise when organizations attempt to open their processes (Wadhwa, Bodas Freitas, &

Sarkar, 2017). A desirable degree of openness can be found by considering the sources of those tensions and by actively discussing and regularly reconsidering them in order to triangulate on an optimal open-organization design. One important tension related to openness is *complexity*. Drawing on modern social systems theory and cognitive psychology, Schreyögg and Sydow (2010) argue that organizations come into existence as complexity-reducing devices. In order to cope with the complexity of the environment and to differentiate themselves from it, organizations constantly adopt complexity-reducing mechanisms, such as developing and maintaining interpretative action patterns, templates, referencing systems, and cognitive frameworks. Such mechanisms allow organizations to exist by establishing boundaries and, thereby, identities (Luhmann, 1995). As opening the innovation process requires making organizational boundaries more permeable, organizations can never completely open up – doing so would make them equal to the environment and they would vanish (Schreyögg & Sydow, 2010). Consequently, an organization can only open itself to a certain extent. The argument also suggests that the more organizations adopt open processes, the more they blur their identities.

Another tension induced by open innovation is *loss of control*. Organizations strive for control in order to gain predictability as well as high reliability and efficiency (Farjoun, 2010). The more external actors are involved in innovation processes, the more difficult it becomes to maintain control of developmental efforts, as each actor may have different ideas and worldviews and therefore different beliefs about what constitutes good and legitimate solutions. It also becomes increasingly difficult to maintain control over the organization's intellectual property because knowledge spillovers can seldom be completely avoided. One way to control tension over intellectual property is to engage in "selective revealing," which Alexy, George, and Salter (2013: 272) define as "the voluntary, purposeful, and irrevocable disclosure of specifically selected resources, usually knowledge based, which the firm could have otherwise kept proprietary, so that they become available to a large share or even all of the general public, including competitors." The sharing of knowledge with the public may yield significant benefits to the organization such as reductions in the costs associated with searching for attractive collaboration partners or the creation of momentum for one's own topics and activities (Henkel, 2006). At the same time, it may reveal weaknesses in the development process and divulge the firm's areas of current interest. Consequently, organizations that engage in selective revealing need to be careful about which knowledge to keep and which knowledge to reveal.

A third tension is *fairness*. "The paradox of openness" (Laursen & Salter, 2014) refers to the fact that organizations need to both share knowledge to maximize value creation and protect knowledge to appropriate value for themselves. The paradox of openness implies tensions between value creation and value capture in open-innovation contexts (Chesbrough, Lettl, & Ritter, 2018). The introduction of open-innovation processes always carries the risk that external contributors may perceive exchanges and processes with the focal organization as unfair. Thus, fairness is a fundamental source of problems in open innovation (Chesbrough et al., 2018; Franke, Keinz, & Klausberger, 2013; Nambisan & Baron, 2010). Colquitt, Greenberg, and Zapata-Phelan (2005) identify three distinct types of fairness in interorganizational relations. *Distributional fairness* refers to the fairness of outcomes relative to contributions. In open innovation, an actor who contributes a great deal to value creation but captures only a small fraction of that value will most likely perceive the outcome as unfair (even though the value for this actor may be positive in a strict value-based analysis). *Procedural fairness* is the fairness of the procedures used to derive certain outcomes. In open innovation, this points to the importance of transparency with respect to selection criteria as well as development and commercialization processes (Franke et al., 2013). It also relates to the provision of appropriate feedback to contributors and the management of disappointments (Piezunka & Dahlander, 2019). *Interactional fairness* refers to the fairness of interpersonal and interorganizational treatment. It is defined as the degree to which actors affected by decisions are treated with dignity and respect (Schermerhorn, Hunt, & Osborn, 1995).

Executives need to proactively deal with the tensions associated with opening up an organization and make the necessary adjustments to the organizational design, especially in critical areas such as strategy, structure, process, and culture. Key openness initiatives may include:

- Strategy – Develop an openness strategy for the entire organization (not just for individual business units). Systematically search for and involve value-enhancing external partners (e.g., lead users, entrepreneurs, complementors, the crowd).

- Structure – Increase the density of linkages with external actors by forming alliances and building open platforms and collaborative communities. Develop synergies among open-innovation activities.
- Process – Search the internal and external environment for resources that can be used in the coproduction of products and services. Train employees to recognize knowledge that can be shared and knowledge that needs to be kept within the organization. Decentralize decision-making rights regarding collaboration with external actors.
- Culture – Create transparency around open-innovation projects. Reward learning from open-innovation experiments. Encourage sharing of open-innovation approaches and best practices.

Collaborative Capabilities: A Relational View

To successfully create and operate an open organization requires a unique set of capabilities. Open organizing assumes that "a firm's critical resources may span firm boundaries and may be embedded in *interfirm* resources and routines" (Dyer & Singh, 1998: 660, italics in original). The relational view of organizing assumes that resources are widely distributed and of generally high quality (Chesbrough, 2006), and a firm should not feel constrained as it searches for resources beyond its formal boundaries.

Over the past couple of decades, proactive, unconstrained search across organizational boundaries had led to a virtual explosion in the means by which organizations began to open up. In East Asia, firms that were latecomers to their industries used their capabilities to pursue "link-and-leverage" strategies, forming alliances with established firms that possessed complementary resources and accelerating innovation (Mathews, 2014). Intel has a history of identifying small, promising technology firms relevant to its core businesses and supporting them in various ways until they can stand on their own and then acquiring or partnering with those firms (Miles & Snow, 1994). Lego, the Danish toy production company, designed and operates a sustainable producer–user ecosystem that provides it with a constant flow of external ideas and suggestions to expand its businesses (Heinerth, Lettl, & Keinz, 2013). Furthermore, there are organizations whose capabilities facilitate open innovation in other organizations. For example, Innocentive is an open innovation and crowdsourcing platform that allows firms with unsolved problems or idle technologies to submit them as "challenges" to be put out to the crowd for solutions.

For many organizations, the space where potentially valuable external resources reside is global, dynamic ecosystems. Learning how to create and capture value in ecosystems is challenging, as no individual firm, or set of firms, can control all the resources. The overall capability that firms need is a means to effectively navigate ecosystems (Ritter, 1999; Ritter & Gemünden, 2003; Ritter, Wilkinson, & Johnston, 2004; Walter, Auer, & Ritter, 2006). One important set of capabilities relates to searching the environment for potential resources while making the firm's own resources visible for others to search. The key is developing a mindset in which organizations feel confident in opening their resources and activity systems to others. An equally important set of capabilities relates to organizing coproduction among diverse actors – for example, building and operating collaborative platforms. Examples range from open-source software projects to large-scale collaboration among competing pharmaceutical companies in the quest for effective COVID-19 vaccines (World Economic Forum, 2020).

Construction and movie industries have for a long time organized production using temporary networks of independent workers (Eccles, 1981; Jones, Hesterly, & Borgatti, 1997). In those industries, autonomous actors constitute resources that can move across locations and projects. The Internet has dramatically increased the ability of integrating various actors into organizational activities irrespective of time and location. This has given rise to a global class of "digital nomads" (Makimoto & Manners, 1997), autonomous actors who move across innovation projects hosted on digital platforms (Richter & Richter, 2020). Firms operating in "nomadic" environments must be able to attract talented workers on an ongoing basis. In Silicon Valley, tech giants such as Google and Facebook rely on a variety of factors to attract and retain talented people, including (1) offering a wide variety of interesting projects, (2) having an attractive digital and physical work environment, (3) providing opportunities to self-develop and implement innovative projects, and (4) fostering an open and transparent culture that values knowledge dissemination and external collaboration (*The Economist*, 2017).

Designing Open Organizations

What are the organizing processes and mechanisms that transform a closed organization into an open one? Although there have been only a few empirical studies of the transformation process (e.g., Chiaroni, Chiesa, & Frattini, 2010), we do have a broad understanding of how the process works. Following the dynamic capabilities (Teece, Pisano, & Shuen, 1997) and open innovation (Zobel & Hagedoorn, 2020) frameworks, a successful transformation from closed to open involves developing the capacity to perform a set of related activities on a continuous basis: sensing, seizing, and aligning.

Sensing

Sensing involves scanning the organization's external and internal environment in search of complementary resources and activities. External relationships are sources of information, opportunities, knowledge, and capabilities, and firms typically use dedicated groups of marketing and technology specialists to identify and forge relationships with external actors who possess complementary activities and resources. Suppliers and customers, as well as universities and commercial research organizations, are important sources of coproducing relationships, and the form and degree of openness depend on the industrial environment in which the firm operates (Pavitt, 1984; Tidd, Bessant, & Pavitt, 1997; Zobel & Hagedoorn, 2020). Opening up implies forming or joining external networks that offer access to valuable resources as well as making the firm's own resources visible to potential partners. In dynamic, "nomadic" environments, network relationships are of greater or lesser permanence depending on the nature of the industrial ecosystem. The choice of collaborating partners, the depth and duration of relationships, the firm's role in the network, and the mechanisms by which the firm controls and coordinates its networks are important design elements.

Seizing

Seizing refers to how firms create and capture value from perceived opportunities. This requires investments in the development of new products and services as well as commercialization activities (Teece, 2007). In open organizing, market, technological, and organizational solutions are pursued through collaborative relationships. Expanding firm boundaries in open, dynamic environments requires relational contracting (Zobel & Hagedoorn, 2020). Unlike formal contracting, which is characterized by the specification of both ends and means (Williamson, 1985), relational contracting is open-ended (Macaulay, 1963; Macneil, 1978). By design, relational contracts are flexible and based on trust; they help to reconcile the inevitable tensions between value creation and value appropriation (Zobel & Hagedoorn, 2020).

Furthermore, effectively collaborating with external actors requires organizational structures and processes that integrate external and internal resources and activities. In open organizations, integration is accomplished by structural elements such as units dedicated to managing external relationships, cross-organizational teams, shared platforms for innovation and collaboration, and incentive systems that stimulate collaboration.

Aligning

Ensuring that the ecosystem of coproducing actors remains viable over time requires continuous alignment of goals, activities, resources, and organizational arrangements. An open organization has a portfolio of collaborative relationships. As firms alter their existing relationships and form new ones, they need to realign their relational contracts in a fair and transparent manner – that is, behave toward collaborating actors in ways that adhere to shared values, norms of reciprocity, trust, and altruism (Ostrom, 1990; Zobel & Hagedoorn, 2020).

Conclusion

In this chapter, we have discussed the challenges that designers face in opening up an organization – how open it should be, the capabilities required to make it work, and how to collaborate with coproducing actors. A move toward openness cannot occur easily or quickly, but research on leading firms shows that opening up is both viable and beneficial.

References

Alexy, O., George, G., & Salter, A. J. 2013. Cui bono? The selective revealing of knowledge and its implications for innovative activity. *Academy of Management Review* 38(2): 270–291.

Barney, J. B. 1991. Firm resources and sustained competitive advantage. *Journal of Management* 17(1): 99–120.

Caves, R. E., & Porter, M. E. 1977. From entry barriers to mobility barriers: Conjectural decisions and contrived deterrence to new competition. *The Quarterly Journal of Economics* 91(2): 241–261.

Chesbrough, H. W. 2003. *Open Innovation: The New Imperative for Creating and Profiting from Technology.* Harvard Business School Press, Boston, MA.

Chesbrough, H. W. 2006. *Open Business Models: How to Thrive in the New Innovation Landscape.* Harvard Business School Press, Boston, MA.

Chesbrough, H. & Bogers, M. 2014. Explicating open innovation: clarifying an emerging paradigm for understanding innovation. In H. Chesbrough, W. Vanhaverbeke, and J. West (eds.), *New Frontiers in Open Innovation*: 3–28. Oxford University Press, Oxford, UK.

Chesbrough, H., Lettl, C., & Ritter, T. 2018. Value creation and value capture in open innovation. *Journal of Product Innovation Management* 35(6): 930–938.

Chiaroni, D., Chiesa, V., & Frattini, F. 2010. Unravelling the process from closed to open innovation: evidence from mature, asset-intensive industries. *R&D Management* 40(3): 222–245.

Colquitt, J. A., Greenberg, J., & Zapata-Phelan, C. P. 2005. What is organizational justice? A historical overview. In J. Greenberg and J. A. Colquitt (eds.), *Handbook of Organizational Justice*, vol. 1: 3–58. Lawrence Erlbaum Associates, New York, NY.

Dyer, J. H. & Singh, H. 1998. The relational view: cooperative strategy and sources of interorganizational competitive advantage. *Academy of Management Review* 23(4): 660–679.

Eccles, R. G. 1981. The quasifirm in the construction industry. *Journal of Economic Behavior & Organization* 2(4): 335–357.

Farjoun, M. 2010. Beyond dualism: stability and change as a duality. *Academy of Management Review* 35(2): 202–225.

Fjeldstad, Ø. D., Snow, C. C., Miles, R. E., & Lettl, C. 2012. The architecture of collaboration. *Strategic Management Journal* 33(6): 734–750.

Franke, N., Keinz, P., & Klausberger, K. 2013. "Does this sound like a fair deal?": antecedents and consequences of fairness expectations in the individual's decision to participate in firm innovation. *Organization Science* 24(5): 1495–1516.

Fuchs, V. 1968. *The Service Economy.* National Bureau of Economic Research, Washington, DC.

Gassmann, O. & Enkel, E. 2004. Towards a theory of open innovation: three core process archetypes. Proceedings of The R&D Management Conference, Lisbon, Portugal, July 6–9.

Greer, C. R., Lusch, R. F., & Vargo, S. L. 2016. A service perspective: key managerial insights from service-dominant (S-D) logic. *Organizational Dynamics* 45: 28–38.

Heinerth, C., Lettl, C., & Keinz, P. 2013. Synergies among producer firms, lead users, and user communities: the case of the LEGO producer-user ecosystem. *Journal of Product Innovation Management* 31(4): 848–866. https://doi.org/10.1111/jpim.12127

Henkel, J. 2006. Selective revealing in open innovation processes: the case of embedded Linux. *Research Policy* 35(7): 953–969.

Jones, C., Hesterly, W. S., & Borgatti, S. P. 1997. A general theory of network governance: exchange conditions and social mechanisms. *Academy of Management Review* 22(4): 911–945.

Keinz, P., Heinerth, C., & Lettl, C. 2012. Designing the organization for user innovation. *Journal of Organization Design* 1(3): 20–36.

Laursen, K. & Salter, A. J. 2014. The paradox of openness: appropriability, external search and collaboration. *Research Policy* 43(5): 867–878.

Luhmann, N. 1995. *Social Systems*. Stanford University Press, Stanford, CA.

Lusch, R. F. & Vargo, S. L. 2014. *Service-Dominant Logic: Premises, Perspectives, Possibilities*. Cambridge University Press, Cambridge, UK.

Macaulay, S. 1963. Non-contractual relations in business: a preliminary study. *American Sociological Review* 28: 1–19.

Macneil, I. R. 1978. Contracts: adjustment of long-term economic relations under classical, neoclassical, and relational contract law. *Northwestern University Law Review* 72: 854–905.

Makimoto, T. & Manners, D. 1997. *Digital Nomad*. Wiley, New Jersey.

Mathews, J. 2014. Entrepreneurial strategies in Asian latecomer firms. In F.-L. Tony Yu and H.-D. Yan (eds.), *Handbook of East Asian Entrepreneurship*: 30–44. Routledge, Abingdon, UK.

Miles, R. E. & Snow, C. C. 1994. *Fit, Failure, and the Hall of Fame: How Companies Succeed or Fail*. Free Press, New York, NY.

Nambisan, S. & Baron, R. A. 2010. Different roles, different strokes: organizing virtual customer environments to promote two types of customer contributions. *Organization Science* 21(2): 554–572.

Normann, R. & Ramirez, R. 1993. From value chain to value constellation: designing interactive strategy. *Harvard Business Review* 71(4): 65–77.

Ostrom, E. 1990. *Governing the Commons: The Evolution of Institutions for Collective Action*. Cambridge University Press, Cambridge, UK.

Pavitt, K. 1984. Sectoral patterns of sectoral change: towards a taxonomy and a theory. *Research Policy* 13: 343–373.

Piezunka, H. & Dahlander, L. 2019. Idea rejected, tie formed: organizations' feedback on crowdsourced ideas. *Academy of Management Journal* 62(2): 503–530.

Ramirez, R. 1999. Value co-production: intellectual origins and implications for practice and research. *Strategic Management Journal* 20(1): 49–65.

Richter, S. & Richter, A. 2020. Digital nomads. *Business & Information Systems Engineering* 62(1): 77–81.

Ritter, T. 1999. The networking company: antecedents for coping with relationships and networks effectively. *Industrial Marketing Management* 28(5): 467–479.

Ritter, T. & Gemünden, H. G. 2003. Network competence: its impact on innovation success and its antecedents. *Journal of Business Research* 56(9): 745–755.

Ritter, T., Wilkinson, I. F., & Johnston, W. J. 2004. Managing in complex business networks. *Industrial Marketing Management* 33(3): 175–183.

Santos, F. M. & Eisenhardt, K. M. 2005. Organizational boundaries and theories of organization. *Organization Science* 16: 491–508.

Schermerhorn, J. R., Hunt, J. G., & Osborn, R. N. 1995. *Basic Organizational Behavior.* Wiley, New York, NY.

Schreyögg, G. & Sydow, J. 2010. Crossroads – organizing for fluidity? Dilemmas of new organizational forms. *Organization Science* 21(6): 1251–1262.

Teece, D. J. 2007. Explicating dynamic capabilities: the nature and microfoundations of (sustainable) enterprise performance. *Strategic Management Journal* 28(13): 1319–1350.

Teece, D. J., Pisano, G., & Shuen, A. 1997. Dynamic capabilities and strategic management. *Strategic Management Journal* 18(7): 509–533.

The Economist. 2017. Google leads in the race to lead artificial intelligence. San Francisco, December 7.

Tidd, J., Bessant, J., & Pavitt, K. 1997. *Managing Innovation: Integrating Technological, Market and Organizational Change.* Wiley, Chichester, UK.

Uhl-Bien, M. 2006. Relational leadership theory: exploring the social processes of leadership and organizing. *Leadership Quarterly* 17(6): 654–676.

Vanhaverbeke, W. 2006. The interorganizational context of open innovation. In H. Chesbrough, W. Vanhaverbeke, and J. West (eds.), *Open Innovation: Researching a New Paradigm*: 205–219. Oxford University Press, Oxford, UK.

von Hippel, E. 1988. *The Sources of Innovation.* Oxford University Press, New York, NY.

von Hippel, E. 2005. *Democratizing Innovation: Users Take Center Stage.* MIT Press, Cambridge, MA.

von Hippel, E. 2016. *Free Innovation.* MIT Press, Cambridge, MA.

Wadhwa, A., Bodas Freitas, I. M., & Sarkar, M. B. 2017. The paradox of openness and value capture protection strategies: effect of extramural R&D on innovative performance. *Organization Science* 28(5): 873–893.

Walter, A., Auer, M., & Ritter, T. 2006. The impact of network capabilities and entrepreneurial orientation on university spin-off performance. *Journal of Business Venturing* 21(4): 541–567.

Williamson, O. E. 1985. *The Economic Institutions of Capitalism*. Free Press, New York, NY.

World Economic Forum. 2020. www.weforum.org/agenda/2020/05/global-science-collaboration-open-source-covid-19

Zobel, A.-K. & Hagedoorn, J. 2020. Implications of open innovation for organizational boundaries and the governance of contractual relations. *Academy of Management Perspectives* 34(3): 400–423.

3 | Actor-Oriented Organizing

ØYSTEIN D. FJELDSTAD AND CHARLES C. SNOW

In August 2004, IBM announced the opening of its BladeCenter architecture. IBM's goal, together with Intel and six other industry leaders, was to form a developer community that could quickly expand the availability of new solutions based on blade technology. Blade.org was launched in early 2006 as an organizational platform that enabled firms in the computer technology industry to collaboratively develop and commercialize computer servers for the large companies that power the Internet, including Internet service providers, telecommunications operators, financial service institutions, e-commerce firms, and search and social media firms. Ultimately, the Blade.org community of more than 300 firms included both technology providers and their key customers (Snow et al., 2011).

A blade computer system consists of a large number of complementary and interoperable hardware, software, and service components. Taking the conventional supply chain approach to the development and sourcing of all the interdependent blade server components was not a viable option because Hewlett Packard and Dell Corporation were well ahead in the race for dominance of this large, rapidly growing market. Blade.org's founding firms sought an organizational approach that would be both faster and more effective than a hierarchically driven supply chain approach. They created a collaborative community of technology firms to develop interoperable solutions that could meet the needs of customers in all industries.

Blade.org member firms self-organized innovation projects, typically involving two to four firms. Before embarking on detailed solution development, a project team uploaded a description of its intended solution to the Blade.org/solutions website. This description was made available to two committees composed of volunteer specialists from member firms. The marketing committee assessed the solution's market potential. The solutions and architecture committee assessed the solution's functionality and compatibility with Blade.org objectives. Once a solution was endorsed, the project team worked with other committees as well, using a standard template to detail business requirements, technical blueprints, and potential customer experience. A complete solution description was made available to all member firms, allowing them to count on the future availability of that solution and adjust their own development efforts accordingly. Thus, Blade.org developed interoperable technologies and solutions via collaboration among self-assembled and mutually adjusting cross-firm innovation teams.

Blade.org is an early and prominent example of *actor-oriented organizing* (Fjeldstad et al., 2012). Actor-oriented organizing is an administrative technology – a set of principles, mechanisms, and tools – that enables organizational actors to self-organize. In this chapter, we present a model of actor-oriented organizing that can be used by organizations to foster self-organized adaptation in complex, dynamic environments. In the first section, we discuss the process of organizational adaptation in order to clarify theoretical issues related to organizing complex, adaptive systems. The adaptive cycle shows how organizations continually solve entrepreneurial, engineering, and administrative problems to maintain fit with a changing environment (Miles & Snow, 1978). We describe how digital technologies affect all aspects of the adaptive cycle, including organizing, in ways that enable organizations to adapt quicker and more effectively. The digitization of products, markets, activities, and resources, coupled with the wide availability of digital infrastructures, supports actor-oriented organizing (Snow, Fjeldstad, & Langer, 2017). In the second section, we describe the elements and principles of actor-oriented organizational design. Actor-oriented organizing is increasingly evident and important as the global economy continues to become more connected and dynamic. We close the chapter with implications for the design and leadership of actor-oriented organizations.

Organizational Adaptation: A Proactive and Reactive Process

An organization is both an articulated purpose and an established mechanism for achieving it (Miles & Snow, 1978). Most organizations engage in an ongoing process of evaluating their purposes – questioning, verifying, and redefining the manner in which they interact with their environments. Effective organizations carve out and maintain a viable market for their goods or services. Ineffective organizations fail at this market alignment task. Organizations must also constantly modify and refine the mechanisms by which they pursue their purposes. Efficient organizations develop mechanisms that complement their market strategy. Inefficient organizations struggle with those mechanisms. For all organizations, the process of adapting to environmental change and uncertainty – of maintaining an effective alignment with the environment while efficiently managing internal interdependencies – is challenging.

Many of the concepts and principles for the design of adaptive organizations can be traced to cybernetics – the transdisciplinary study of control and coordination of purposeful human and machine systems (Ashby, 1956, 1958; Wiener, 1950). Organizations are complex, dynamic systems that must be able to take appropriate action relative to both the current and future states of their environment. An organization must have a repertoire of capabilities that corresponds to the environmental conditions that it may face – in cybernetic terms, the variety of the internal environment must match the variety of the external environment (Ashby, 1956). An organization's ability to remain viable over time requires it to be able to adapt its repertoire of capabilities to match a changing environment. This entails balancing what the organization currently does well with what it needs to do next (Beer, 1972). A balanced adaptive process is seldom seamless, requiring a continuous stream of individual and team decisions to be made across time and geographies.

Organizations use information to direct their efforts; they process information from both their external and internal environments and take action (Ashby, 1956). Some actions are guided by feedback – the assessment of results or performance in relation to organizational goals. Other actions feed forward – they are taken to achieve a desired future state (Simon, 1969). The communication of organizational information is called "messaging" (Wiener, 1950). Messages contain information that reduce uncertainty and therefore help to direct action toward achieving goals (Shannon & Weaver, 1949). An organization is aligned with its environment when its capabilities allow effective responses to environmental problems or opportunities. When a misalignment occurs, reorganization is required to maintain organizational viability. Reorganization may entail modification of the existing system or, more radically, changes in the basic principles by which the system is organized.

In complex organizing – characterized by a large number of elements and interdependencies among them – grouping and connecting actors is challenging (Ethiraj & Levinthal, 2004). In hierarchical organizations, reorganizing requires executive action to alter control and coordination relationships (Barnard, 1938). The more dynamic the environment, the more frequently reconfiguration of internal and external relationships will occur (Ciborra, 1996; Girod & Whittington, 2015, 2017; Kellogg, Orlikowski, & Yates, 2006). High dynamism coupled with high complexity severely challenges hierarchical organization designs because hierarchy tends to distort information flows and slow down decision-making (Thompson, 1967). Self-organizing, in contrast, implies the ability to spontaneously reorganize and realign the organization in response to changes in the environment (Ashby, 1947). Following von Foerster (1960), in order for self-organizing to work, new resource varieties must be generated and new relationships among the resources must be formed. The search for and selection of resources, and the development of new relationships, are best done by organization members themselves because they possess knowledge about their specific situation and compatibilities (Hayek, 1945). Because organizational actors are boundedly rational, their search is not exhaustive, and their responses are satisfactory rather than optimal (March & Simon, 1958; Simon, 1947).

Miles and Snow (1978) conceptualized organizations adapting to a changing environment as a perpetual cycle in which the internal pace of change must be synchronized with the pace of change in the environment. Their adaptive cycle portrays firms as continually solving three interrelated problems: entrepreneurial, engineering, and administrative. As shown in Figure 3.1, solving the entrepreneurial problem refers to creating the domains in which the organization will operate – its products, services, and markets. Solving the engineering problem involves configuring the organization's activities and resources. Solving the administrative problem ensures that the organization remains viable over time by balancing its exploitation and exploration efforts. Exploitation is rationalizing and improving the structures and processes that have been established, helping the organization become more efficient. Exploration entails developing the capabilities necessary to remain effective in a changing environment (March, 1991;

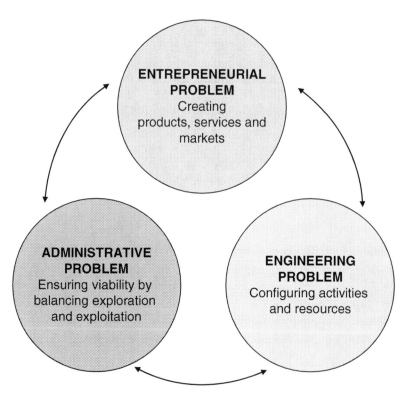

Figure 3.1 The adaptive cycle
From Miles and Snow (1978). Used with permission of Stanford University Press; permission conveyed through Copyright Clearance Center, Inc.

Miles & Snow, 1978). For a given organization, environmental dynamism is essentially captured by changes in customer needs and preferences, actions taken by competitors in the industry, and technological progress (Bourgeois & Eisenhardt, 1988).

Miles and Snow (1978) showed that how a firm goes about solving its adaptive problems is its strategy. Firms that are adept at exploitation refine their existing solutions based on feedback from the market. Exploiters follow a classic planning sequence of Plan -> Act -> Evaluate, in which the evaluation of results from previous plans feeds back into the next planning cycle. Firms that are adept at exploration engage with a new challenge or opportunity before undertaking detailed planning. Experimental action calls for a process that does not lock the organization into a particular direction until the shape of future events comes into clearer focus. Thus, explorers' behavior follows a sequence of Act -> Evaluate -> Plan. The process feeds forward – experimental actions are taken for the purpose of learning, which in turn is used to guide further actions.

An organization's adaptive solutions are constrained by the state of technology (Arthur, 2009), institutions such as laws and regulations (Williamson, 1985), and norms (Crawford & Ostrom, 1995) as well as by the availability of infrastructures such as communications, transportation, and transaction services (North & Wallis, 1994). The advent of digitization – computer hardware, software, transmission networks, protocols, programming languages, very large-scale integrated circuits, algorithms, and all the components and practices that belong to these various technologies – enables new solutions to all three adaptive problems and, in turn, new approaches to organizing. Moreover, because new solutions are based on the combinatorial and exponential properties of digital technologies (Brynjolfsson & McAfee, 2014), the speed at which adaptation takes place can increase dramatically.

The Entrepreneurial Problem: Creating Products and Markets

Digitization affects the very nature of products and services as well as how they are developed, produced, distributed, and maintained/ upgraded. Digital technologies can be combined and recombined endlessly for fresh purposes as in, for example, iPhones and autonomous vehicles. Digital technologies also enable replication and global distribution of products and services at close to zero marginal cost (Shapiro & Varian, 1999; Varian, 2000), as in Google search, Facebook messaging, and Netflix streaming services. Furthermore, digitally embedded products can be monitored, maintained, and upgraded in real time, as Tesla does with its vehicles.

Digitization similarly affects customer creation and development. As originally argued by Drucker (1954), the purpose of business is to create a customer. Customers and markets are created by developing and making available products and services that customers value and will pay for. In a digital world, a firm's offerings can be continuously adapted to customer preferences as revealed through their use of those products and services. Netflix, for example, customizes the content available to its individual users by applying machine learning algorithms that analyze rich customer data. Similarly, in open-source software development, users collaboratively create the software they want (von Hippel & von Krogh, 2003).

A firm's choice of market scope can be significantly affected when its products and services are digital. Google, for example, can rapidly expand the markets in which its products are available provided that customers have an Internet connection. The diffusion of Facebook illustrates how customers, by recruiting each other onto the social media platform, create an emergent process that determines the scope of the market served by the company.

The Engineering Problem: Configuring Activities and Resources

Digital technologies change the nature of activities and resources as well as how they can be organized. Digitization enables the customization of activities to particular situations. In Guatemala, for example, the nonprofit organization LifeNabled uses 3D scanners to create templates for prosthetic limbs. The digital templates are fed into additive printers that produce perfectly customized artificial limbs for patients who otherwise could not afford them (Peters, 2019). In addition, digitized activities can be performed autonomously, for example, chatbots or other robotic processes. Activities can even modify themselves by using machine learning algorithms and feedback on their performance. At Tesla's manufacturing facility in California, technicians work alongside hundreds of collaborative robots made by the German firm Kuka Robotics to assemble electric cars. By using artificial intelligence reinforcement learning algorithms, the robots are able to switch tools and perform certain tasks far better and faster than their human coworkers (Gershgorn, 2016). Furthermore, physical assets, such as a plant or complex equipment, are increasingly complemented with digital twins – rich digital replicas that can be used for monitoring, simulation, predictive maintenance, control, and coordination. The Norwegian company Arundo develops software that is used to optimize the operation and maintenance of physical assets and processes across a wide variety of industrial sectors.

Interaction with customers, suppliers, and partners is increasingly done via various types of digital platforms. Such platforms enable cocreation and coproduction of products and services (Cusumano, Gawer, & Yoffie, 2019; Gawer & Cusumano, 2014; Greer, Lusch, & Vargo, 2016). For example, NikebyYou allows customers to codesign their own shoes. Furthermore, digital resources are important to the performance of a firm's activities and are highly conducive to being shared. Digital resource sharing allows firms of any size to benefit from global scale in communicating, processing, and storing data. Amazon Web Services, for example, allows customers anywhere in the world access to large amounts of computing power. Physical resources can also be shared via low-cost digital platforms. For example, hubs that offer companies shared access to 3D printing are emerging globally (Piller, Weller, & Kleer, 2015).

The digitization of activities and resources offers alternative means of control and coordination (Setia, Venkatesh, & Joglekar, 2013). Maintenance of the Hong Kong subway system relies heavily on artificial intelligence algorithms to schedule all maintenance tasks. In a typical week, more than 10,000 people carry out 2,600 work orders generated by the system (Hodson, 2014). Autodesk's BIM 360 Building Information Modelling platform enables multidisciplinary actors to self-coordinate design and implementation activities using shared 3D models of construction projects. Overall, the digitization of activities and resources gives firms immediate, scalable access to a variety of digital, physical, and human resources and therefore increases the speed with which new solutions to the engineering problem can be implemented, controlled, and coordinated.

The Administrative Problem: Ensuring the Viability of the Organization over Time

Solving the administrative problem involves formulating and implementing processes that enable the organization to continue to adapt (Miles & Snow, 1978). Organizational viability requires dynamic fit, the maintenance of internal and external fit over time (Miles & Snow, 1984). Maintaining dynamic fit means balancing forward-looking and backward-looking processes such that organizational change synchronizes with the pace of change in the environment (Miles & Snow, 1994). Exploratory or forward-looking processes seek to "anticipate the shape of an uncertain future" (Simon, 1993) and generate variety by developing novel product/market and activity/resource solutions. Exploitative or backward-looking processes refine and reuse existing solutions.

Digitization affects both the nature and pace of exploration. In a digital world, experimentation, simulation, prototyping, and design can all be performed on digital representations. New digital representations can be rapidly created and modified by adjusting and recombining existing elements. Digital representation can also be used to increase the variety of actors participating in exploratory activities (Benkler, 2002). When the objects being worked on are digital – for example, digital representations of both genetic structures and the molecules targeting them – it is possible to collaborate widely in therapeutic drug discovery (Kolbjørnsrud, 2018). Increasingly, digital representation enables digital agents to collaborate with human actors. For example, Autodesk's collaborative design platform includes intelligent "generative design" software that creates and evaluates numerous alternative engineering models based on criteria provided by engineers who, in turn, choose among a set of viable solutions. Participation in these various forms of "open innovation" sensitizes organization members that concepts, technologies, and other resources are plentiful and that the organization has to be open to learning about and experimenting with them (Chesbrough & Rosenbloom, 2002).

Exploitation entails refining and reusing existing solutions (March 1991; Miles & Snow, 1978). Digital refinement is exemplified by the frequent operating system upgrades provided by companies such as Microsoft and Tesla. Similarly, digital twins – digital replicas of physical entities such as machines or buildings – are used to optimize the operating performance of their corresponding physical entities. Siemens applies digital twins along its entire value chain in order to improve efficiency and minimize failure rates. Digital reuse of existing solutions is exemplified by the distribution of software and other forms of digital content, such as music and video, to hundreds of millions of users by Apple, Netflix, and Spotify at close to zero marginal cost. Furthermore, the proliferation of software and the exchange of digital content are often fueled by network effects – the value to users increases with adoption by other users (Katz & Shapiro, 1985). Network effects can provide firms with substantial exploitation gains.

Balancing exploration and exploitation is crucial to organizational survival and performance (March, 1991). Organizations that emphasize exploration to the detriment of exploitation may fail to appropriate value from their search for new solutions, whereas organizations that overexploit face technological obsolescence (Christensen & Bower, 1996; March, 1991; Miles & Snow, 1978). Furthermore, concentrating too heavily on exploitation carries a hidden cost – it reduces the likelihood of finding new solutions (Holland, 1992). Generally speaking, digitization accelerates the pace of change. Therefore, the need for organizations to adapt faster in order to maintain dynamic fit tilts the optimal balance in favor of exploration over exploitation.

Actor-Oriented Organizing

An organization's ability to adapt is a function of its design. Organizing involves grouping and integrating resources in structures and processes that allow the control and coordination of activities (Lawrence & Lorsch, 1967; Puranam, 2018). Control entails setting goals, monitoring progress toward achievement of those goals, and allocating resources. Coordination refers to managing activity and resource interdependencies. A traditional organization is arranged hierarchically – that is, control and coordination are achieved through an authority structure in which superiors plan and coordinate the activities of subordinates, allocate resources, and resolve problems and conflicts (Simon, 1962). A hierarchical organization can be effective in stable and predictable environments but not in high-velocity, uncertain, complex, and ambiguous environments that require greater organizational adaptability (Davis, Eisenhardt, & Bingham, 2009; Sull & Eisenhardt, 2015). In those environments, we observe the emergence of actor-oriented forms of organizing, which minimize the use of hierarchical mechanisms to achieve control and coordination of groups of actors (Fjeldstad et al., 2012). For example, during Hurricane Katrina in 1995, the centralized response of the Federal Emergency Management Agency was late and insufficient, whereas effective relief came from emergent groups that used social media to organize resources and coordinate activities (Majchrzak, Jarvenpaa, & Hollingshead, 2007).

Actor-Oriented Organizational Architecture

Actor-oriented organizing is an administrative technology centered on actors and their means of organizing relationships with other actors (Fjeldstad et al., 2012). An actor is any entity capable of acting intentionally, for example, an individual, group, or organization (King, Felin, & Whetten, 2010). The actor-oriented organizational approach has three elements: (1) *actors* who have the capabilities and values to self-organize; (2) *commons* shared by the actors; and (3) *protocols, processes,* and *infrastructures* that enable multiactor collaboration. By focusing on actors and their means of interaction, actor-oriented organizing enables organizations to continuously adapt to the opportunities and challenges arising in their environments. In actor-oriented organizing, control and coordination are achieved through both direct and indirect interactions among the actors rather than through hierarchical planning, delegation, and integration.

In contrast to hierarchical organizing, in which superiors assemble and allocate resources, in actor-oriented organizing, actors must possess the capabilities and values to self-organize. They identify and connect with potential collaborators, create a shared understanding of their situation, mutually align their goals, and jointly coordinate their activities. Competent actors who treat each other fairly and value their relationship as much as their own self-interest can collaborate effectively (Snow, 2015). When actors share collaborative values, employ the norm of reciprocity in their relationships, and trust one another in the self-governance process, they can self-organize resources with only minimal use of hierarchical mechanisms (Hess & Ostrom, 2006; Ostrom, 1990, 2010; Wilson, Ostrom, & Cox, 2013). Increasingly, physical and virtual digital agents complement human actors in the performance of activities. Equipping digital agents with artificial intelligence – the ability of machines to sense, comprehend, act, and learn (Simon & Newell, 1958; Winston, 1992) – enables them to collaborate with both human and other digital actors.

In actor-oriented organizing, actors connect using protocols and infrastructures (Dahl & Nygaard, 1966; Fjeldstad et al., 2012; Hewitt, 1977). A protocol is a widely understood set of rules that guide actors in their communications and transactions. Protocols and processes, frequently embedded in software as interfaces and algorithms, guide the self-assembly of actors around tasks and the mutual adjustment of their behavior. For example, in Accenture's processes for team formation, senior consultants post projects that potential participants from the global pool of more than 500,000 employees can join. Furthermore, consultants can search for colleagues with relevant capabilities for a particular task or project.

Commons are resources collectively owned and shared by actors. Commons can be physical resources, intangible resources such as knowledge, or task environment representations that support shared situation awareness (Ziemke, Schaefer, & Endsley, 2017). Ostrom (2000) showed that commons can be governed collectively when users have a shared understanding of the consequences of their actions, follow common rules for resource use, and are transparent in their behavior. A commons of particular importance to large-scale modern organizing is a digital representation of the task environment, which serves as the basis of actors' situation awareness – an up-to-date understanding of problems and opportunities as well as the availability of resources to address them. Situationally aware actors have a greater likelihood of making appropriate decisions and performing well, particularly in complex, dynamic environments (Endsley, 1995). Shared situation awareness is a group concept. It captures overlap in actors' understanding of their situation and is critical to their ability to self-coordinate (Endsley & Jones, 1997). Shared digital task environment representations enable situation awareness among large groups of dispersed human and digital actors. Computer scientists have developed "blackboard systems" – digital task environment representations and associated algorithms – that enable digital actors to assess situations using digital sensors for perceptual inputs and artificial intelligence for interpretation (Pew & Mavor, 1998).

In summary, actor-oriented organizational architecture is focused on the organization's actors: the work they perform and the principles and processes by which they directly and indirectly interact with other internal and external actors. Digital representation of the task environment contributes to shared situation awareness among collaborating actors. Actors use protocols and their associated processes to reduce ambiguity and increase the efficiency and effectiveness of collaboration. The high connectivity and conductivity made possible by the proliferation of the Internet and coevolving communications, transportation, and transaction technologies support the operations of actor-oriented organizations (Chong et al., 2019; Kanter, 2019). Using actor-oriented mechanisms, competent actors pursuing shared goals self-organize with limited need for hierarchical control and coordination (Massa & O'Mahony, 2021)

Table 3.1 *Actor-oriented organizing principles*

Principle	Definition
Self-assembly	Autonomous organizing of actors into teams using advertising and search protocols
Stigmergy	Continuous actor-determined adjustments made to achieve consistency among goals and actions
Algorithmic information processing	Use of algorithms to perform repetitive and computationally intensive tasks
Complementary hierarchical control	Resolving inconsistencies and conflicts by hierarchical means when required

Source: Author original

Principles of Actor-Oriented Organizing

Actor-oriented organizing is based on core principles of cybernetics and computer science, specifically self-assembly of agents and resources, mutual adjustment based on feedback from a shared representation of the task environment, and distributed control and coordination among autonomous agents (Ashby, 1956, 1962; Axelrod, 1984; Dahl & Nygaard, 1966; von Foerster, 1960; Wiener, 1950). The focus of design in actor-oriented organizing is actors and the properties of the relationships that they dynamically form, maintain, and dissolve (Fjeldstad et al., 2012). Designing in this context means creating the specific commons, protocols and procedures, and infrastructures that actors will use to collaborate. See Table 3.1 for a summary of the principles underlying actor-oriented organizing.

Self-assembly. In actor-oriented organizing, actors autonomously form functional relationships. Self-assembly has been extensively studied in science and engineering. It is a central focus in computer science research on intelligent adaptive systems, especially in actor-oriented programming (Hewitt, 1977). Self-assembly requires that actors and other entities have the information necessary to determine the relevance of relationships and can freely form and dissolve relationships as needed (Whitesides & Grzybowski, 2002). When actors are omniscient – that is, they share a complete representation of their situation and can search globally – adaptation to complex environments is greatly simplified (Levinthal & Warglien, 2011).

Increasingly, organizations rely on flexible, temporary teams composed of experts from a variety of disciplines to identify and address emerging problems and opportunities (McChrystal et al., 2015). Adaptation to complex, dynamic conditions requires teams that can work across internal and external environments and have the ability to rapidly reconfigure and change direction (Carboni, Cross, & Edmondson, 2021; Edmondson, 2012). Many teams in the creative arts, engineering, consulting, and research self-assemble, which has been shown to positively affect team performance (Guimera et al., 2005). In actor-oriented organizing, effective self-assembly is supported by advertising and search mechanisms such as actor profiles, custom search engines, and shared task environment representations.

Stigmergy. Actors use stigmergy – the mutual adjustment of actions and goals based on feedback from the task environment – to coordinate and control their activities (Grassé, 1959; Heylighen, 2016). Complex, dynamic environments increase the need for mutual adjustment among actors (Thompson, 1967). Moreover, digital technologies lower the costs of communication among actors and can increase the scope of their interactions and information sharing (Crowston, 1997; Malone & Crowston, 1994), thereby making stigmergic coordination and control increasingly feasible and useful. Stigmergy complements direct communication among actors (Foss, Fredriksen, & Rullani, 2016) and is exemplified by open-source software development where programmers share access to the source code and can adapt their own activities to the current state of the software (Bolici, Howison, & Crowston, 2016). It is also exemplified by large, complex construction projects in which engineers from different disciplines work on a single digital model of the project as it emerges (Saieg et al., 2018) or by firms in the Blade.org community coordinating their actions to achieve interoperability of their respective solutions via the solution repository (Snow et al., 2011). Stigmergic setting of goals is exemplified by Swarm AI$^{©}$, a system that enables a large number of human actors to negotiate goals by indicating and continuously updating their preferences using a game-like graphical computer interface until consensus has been reached. In addition to the human inputs, an intelligent digital agent observes and processes information about preference development and provides feedback to help guide the process toward consensus around a goal (Metcalf, Askey, & Rosenberg, 2019). In summary, stigmergy allows actors to collectively control and coordinate their goals and actions by using a shared representation of the task environment.

Algorithmic information processing. In actor-oriented organizing, digital actors assume tasks that can be performed algorithmically. An algorithm is a step-by-step procedure for processing information. Emerging technologies such as sensors, high-speed mobile data connectivity, artificial intelligence, and cloud computing remove many information-processing constraints and enable algorithmic information processing. Tasks that can be performed algorithmically include inferring patterns in large amounts of data and solving computationally intensive problems. In actor-oriented organizing, algorithms are used in both coordination and control. With respect to coordination, algorithms are used in the division of labor and integration of work (Faraj, Pachidi, & Sayegh, 2018). For control, they are used for purposes such as directing, evaluating, and disciplining actors (Kellogg, Valentine, & Christin, 2020).

Complementary hierarchical control. In actor-oriented organizing, hierarchy is primarily used to create new organizations and support their continued operation and development. Actors with authority launch new initiatives, design their specific elements, and make enabling resources available to other actors. Actors vary with respect to their degree of ownership of the resources used in pursuit of organizational goals. When resources are largely owned by the actors themselves, as found in professional services and creative industries, the actors retain considerable control over their use (Jones et al., 1998; Løwendahl, Revang, & Fosstenløkken, 2001). Resources organized as commons are collectively owned and can be managed by collective rather than hierarchical decision-making (Ostrom, 1990, 2010).

Designing and Leading Actor-Oriented Organizations

With their reliance on self-assembly, mutual adjustment, and algorithmic information-processing, actor-oriented organizations are complex adaptive systems where actors learn and adapt in response to interactions with other actors. How can organization designers turn this abstract concept into workable organizations? Some of the best examples of actor-oriented organizing have developed from existing organizations. For example, when Blade.org was launched in 2006, its purpose was to accelerate the development and commercialization of solutions based on IBM's blade server technology. Blade.org became an organization when eight founding firms (IBM, Intel, and six other computer companies) created an organizational platform that would allow firms in the computer server industry to collaborate with one another in developing interoperable solutions. The founding firms invited twenty-seven prominent technology firms to establish the community. Subsequently, another forty-three firms were accepted into Blade.org from nominations and applications. Firms were nominated and invited based on their technical competence and business reputation. Because all seventy of Blade.org's core firms were competent and trustworthy, the community was able to quickly begin collaborating by using the platform's protocols, processes, and commons. After one year of operation, Blade.org member firms had obtained over a billion dollars in venture funding (Mullins, 2007). Having achieved its mission of quickly establishing a vibrant blade server community, Blade.org ceased operations in 2011. The member firms continued developing and offering their solutions in the blade server marketplace.

Haier, a rapidly growing Chinese multinational corporation in major home appliances, healthcare, and other sectors, exemplifies actor-oriented organizing at large scale. In 2012, Haier initiated a transformation of its hierarchical organization of departments into a group of more than 4,000 self-organizing "microenterprises" (Fischer, Lago, & Liu, 2013; Jiang, Hu, & Wang, 2019; Reeves, Haanæs, & Sinha, 2015). According to CEO Ruimin Zhang, "We replaced the bureaucratic model with a model based on self-employment, self-motivation, and self-organization" (China.org.cn, 2018). Inspired by the idea of an internet-based economy, Zhang designed the Haier organization around platforms that enabled independent microenterprises of ten to fifteen people to form collaborative relationships. Over time, Haier developed more than twenty organizational platforms in diverse categories and services. Microenterprise entrepreneurs were invited to come forward with proposals to join one of the platforms. Accepted proposals included funding supplied by both Haier and the microenterprises. Microenterprises have the freedom and incentives to choose their customers and adapt their network of collaborators to develop and deliver products and services that meet customers' needs. Platforms include a custom search engine that supports the self-assembly of collaborators as well as tools for self-coordination (Li et al., 2020). Product ideas are solicited from users via social media such as Facebook and Twitter. The distribution of rewards among collaborators takes multiple forms, including buyer–seller relationships, joint ownership of patents and other intellectual property, and profit sharing according to predefined formulas (Nunes & Downes, 2016).

ImproveCareNow (ICN) is one of nine large actor-oriented learning healthcare systems in which researchers, clinicians, patients, and parents/caretakers collaborate to cocreate and coproduce care for children with inflammatory bowel disease (Batalden et al., 2016; Britto et al., 2018). ICN's purpose is to improve the effectiveness and efficiency of care for children who have this particular disease. ICN currently includes more than 105 member hospitals in the United States and internationally. It was initiated by Cincinnati Children's Hospital in 2007 in response to a call from the US National Academy of Medicine for the development of learning health systems in which patients and clinicians collaborate to ensure innovation, quality, and value of care (McGinnis, Michael, & Olsen, 2007). Members of ICN have access to a variety of tools that support collaborative development of evidence-based treatments and best practices as well as knowledge sharing across the network. From an actor-oriented perspective, shared goals and values, a common language, a collective mindset, and shared situation awareness allow ICN members to self-organize their activities. Over a five-year period, ICN increased the proportion of patients in remission from 55 percent to 77 percent, thus significantly improving the quality of life for more than 25,000 children (Forrest et al., 2014).

Actor-oriented organizations such as Blade.org, Haier, and ICN are complex adaptive systems. In such organizations, leadership is exercised by "enabling adaptive space" for innovative ideas (Uhl-Bien & Arena, 2017) and by helping actors make sense of emerging events (Weick, 1979). Specifically, Hazy and Uhl-Bien (2015) identify five leadership functions in complex adaptive systems: *generative* – creating aspirations and encouraging experimentation; *administrative* – establishing goals and ensuring that actors have the necessary resources; *community building* – creating a shared sense of identity and purpose; *information gathering* – collecting and synthesizing relevant information from both the external and internal environments; and *information using* – taking actions that contribute to reconfiguring the organization. In Blade.org, committees consisting of representatives from the member firms exercised collective leadership by making sense of solutions emerging from interfirm collaborations and by taking actions that leveraged the future value of those solutions to other member firms. Thus, Blade.org facilitated member firms' coordinated development and commercialization of complex solutions to which the collaborating firms contributed complementary pieces. The Haier example illustrates the substitution of a flat, self-organizing, and continuously adaptable model for a hierarchical model with numerous levels and cumbersome governance processes. In ICN, medical professionals and parents of chronically ill children use actor-oriented principles and processes to organize the development of effective medical treatments and practices.

Conclusion

We believe that a new design paradigm, where the focus is on the individual elements of a system and the nature of their interactions, is becoming increasingly visible across a diverse set of scientific fields. This emerging paradigm reflects the cybernetic concepts of self-assembly of compatible elements and self-coordination via interaction and feedback (Ashby, 1956, 1958; von Foerster, 1960; Wiener, 1950). In science and engineering, the paradigm is seen in systems ranging from nanostructures to self-configuring robots (Whitesides & Grzybowski, 2002). In biology, research scientists have designed cells with a propensity to cooperate in groups and form functional structures adapted to novel circumstances (Kriegman et al., 2020). In computer science, the new paradigm is seen in object- and actor-oriented programming and in the design of the Internet (Dahl & Nygaard, 1966; Hewitt, 1977; Licklider, 1960). Computer science also serves as a source of conceptual models for human organizing (Benkler, 2002), and digital technologies allow for new ways of thinking about how to organize (Snow et al., 2017).

In organization theory, the new design paradigm is evidenced in actor-oriented organizing (Fjeldstad et al., 2012), which relies on enabling protocols and processes to guide collaboration. Actors that are able to continuously self-organize into temporary teams are the key to understanding actor-oriented organizing and its adaptive properties. As the environment changes, presenting new problems and opportunities, actors form new complementary relationships with one another. When particular relationships are no longer functional, the actors dissolve those relationships and form new ones. Infrastructures that connect actors, along with shared representations of task environments, support actor-oriented organizing. The resulting organizations are complex adaptive systems characterized by emergence – they exhibit properties and behaviors that emerge only when the parts interact in a wider whole (Goldstein, 1999). Leadership in an emergent organization is exercised through sensemaking and generative processes (Garud, Kumaraswamy, & Sambamurthy, 2006; Uhl-Bien & Arena, 2017).

Alfred Chandler, in his classic book *Strategy and Structure* (1962), stated that structure follows strategy. In a highly connected, rapidly changing world, we need dynamic conceptualizations of both strategy and organization. It therefore seems natural, with paradigmatic analogies in biology and technology, to focus on strategizing that guides adaptation and designs that enable continuous organizing of activities and resources.

References

Arthur, W. B. 2009. *The Nature of Technology: What It Is and How It Evolves*. Free Press, New York, NY.

Ashby, W. R. 1947. Principles of the self-organizing dynamic system. *Journal of General Psychology* 37: 125–128.

Ashby, W. R. 1956. *An Introduction to Cybernetics*. Wiley, New York, NY.

Ashby, W. R. 1958. Requisite variety and its implications for the control of complex systems. *Cybernetica* 1(2): 83–99.

Ashby, W. R. 1962. Principles of the self-organizing system. In H. von Foerster and G. J. Zopf (eds.), *Principles of Self-Organization: Transactions of the University of Illinois Symposium*: 255–278. Pergamon Press, London, UK.

Axelrod, R. M. 1984. *The Evolution of Cooperation*. Basic Books, New York, NY.

Barnard, C. I. 1938. *The Functions of the Executive*. Harvard University Press, Cambridge, MA.

Batalden, M., Batalden, P., Margolis, P., Seid, M., Armstrong, G., Opipari-Arrigan, L., & Hartung, H., 2016. Coproduction of healthcare service. *BMJ Quality & Safety* 25(7): 509–517.

Beer, S. 1972. *Brain of the Firm: The Managerial Cybernetics of Organization*. Penguin Press, London, UK.

Benkler, Y. 2002. Coase's penguin, or, Linux and the nature of the firm. *Yale Law Journal* 112(3): 369–446.

Bolici, F., Howison, J., & Crowston, K. 2016. Stigmergic coordination in FLOSS development teams: integrating explicit and implicit mechanisms. *Cognitive Systems Research* 38: 14–22.

Bourgeois III, L. J. & Eisenhardt, K. M. 1988. Strategic decision processes in high-velocity environments: four cases in the microcomputer industry. *Management Science* 34(7): 816–835.

Britto, M. T., Fuller, S. C., Kaplan, H. C., et al. 2018. Using a network organisational architecture to support the development of Learning Healthcare Systems. *BMJ Quality & Safety* 27(11): 937–946.

Brynjolfsson, E. & McAfee, A. 2014. *The Second Machine Age: Work, Progress, and Prosperity in a Time of Brilliant Technologies.* W. W. Norton, New York, NY.

Carboni, I., Cross, R., & Edmondson, A. C. 2021. No team is an island: how leaders shape networked ecosystems for team success. *California Management Review* 64(1): 5–28.

Chandler, A. D. 1962. *Strategy and Structure: Chapters in the History of the Industrial Enterprise.* MIT Press, Cambridge, MA.

Chesbrough, H. & Rosenbloom, R. S. 2002. The role of the business model in capturing value from innovation: evidence from Xerox Corporation's technology spin-off companies. *Journal of Industrial and Corporate Change* 11(3): 529–555.

China.org.cn 2018. Zhang Ruimin lights the fire of management change.

Ciborra, C. U. 1996. The platform organization: Recombining strategies, structures, and surprises. *Organization Science* 7(2): 103–118. www .china.org.cn/business/2018-12/03/content_74233673.htm

Chong, A. Y. L., Lim, E. T. K., Hua, X., Zheng, S., & Tan, C.-W. 2019. Business on chain: a comparative case study of five blockchain-inspired business models. *Journal of the Association for Information Systems* 20(9): 1310–1399.

Christensen, C. M. & Bower, J. L. 1996. Customer power, strategic investment, and the failure of leading firms. *Strategic Management Journal* 17(3): 197–218.

Crawford, S. E. & Ostrom, E. 1995. A grammar of institutions. *American Political Science Review* 89(3): 582–600.

Crowston, K. 1997. A coordination theory approach to organizational process design. *Organization Science* 8(2): 157–175.

Cusumano, M. A., Gawer, A., & Yoffie, D. B. 2019. *The Business of Platforms: Strategy in the Age of Digital Competition, Innovation, and Power.* HarperCollins, New York, NY.

Dahl, O.-J. & Nygaard, K. 1966. SIMULA: an ALGOL-based simulation language. *Communications of the ACM* 9(9): 671–678.

Davis, J. P., Eisenhardt, K. M., & Bingham, C. B. 2009. Optimal structure, market dynamism, and the strategy of simple rules. *Administrative Science Quarterly* 54(3): 413–452.

Drucker, P. F. 1954. *The Practice of Management: A Study of the Most Important Function in American Society.* Harper & Brothers, New York, NY.

Edmondson, A. C. 2012. Teamwork on the fly. *Harvard Business Review* 90(4): 72–80.

Endsley, M. R. 1995. Toward a theory of situation awareness in dynamic systems. *Human Factors* 37(1): 32–64.

Endsley, M. R. & Jones, W. M. 1997. *Situation Awareness, Information Dominance, and Information Warfare.* Technical Report 97–01. Endsley Consulting, Belmont, CA.

Ethiraj, S. K. & Levinthal, D. 2004. Bounded rationality and the search for organizational architecture: an evolutionary perspective on the design of organizations and their evolvability. *Administrative Science Quarterly* 49(3): 404–437.

Faraj, S., Pachidi, S., & Sayegh, K. 2018. Working and organizing in the age of the learning algorithm. *Information and Organization* 28(1): 62–70.

Fischer, B., Lago, U., & Liu, F. 2013. *Reinventing Giants: How Chinese Global Competitor Haier Has Changed the Way Big Companies Transform.* Jossey-Bass, San Francisco, CA.

Fjeldstad, Ø. D., Snow, C. C., Miles, R. E., & Lettl, C. 2012. The architecture of collaboration. *Strategic Management Journal* 33(6): 734–750.

Forrest, C. B., Margolis, P., Seid, M., & Colletti, R. B. 2014. PEDSnet: how a prototype pediatric learning health system is being expanded into a national network. *Health Affairs* 33(7): 1171–1177.

Foss, N. J., Frederiksen, L., & Rullani, F., 2016. Problem-formulation and problem-solving in self-organized communities: How modes of communication shape project behaviors in the free open-source software community. *Strategic Management Journal* 37(13): 2589–2610.

Furr, N., Ozcan, P., & Eisenhardt, K. M. 2022. What is digital transformation? Core tensions facing established companies on the global stage. *Global Strategy Journal* 12(4): 595–618.

Garud, R., Kumaraswamy, A., & Sambamurthy, V. 2006. Emergent by design: performance and transformation at Infosys Technologies. *Organization Science* 17(2): 277–286.

Gawer, A. & Cusumano, M. A. 2014. Industry platforms and ecosystem innovation. *Journal of Product Innovation Management* 31(3): 417–433.

Gershgorn, D. 2016. Elon Musk's artificial intelligence group opens a "gym" to train A.I. Popular Science. April 27. www.popsci.com/elon-musks-artificial-intelligence-group-opens-gym-to-train-ai/.

Girod, S. J. G. & Whittington, R. 2015. Change escalation processes and complex adaptive systems: from incremental reconfigurations to discontinuous restructuring. *Organization Science* 26(5): 1520–1535.

Girod, S. J. G. & Whittington, R. 2017. Reconfiguration, restructuring and firm performance: dynamic capabilities and environmental dynamism. *Strategic Management Journal* 38(5): 1121–1133.

Goldstein, J. 1999. Emergence as a construct: history and issues. *Emergence* 1(1): 49–72.

Goldstein, J. 2007. A new model of emergence and its leadership implications. In J. Hazy, J. Goldstein, and B. Lichtenstein (eds.), *Complex Systems Leadership Theory*: 61–92. ICSE Publishing, Mansfield, MA.

Grassé, P. P. 1959. La reconstruction du nid et les coordinations interindividuelles chez Bellicositermes natalensis et Cubitermes sp. la théorie de la stigmergie: Essai d'interprétation du comportement des termites constructeurs. *Insectes Sociaux* 6(1): 41–80.

Greer, C. R., Lusch, R. F., & Vargo, S. L. 2016. A service perspective. *Organizational Dynamics* 1(45): 28–38.

Guimera, R., Uzzi, B., Spiro, J., & Amaral, L. A. N. 2005. Team assembly mechanisms determine collaboration network structure and team performance. *Science* 308(5722): 697–702.

Hayek, F. A. 1945. The use of knowledge in society. *American Economic Review* 35(4): 519–530.

Hazy, J. K. & Uhl-Bien, M. 2015. Towards operationalizing complexity leadership: how generative, administrative and community-building leadership practices enact organizational outcomes. *Leadership* 11(1): 79–104.

Hess, C. & Ostrom, E. 2006. *Understanding Knowledge as a Commons: From Theory to Practice*. MIT Press, Cambridge, MA.

Hewitt, C. 1977. Viewing control structures as patterns of passing messages. *Artificial Intelligence* 8(3): 323–364.

Heylighen, F. 2016. Stigmergy as a universal coordination mechanism I: definition and components. *Cognitive Systems Research* 38: 4–13.

Hodson, H. 2014. The AI boss that deploys Hong Kong's subway engineers. *New Scientist*. July 2. www.newscientist.com/article/mg22329764-000-the-ai-boss-that-deploys-hong-kongs-subway-engineers.

Holland, J. H. 1992. Genetic algorithms. *Scientific American* 267(1): 66–73.

Jiang, S., Hu, Y., & Wang, Z. 2019. Core firm based view on the mechanism of constructing an enterprise innovation ecosystem: a case study of Haier Group. *Sustainability* 11: 3108–3144.

Jones, C., Hesterly, W. S., Fladmoe-Lindquist, K., & Borgatti, S. P. 1998. Professional service constellations: how strategies and capabilities influence collaborative stability and change. *Organization Science* 9(3): 396–410.

Kanter, R. M. 2015. *Move: Putting America's Infrastructure Back in the Lead*. W. W. Norton, New York, NY.

Kanter, R. M. 2019. The future of bureaucracy and hierarchy in organizational theory: a report from the field. In P. Bourdieu, J. S. Coleman, and Z. W. Coleman (eds.), *Social Theory for a Changing Society*: 63–93. Routledge, New York, NY.

Katz, M. L. & C. Shapiro. 1985. Network externalities, competition, and compatibility. *American Economic Review* 75(3): 424–440.

Kellogg, K. C., Orlikowski, W. J., & Yates, J. 2006. Life in the trading zone: structuring coordination across boundaries in postbureaucratic organizations. *Organization Science* 17(1): 22–44.

Kellogg, K. C., Valentine, M. A., & Christin, A. 2020. Algorithms at work: the new contested terrain of control. *Academy of Management Annals* 14(1): 336–410.

King, B. G., Felin, T., & Whetten, D. A. 2010. Perspective – finding the organization in organizational theory: a meta-theory of the organization as a social actor. *Organization Science* 21(1): 290–305.

Kolbjørnsrud, V. 2018. Collaborative organizational forms: on communities, crowds, and new hybrids. *Journal of Organization Design* 7(1): 1–21.

Kriegman, S., Blackiston, D., Levin, M., & Bongard, J. 2020. A scalable pipeline for designing reconfigurable organisms. *Proceedings of the National Academy of Sciences* 117(4): 1853–1859.

Lawrence, P. R. & Lorsch, J. W. 1967. Differentiation and integration in complex organizations. *Administrative Science Quarterly* 12(1): 1–47.

Levinthal, D. A. & Warglien, M. 1999. Landscape design: designing for local action in complex worlds. *Organization Science* 10(3): 342–357.

Li, X., Cao, J., Liu, Z., & Luo, X. 2020. Sustainable business model based on digital twin platform network: The inspiration from Haier's case study in China. *Sustainability* 12(3): 936.

Licklider, J. C. R. 1960. Man-computer symbiosis. *IRE Transactions on Human Factors in Electronics* HFE-1: 4–11.

Løwendahl, B. R., Revang, Ø., & Fosstenløkken, S. M. 2001. Knowledge and value creation in professional service firms: a framework for analysis. *Human Relations* 54(7): 911–931.

Majchrzak, A., Jarvenpaa, S. L., & Hollingshead, A. B. 2007. Coordinating expertise among emergent groups responding to disasters. *Organization Science* 18(1): 147–161.

Malone, T. W. & Crowston, K. 1994. The interdisciplinary study of coordination. *ACM Computing Surveys* 26(1): 87–119.

March, J. G. 1991. Exploration and exploitation in organizational learning. *Organization Science* 2(1): 71–87.

March, J. G. & Simon, H. A. 1958. *Organizations*. Wiley, New York, NY.

Massa, F. G. & O'Mahony, S. 2021. Order from chaos: how networked activists self-organize by creating a participation architecture. *Administrative Science Quarterly* 66(4): 1037–1083.

McChrystal, G. S., Silverman, D., Collins, T., & Fussell, C. 2015. *Team of Teams: New Rules of Engagement for a Complex World*. Penguin Random House, New York, NY.

McGinnis, J., Michael, D. A., & Olsen, L. A. eds. 2007. *The Learning Healthcare System: Workshop Summary*. National Academies Press.

Metcalf, L., Askay, D. A., & Rosenberg, L. B. 2019. Keeping humans in the loop: pooling knowledge through artificial swarm intelligence to improve business decision making. *California Management Review* 61(4): 84–109.

Miles, R. E. & Snow, C. C. 1978. *Organizational Strategy, Structure, and Process*. McGraw-Hill, New York, NY.

Miles, R. E. & Snow, C. C. 1984. Fit, failure and the hall of fame. *California Management Review* 26(3): 10–28.

Miles, R. E. & Snow, C. C. 1994. *Fit, Failure, and the Hall of Fame: How Companies Succeed or Fail*. Free Press, New York, NY.

Mullins, R. 2007. IBM's Blade.org group attracts investors. IDG News Service. www.networkworld.com/article/2295419/ibm-s-blade-org-group-attracts-investors.html

North, D. C. & Wallis, J. J. 1994. Integrating institutional change and technical change in economic history: a transaction cost approach. *Journal of Institutional and Theoretical Economics (JITE)/Zeitschrift für die gesamte Staatswissenschaft* 150(4): 609–624.

Nunes, P. & Downes, L. 2016. At Haier and Lenovo, Chinese-style open innovation. Forbes.com, 26 Sept.

Ostrom, E. 1990. *Governing the Commons: The Evolution of Institutions for Collective Action*. Cambridge University Press, Cambridge, UK.

Ostrom, E. 2000. Collective action and the evolution of social norms. *Journal of Economic Perspectives* 14(3): 137–158.

Ostrom, E. 2010. Beyond markets and states: polycentric governance of complex economic systems (2009 Nobel Prize Lecture). *Transnational Corporations Review* 2(2): 1–12.

Peters, A. 2019. How 3D printing is making prosthetics cheap and accessible, even in remote places. *Fast Company*. June 4. www.fastcompany.com/90358495/how-3d-printing-is-making-prosthetics-cheap-and-accessible-even-in-remote-places.

Pew, R. W. & Mavor, A. S. 1998. *Modeling Human and Organizational Behavior: Application to Military Simulations*. The National Academies Press, Washington, DC.

Piller, F. T., Weller, C., & Kleer, R. 2015. Business models with additive manufacturing – opportunities and challenges from the perspective of economics and management. In C. Brecher (ed.), *Advances in Production Technology*: 39–48. Springer, New York, NY.

Puranam, P. 2018. *The Microstructure of Organizations*. Oxford University Press, Oxford, UK.

Reeves, M., Haanæs, K., & Sinha, J. 2015. *Your Strategy Needs a Strategy: How to Choose and Execute the Right Approach*. Harvard Business Review Press, Boston, MA.

Saieg, P., Sotelino, E. D., Nascimento, D., & Caiado, R. G. G. 2018. Interactions of building information modeling, lean and sustainability on the architectural, engineering and construction industry: a systematic review. *Journal of Cleaner Production* 174: 788–806.

Seid, M., Hartley, D. M., Dellal, G., Myers, S., & Margolis, P. A. 2019. Organizing for collaboration: an actor-oriented architecture in ImproveCareNow. *Learning Health Systems* 4(1): e10205.

Setia, P., Venkatesh, V., & Joglekar, S. 2013. Leveraging digital technologies: how information quality leads to localized capabilities and customer service performance. *MIS Quarterly* 37(2): 565–590.

Shannon, C. E. & Weaver, W. 1949. *A Mathematical Theory of Communication*. University of Illinois Press, Urbana, IL.

Shapiro, C. & Varian, H. R. 1999. *Information Rules: A Strategic Guide to the Network Economy*. Harvard Business School Press, Boston, MA.

Simon, H. A. 1947. *Administrative Behavior: A Study of Decision-Making Processes in Administrative Organizations*. Macmillan, New York, NY.

Simon, H. A. 1962. The architecture of complexity. *Proceedings of the American Philosophical Society* 106(6): 467–482.

Simon, H. A. 1969. *The Sciences of the Artificial*. The MIT Press, Cambridge, MA.

Simon, H. A. 1993. Strategy and organizational evolution. *Strategic Management Journal* 14(S2): 131–142.

Simon, H. A. & Newell, A. 1958. Heuristic problem solving: the next advance in operations research. *Operations Research* 6(1): 1–10.

Snow, C. C. 2015. Organizing in the age of competition, cooperation, and collaboration. *Journal of Leadership & Organizational Studies* 22(4): 433–442.

Snow, C. C., Fjeldstad, Ø. D., & Langer, A. M. 2017. Designing the digital organization. *Journal of Organization Design* 6(1): 1–13.

Snow, C. C., Fjeldstad, Ø. D., Lettl, C., & Miles, R. E. 2011. Organizing continuous product development and commercialization: the collaborative community of firms model. *Journal of Product Innovation Management* 28(1): 3–16.

Sull, D. & Eisenhardt, K. M. 2015. *Simple Rules: How to Thrive in a Complex World*. Houghton Mifflin Harcourt, Boston.

Thompson, J. D. 1967. *Organizations in Action: Social Science Bases of Administrative Theory*. McGraw-Hill, New York, NY.

Uhl-Bien, M. 2021. Complexity and COVID-19: leadership and followership in a complex world. *Journal of Management Studies* 58(5): 1400–1404.

Uhl-Bien, M. & Arena, M. 2017. Complexity leadership: enabling people and organizations for adaptability. *Organizational Dynamics* 46: 9–20.

Uhl-Bien, M. & Arena, M. 2018. Leadership for organizational adaptability: a theoretical synthesis and integrative framework. *The Leadership Quarterly* 29: 89–104.

Uhl-Bien, M., Marion, R., & McKelvey, B. 2007. Complexity leadership theory: shifting leadership from the industrial age to the knowledge era. *The Leadership Quarterly* 18(4): 298–318.

Varian, H. R. 2000. Buying, sharing and renting information goods. *Journal of Industrial Economics* 48(4): 473–488.

von Foerster, H. 1960. On self-organizing systems and their environments. In H. von Foerster (ed.), *Understanding Understanding: Essays on Cybernetics and Cognition*: 1–20. Springer, New York, NY.

von Hippel, E. & von Krogh, G. 2003. Open source software and the "private-collective" innovation model: issues for organization science. *Organization Science* 14(2): 209–223.

Weick, K. E. 1979. *The Social Psychology of Organizing*, 2nd ed. Addison-Wesley, New York, NY.

Whitesides, G. M. & Grzybowski, B. 2002. Self-assembly at all scales. *Science* 295(5564): 2418–2421.

Wiener, N. 1950. *The Human Use of Human Beings: Cybernetics and Society*. Houghton Mifflin, Boston, MA.

Williamson, O. E. 1985. *The Economic Institutions of Capitalism: Firms, Markets, Relational Contracting*. Free Press, New York, NY.

Wilson, D. S., Ostrom, E., & Cox, M. E. (2013). Generalizing the core design principles for the efficacy of groups. *Journal of Economic Behavior & Organization* 90: S21–S32.

Winston, P. H. 1992. *Artificial Intelligence*, 3rd ed. Addison-Wesley, Reading, MA.

Ziemke, T., Schaefer, K. E., & Endsley, M. 2017. Situation awareness in human-machine interactive systems. *Cognitive Systems Research* 46(1): 1–2.

4 | *Collaborative Conflict Management*

VIVIANNA FANG HE AND PHANISH PURANAM

The Borg Collective from the science fiction television series *Star Trek* is a single "hive mind" that inhabits multiple bodies. All species the Collective encounters are assimilated into it, and resistance, as the Collective frequently points out, is futile. Once assimilated, all agents lose their individual distinctiveness (i.e., they then know and want the same things). With identical knowledge and perfectly aligned goals, working together becomes easy and organization design unnecessary. For us humans, neither is true – we know and want different things. We live in a world where aspirations to collectively do more than what any one of us can individually accomplish coexist with large differences in information and interests across individuals.

Organizations can be viewed as goal-directed systems of collaboration. Organizing is a technology – perhaps humanity's oldest one – that allows us to structure collaboration among individuals with diverse knowledge and interests in order to achieve a goal. Collaboration occurs both within and across organizations. Within firms and other types of organizations, collaboration is manifested in intra- and inter-team departmental or divisional work. Between organizations, collaboration occurs in strategic alliances, joint ventures, partnerships, consortia, and ecosystems (Gulati, Puranam, & Tushman, 2012). In all cases, collaboration is motivated by potential synergies from acting together.

When collaboration succeeds in creating the "unity of effort required by the demands of the environment" (Lawrence & Lorsch, 1967: 11), effective integration of effort has occurred. However, two potential problems may prevent the achievement of unified effort. First, personal agency may inhibit the willingness to cooperate (Prendergast, 1999). Shirking and free-riding are extreme manifestations of cooperation problems. Second, collaboration can be impeded by knowledge-related coordination problems. Differences in what people know and believe – knowledge gaps – can lead to breakdowns in collaboration even when everybody is motivated to contribute to a desired collective outcome (Camerer & Knez, 1996; Heath & Staudenmayer, 2000). Both sets of challenges may coexist, with one amplifying the other (Kogut & Metiu, 2001).

Authority has provided the standard solution to overcome cooperation and coordination challenges, at least in the economic sphere (Coase, 1937; Freeland & Zuckerman, 2018; Lee & Edmondson, 2017). Authority is the legitimate ability of A to demand obedient behavior from B within a specified realm of actions (Barnard, 1938; Simon, 1947; Weber, 1922). The source of the legitimacy and enforcement distinguishes formal from informal authority. Formal authority relies on norms outside the focal organization for their legitimacy and enforcement. However, exceptions that do not seem to rely on either form of authority do exist. In organizations such as "boss-less" firms, online communities, and common-pool resource communities, members collaborate with limited or no dependence on authority (superiors in a hierarchy). These and similar types of organizations can be viewed as examples of collaborative, nonhierarchical organizing (Adler & Heckscher, 2018; Heckscher & Adler, 2006; Morgan, 2012).

Our survey of the research literature, as well as our experience with and observations of organizations, leads us to two broad conclusions. First, to understand why authority has been the usual solution to collaboration at scale requires us to examine its critical role in managing conflicts. Conflicts can be broadly viewed as breakdowns, either implicit or explicit, in coordination and cooperation. This implies that *organizing without authority is fundamentally about managing conflicts without recourse to authority*. Second, across collaborative organizations in a variety of contexts, we observe that strategies to manage conflicts focus heavily on *prevention* as well as *resolution*. Leveraging authority to design in a way that reduces the need for active intervention constitutes a "hidden hand" approach to producing order, distinct from both the "visible hand" in managerial hierarchies and the "invisible hand" in markets. We draw on the actor-oriented framework introduced by Fjeldstad et al. (2012), who distinguish between modifying the *properties of actors* within the system and modifying the *properties of interactions among actors* as a basis to manage conflict. Moreover, we point to the specific ways in which those modifications can help manage conflict through prevention as against resolution.

Our chapter is organized as follows. We begin to answer our central question – how can organizations engage in collaboration without relying on authority – by discussing the problems caused by authority and the importance of searching for viable alternatives. This is followed by a discussion of the relationship between authority and collaboration. For collaboration to be effective, authority must be able to resolve conflicts when they occur or prevent conflicts from occurring in the first place. We compare hierarchical and nonhierarchical conflict management mechanisms. We then discuss studies that have examined the problem of collaboration without authority in different empirical contexts, specifically boss-less firms, online communities, and common-pool resource communities. We close with a synthesis of what we have learned about collaborative conflict management and implications of these lessons for organization design.

Why the Search for Alternatives to Authority Is Worthwhile

Hierarchies of authority have provided the foundation for work relationships for millennia, reaching unprecedented levels of complexity, scale, and scope after the Industrial Revolution (Chandler, 1962). Even though a primary function of multilayered authority structures is to manage conflicts, their "multilayered" nature may inhibit their ability to do so (Puranam, 2018). Information is distorted or lost in multilayered systems through filtering, and control is impeded by passing through layers of hierarchical delegation (March & Simon, 1958). Information and control losses lie at the root of common complaints about hierarchies such as their slow responses and adaptation to changes in the environment (Mortensen & Haas, 2018).

According to evolutionary psychology, hierarchical organizing is alien to the social organizations of our ancestors (Nicholson, 1997; Van Vugt, 2006). Although culturally conditioned over time and across contexts (Henrich, 2017), universal human values lean toward egalitarianism and autonomy (Brown, 1991; Pittman & Zeigler, 2007; Ryan & Deci, 2018). While various types of hierarchical organizations, including families, churches, militaries, and corporations, have appeared and flourished, it is unlikely that the biological basis of human psychology has changed much (Cosmides & Tooby, 1997; Van Vugt, 2017; Van Vugt & Ahuja, 2011). Thus, human preferences for egalitarianism, autonomy, and fairness appear to be misaligned with hierarchical organizing. Moreover, aspects of today's organizational environments appear to justify a search for alternatives to hierarchy. First, collaborative, nonhierarchical organizations are growing in prominence. We need to understand these organizations as possible alternatives to hierarchical organizing. Second, for an increasing proportion of participants in the labor force, such as Millennials, it is important to find ways to organize outside the shadow of authority (Laloux, 2014; Lee & Edmondson, 2017). Third, digital technologies enable large-scale collaboration that does not rely heavily on authority. Those technologies include tools for online collaboration as well as algorithms that can perform managerial functions, including monitoring and coordination (Aggarwal, Posen, & Workiewicz, 2017; Malone, 2016).

We have more or less come to terms with working in and being surrounded by hierarchical organizational structures. That said, factors such as a rise in living standards, the availability of alternative economic opportunities, and changing attitudes about wealth and power inequality are stimulating more expressions of the desire to escape the stifling aspects of authority. In fact, even modern corporations, despite all the negative imagery that bureaucracy evokes, are quite different in their use of authority than their earlier brethren – governance of the modern corporation typically combines hierarchy and consent (Freeland, 1996).

Key to Successful Collaboration: Managing Conflicts

Collaboration requires cooperation and coordination across multiple actors. Impediments to collaboration can arise in the form of limited motivation (agency problems and cooperation failures) and information availability (knowledge gaps and coordination failures). Insofar as collaboration is instantiated by unity of action (Lawrence & Lorsch, 1967), it is useful to conceptualize breakdowns of collaboration – due to either limited motivation or limited information, or a combination of both – as conflicts. For our purposes, we do not distinguish between different forms of conflict (e.g., process, task, or relationship conflict) (DeChurch, Mesmer-Magnus, & Doty, 2013). We consider all breakdowns in collaboration to manifest as conflicts, which include disagreements and disputes that may be explicit (e.g., disputes arising from coordination or cooperation failures) or implicit (e.g., withholding of effort or undetected misunderstandings). A conflict is, thus, synonymous with a failure in collaboration.

Why Large-Scale Collaboration Is Hard to Sustain

It is a well-known property of groups that their ability to function cohesively is adversely affected by large size. The impact of group size on the cumulation of challenges to collaboration typically increases exponentially. To see this, consider that as the number of interacting peers increases, the number of potential dyadic interactions increases as a quadratic function. Furthermore, the probability that any given interaction suffers a breakdown in peer-to-peer collaboration because of motivation and/or information-related reasons will also increase with group size. One reason this occurs is that the possibility of free-riding increases if rewards are held constant while increasing the number of contributors (Kollock, 1998; Prendergast, 1999). Another reason is that trust and reciprocity norms may be harder to maintain in larger groups, given the limits of human capacity to keep track of large numbers of individuals in their social environment (Dunbar, 1992). In sum, increasing group size increases the number of interactions as well as the risk that each interaction experiences a collaboration failure. Both act as constraints on scaling collaboration.

As group size increases, so does the cumulative number of failures of collaboration the group experiences. This is always problematic for group performance that depends on collaborative interactions but particularly so if group performance requires all (or a significant majority) of interactions to be effective in terms of collaboration. Consider the original example provided by Adam Smith (1776: 5): Pin making can be divided into "eighteen distinct operations, which, in some manufactories are all performed by distinct hands." Prior to specialization – each individual performs all eighteen operations – group output was simply a linear increase in individual output with no need for collaboration (i.e., neither cooperation nor coordination is required). But with specialization, the output of the eighteen individuals each performing one specific task depended on a large amount of collaboration between them (the different parts must fit each other and be produced in volumes that prevent idle time, etc.). Total output thus becomes vulnerable to effective collaboration between many (if not all) of the eighteen actors (Puranam, Raveendran, & Knudsen, 2012).

How Authority Can Facilitate Collaboration at Scale

Authority can play a useful role in avoiding collaboration failures, either (1) by lowering, through redesign and reorganization, the risk that an interaction experiences a failure of collaboration (prevention) or (2) by acting as a mechanism for conflict resolution when conflicts inevitably arise (resolution). Authority can prevent conflict by reducing the chances that any interaction ends in collaboration failure. Giving one agent the authority to monitor and reward (or sanction) other agents who may be tempted to shirk or free-ride can mitigate agency and cooperation problems (Alchian & Demsetz, 1972; Williamson, 1975). By making the knowledgeable individual in a domain the authority figure for that domain (Demsetz, 1988), and letting this individual direct the actions of others, their efforts will be effectively integrated. Similarly, by imposing the same decision premises or assumptions on multiple agents, their actions can effectively be coordinated without the need for them to communicate directly with one another (March & Simon, 1958). Such manifestations of authority can prevent conflicts from arising in the first place.

If conflicts do arise, authority can remedy the limits of peer-to-peer dispute resolution. At the dyadic level, it is easy to imagine most conflicts being resolved bilaterally by peers. With large numbers of individuals, however, peer-to-peer resolution of conflict becomes problematic. Often, it is useful to authorize an individual to decide. The role of authority as "referee" is an alternative to peer-to-peer consensus (in any form, including voting) in conflict resolution (March & Simon, 1958).

To summarize, authority helps to scale collaboration by either preventing disputes and conflicts from arising in the first place or, alternatively, resolving them when peer-to-peer dispute resolution proves insufficient. This leads to an important implication: For collaborative organizing to work, conflicts must be rare or peer-to-peer conflict resolution mechanisms must be highly effective (or both). With this insight in mind, we now turn to a diverse set of examples for lessons on how to organize collaboration – specifically, how to manage conflicts without relying on authority.

A Survey of Collaborative Organizing

Organizational scholars have long recognized that culture is a potentially viable alternative to hierarchical control to achieve collaboration in formal organizations (O'Reilly & Chatman, 1996; Ouchi, 1980). When bureaucracy fails to induce individuals to accomplish coordination and cooperation through hierarchy, collaboration may result from leveraging a variety of social mechanisms such as values and norms (Adler & Heckscher, 2018; Ostrom, 2005). Accordingly, when examining the literature on collaborative conflict management, we were particularly sensitive to the role of cultural elements that might serve as substitutes to authority. Specifically, we looked at scope (what aspects of culture are important for collaboration?) and designability (despite being an emergent phenomenon, can cultural elements be designed to some extent?) (Schein, 2004). We were particularly concerned with possible design interventions that produce cultural elements supportive of collaboration. In Table 4.1, we present a summary of our findings regarding collaborative versus authority-based conflict management.

Boss-Less Firms

There has been recent scholarly interest in organizations that operate without managerial hierarchies (Freeland & Zuckerman, 2018; Lee & Edmondson, 2017; Puranam, Alexy, & Reitzig, 2014). There is as yet no consensus on the viability and scalability of such forms, and opinions vary widely (Burton et al., 2017; Foss & Dobrajska, 2015; Laloux, 2014; Malone, 2004; Turco, 2016; Zenger, 2015). Nevertheless, a close look at some of the notable examples may provide insights into how conflict is managed in boss-less organizations. Such organizations include firms producing software (Valve Corporation, Spotify), industrial materials (W. L. Gore, FAVI), consumer goods (Zappos), food products (Morningstar), and nursing services (Buurtzorg). The data on these organizations is largely case-based accounts, including some that rely solely on secondary sources (Askin & Petriglieri, 2016; Felin, 2015; Puranam & Håkonsson, 2015). Nevertheless, it points to some interesting indicators about how conflict may be managed in a nonhierarchical system.

The presumption in many nonhierarchical firms is that conflicts must be resolved primarily through informal, peer-to-peer interaction.

Table 4.1 Collaborative conflict prevention and resolution

Organizational form	Key studies	Scale	Prevention mechanisms		Resolution mechanisms
			Value alignment	Interdependence management	
Hierarchical (authority-based) organizations	Chandler (1962); March and Simon (1958); Mintzberg (1979); Williamson (1975)	All sizes	Incentives	Structuring of workflows; Coordination by plan and standardization	Managerial direction and monitoring; Conflicts resolved by managerial superiors
Boss-less firms	Laloux (2014); Lee & Edmondson (2017); Puranam & Håkonsson (2015)	Small to medium	Self-selection based on values and interests; Maintenance of personal reputation	Modularization of work; Mutual adjustment	Peer-to-peer conflict resolution; Lateral escalation to a wider circle of peers; Process coaches; Withdrawal from the team
Online communities	Jeppesen & Lakhani (2010); Lee & Cole (2003); Piskorski & Gorbatai (2017); Klapper & Reitzig (2018)	All sizes	Self-selection based on values and interests; Maintenance of personal status	Modularization of work; Discussions and actions visible to all participants	Requests for comments in a public forum; Volunteer mediation committee; Formally elected arbitration committee
Common-pool resource communities	Dietz, Ostrom, & Stern (2003); Lansing (1987); Ostrom (1990); Ostrom et al. (1994); Wilson, Ostrom, & Cox (2013)	Medium to large	Shared sense of belonging and common goals; Shared moral and ethical standards	Procedures and rituals; Common knowledge of how actions affect each other	Grievance airing at communal gatherings; Collective choice; Arbitration by chiefs or syndics

Source: Author original

Conflict resolution at Valve Corporation, the Seattle-based video game developer, is reported to largely occur through a consensus process. Teams at Valve are formed through self-selection, with individuals free to choose which teams to join (as well as leave). Valve is also famous for its intense screening processes for recruitment and selection. Its two-stage approach to selection – first into the company and then into teams – produces a high degree of alignment between individuals in terms of goals and mental models. Nonetheless, conflicts may still arise. A Valve employee stated on a blog:

We're all human, so teams sometimes argue (and sometimes passionately) about what to do and how to do it, but people are respectful of each other, and eventually get to a consensus that works. There are stresses and more rigid processes when products are close to shipping, especially when there are hard deadlines for console certification (although shipping for the PC is much more flexible, thanks to Steam). Sometimes people or teams wander down paths that are clearly not working, and then it's up to their peers to point that out and get them back on track.

When conflict arises within teams, resolution is initially attempted within the team, then the next circle of peers, and so radiates outward until the dispute is resolved. This process is described as "lateral escalation" and is not necessarily rapid or always effective (Puranam & Håkonsson, 2015). However, its feasibility may depend on the possible adverse consequences to an individual's reputation and, therefore, to the likelihood of participating in future projects. Reputational forces act against adopting unreasonable positions and may serve as a conflict resolution mechanism. They may also act as a mechanism that prevents the emergence of conflicts in the first place. A concern for one's reputation is an important cultural element in an organization that has under 500 employees, where the probability of encountering each other repeatedly across projects is high. If all else fails, the team can disband, as entry and exit into the team is voluntary. Similar practices have been reported at software developers Menlo Innovations and GitHub (prior to its scaling up through venture capital investment) as well as W. L. Gore, which makes the chemical polymer known as Gore-Tex (Puranam & Håkonsson, 2015).

At Morningstar, the California-based tomato paste processing company, FAVI, the French autoparts maker, and SEMCO, the Brazilian manufacturing company, disputes between colleagues are expected to be resolved peer to peer, with the CEO becoming involved only as a last resort (Laloux, 2014). The reputational consequences of escalation to the CEO are seen as negative. A similar principle was recorded in Procter & Gamble's Organization 2005, an initiative that was put in place in 1996 by then-CEO Edward Lafley (Piskorski & Spadini, 2007). This structure rejected the matrix form and instead created large groupings by geography, function, and product. When conflicts arose, triggered by interdependencies between any of these axes, the first common boss employees in each of the groupings might encounter was Lafley himself. In practice, managers felt pressured to resolve issues bilaterally, as Lafley had apparently indicated that he would intervene the first time a conflict reached him but "find new managers" the second time.

Holacracy is a system for reorganizing hierarchies to increase employee empowerment (Robertson, 2015). One of its consequences is diminished reliance on authority for conflict resolution. Instead, employees working in teams ("circles" in holacracy terminology) follow strict discussion protocols that attempt to produce consensus by systematic iteration of talking turns and information sharing until objections and issues have died down. An escalation process to the next level in the hierarchy exists, but its use is strongly discouraged. As with Valve Corporation, adopters of holacracy also seem to rely on sorting into the company as an important source of alignment on values and attitudes (Askin & Petriglieri, 2016). Zappos, the retail shoe company that is now part of Amazon, reportedly offered a USD 3,000 "bonus" for quitting during the four-week probation period as a way to enhance self-sorting (Laloux, 2014).

Some nonhierarchical organizations create formal roles such as "process coaches." Coaches are not part of the authority structure but instead offer mediation services to manage conflicts. This role has been observed in Buurtzorg, the Dutch nursing services organization that comprises largely autonomous self-managed local teams, as well as in the practice of agile software development, such as practiced at Spotify or ING Group (Laloux, 2014). The advice of process coaches is not binding, but the norm of deference to them seems to be important.

Beyond promoting norms that are conducive to conflict prevention and resolution, it is also noteworthy that boss-less firms go to great lengths to organize workflows in ways that minimize the possibility of conflicts occurring in the first place. A commonality across the aforementioned examples is that, with the exception of Morningstar, every nonhierarchical firm has adopted a team-based organizational structure. The team structure is modular – it comprises multiple teams that are weakly interdependent with each other but strongly interdependent within. This organizing principle is taken seriously enough to avoid centralizing most functions, actively ignoring potential synergies and economies of scale at the expense of keeping interdependencies between teams as small as possible (Laloux, 2014). Put differently, the workflow of these organizations is designed to minimize the occurrence of conflicts between teams, with cultural elements such as values, norms, and concern for reputation helping to manage intrateam conflicts and easing the formation of future teams when that occurs through self-selection (e.g., Valve Corporation, Menlo Innovations, W. L. Gore).

Online Communities

In online communities, traditional bureaucratic features such as employment contracts, reporting relationships, and span of control are absent (Faraj & Johnson, 2011; Faraj et al., 2016; Gulati et al., 2012). Interactions in online communities have a few distinct features. As summarized by He et al. (2020), such interactions are anonymous, simultaneous (i.e., many participants can interact at the same time), transparent (i.e., discussion and actions are often documented permanently and visible to all), and low in media richness (i.e., affords no transmission of facial expression or body language). Moreover, the borders of online communities are unbounded in that participants can enter and exit at will. Individuals self-select into online communities based on similar ideology (a set of beliefs and values), resulting in the prealignment of values (Stewart & Gosain, 2006). Put differently, online communities consist of members who voluntarily assemble and contribute to a common goal (e.g., developing open-source software). Sorting, predominantly at joining, constitutes the basis of strong social norms in online communities.

Community norms such as openness, egalitarianism, and decision-making through consensus tend to prevent conflicts over fundamental values from emerging and escalating. For example, even when online community members are debating as contentious a matter as a license decision, high value alignment allows such debate to be handled with a problem-solving approach and not digressing into endless bargaining (He et al., 2020). Concurrently, modularized product development (Langlois & Garzarelli, 2008), together with a sophisticated "version control" system to track design changes (MacCormack, Rusnak, & Baldwin, 2006), keeps interdependence among agents predictable (Puranam et al., 2012) and helps to curtail conflicts at the operational level.

Nevertheless, because contributors in online communities differ in terms of knowledge, experience, and values, it is inevitable that they will experience conflict. Tensions among developers of the Linux kernel and Firefox (Lee & Cole, 2003; Wang, Shih, & Carroll, 2015), as well as the "edit wars" among Wikipedia editors (Arazy et al., 2015; Kane, Johnson, & Majchrzak, 2012), indicate the potential for conflicts to erupt. Therefore, online communities such as Wikipedia (Forte, Larco, & Bruckman, 2009; Klapper & Reitzig, 2018; Piskorski & Gorbatai, 2017) and NetBeans, a large open-source software community sponsored by Sun Microsystems (Jensen & Scacchi, 2005), have an explicit third-party conflict intervention mechanism in place. When a dispute occurs, the involved parties typically post a "request for comment" in a public forum, inviting all contributors to present their views on how the dispute should be resolved. If those measures prove insufficient, contributors can resort to a volunteer-run mediation committee. Neither the public forum nor the committee can enforce a binding resolution, but they can provide suggestions of what the involved parties could/should do. If both the public forum and mediation committee fail to resolve the dispute, it is escalated to an arbitration committee consisting of formally elected members. The duty of the arbitration committee is to thoroughly investigate the issue and make a public decision (Kittur et al., 2007; Piskorski & Gorbatai, 2017). Failure to follow the arbitration committee's decision is a violation of community norms, thereby threatening the parties' reputation.

Despite the availability of third-party interventions, members of online communities seldom invoke any committee for the purpose of resolving conflict. As Jensen and Scacchi (2005) reported, in the NetBeans community's entire history the board has never acted, and disputes always dissolved before reaching the board. Similarly, observing the Wikipedia community's conflict history, Forte, Larco, and Bruckman (2009: 50) noted, "it seems almost miraculous that editors do not get permanently bogged down in 'edit wars' and that real work gets done at all. Yet somehow, despite common episodes of controversy and disagreement among authors, it does." Given these observations, it appears that online communities have effective mechanisms to prevent conflict from escalating to a point that requires arbitration.

Common-Pool Resource Communities

In communities that organize around particular common pool-resources, members mutually depend on each other and share a goal of preserving the natural resources they rely upon. Despite a superordinate goal shared among members, differences in values and power make disputes likely to occur given the strong interdependencies within those communities. Elinor Ostrom and colleagues (e.g., Dietz et al., 2003; Ostrom, 1990; Ostrom et al., 1994) have provided rich accounts of multilateral dispute resolution in such communities. One prominent example is that of the Horta de Valencia, the irrigation community covering 16,000 hectares of farmland around Valencia (Spain), which has informal courts for conflict resolution (Ostrom, 1990). For centuries, syndics – the chiefs of the irrigation communities – met on Thursday mornings, forming a water court called Tribunal de las Aguas de Valencia. Syndics had the power to arbitrate day-to-day disputes in their local administrative region and levy fines on those they deemed at fault (though the fines are not legally binding). In modern times, a locally elected executive committee provides consultation to the syndics. When large disputes over water rights occurred, they would be settled following an established procedure at Tribunal de las Aguas de Valencia: A presiding officer first questioned those involved and others who might be able to provide additional information, then the members of the court, excluding any syndics whose canals were involved, would make a decision based on the facts of the case. Fines and decisions issued by the water court were recorded.

On the face of it, such institutions represent a form of authority even though they have no basis in the legal regime of the land. However, we nevertheless see such social systems as essentially collaborative because their conflict resolution mechanisms are not used very often. Given the detailed court records from 1443 to 1486, and the estimated potential instances for water disputes to escalate, Ostrom (1990) concluded that formal resolution accounted for a mere 0.8 percent of all possible disputes over water rights in those years. Further, she points out a somewhat puzzling fact in these communities: "there is considerable potential for violence among irrigators and between irrigators and their agents." Actual violence, however, "never approached the potential" (Ostrom, 1990: 74). Evidence suggests that in addition to informal and formal conflict resolution mechanisms, common-pool resource communities also have in place effective conflict prevention mechanisms.

In addition to cultural norms that effectively prevent conflict, prevention mechanisms may also involve workflows that minimize interdependence (Wilson et al., 2013), an approach that reduces the likelihood of conflict-producing interactions among agents. Take the procedure for cutting trees for timber in Törbel (Switzerland), an alpine village of approximately 600 residents. The villagers of Törbel first make a collective decision on the timing of the harvest and the trees that are mature enough to be cut. Then each family eligible to receive timber sends somebody to form work teams and equitably divide the work, which ranges from cutting trees and hauling logs to piling the logs into equal stacks. At the end of a workday, which is typically timed according to local festivities, the stacks are assigned to families based on the result of a lottery. This procedure defines the timing and scope of logging activities, preventing the problem of overusing the resources (Ostrom, 1990). In combining peer monitoring and randomized allocation of timber stacks, it also reduces the potential for conflict over the compensation of labor.

Traditional rice-farming communities on the island of Bali (Indonesia) offer another illustration. Over the past thousand years, the Balinese have transformed the local landscape into terraces of rice fields that depend on water from irrigation systems. With such dependence, conflict between the upstream farmers who have advantage over water usage and downstream farmers who count on the generosity of their upstream neighbors seems inevitable. However, the Balinese have devised a "ritual technology" – a religion based on the Goddess of the Crater Lake and manifested as a network of water temples – to temporally and spatially coordinate the irrigation schedule (Lansing, 1987, 1991; Lansing & Kremer, 1993). Guided by the ritual calendar set by the temples, farmers follow a cropping pattern and agricultural schedule. The synchronized planting and harvesting also serves a critical function of pest control. Although the farmers may not be aware of the exact causal relationship behind the practice, the consequence of occasional violation of the local norms (i.e., outbreak of pests), together with superstitious learning (i.e., association between the outbreak and punishment by the Goddess), facilitates the establishment of a strong local norm. The observance of this irrigation schedule minimizes conflict over water rights and maintains an ecological balance between pest and water levels (Lansing et al., 2017).

These various conflict prevention mechanisms notwithstanding, conflicts do arise occasionally in common-pool resource communities. Ostrom (1990) argued that one of the key differences between successful and less successful communities is that the former has effective informal mechanisms to manage conflict without resorting to formal legal procedures (e.g., contracts, the courts, or arbitration). This is because outside intervention may destroy the legitimacy of the informal mechanisms that rest on norms. Such informal mechanisms can range from ballots and polls where multiple participants are engaged (perhaps passively) to communal participation such as village gatherings and festivities where not only disputants but many community members also actively provide input, aiming at a solution acceptable to all participating members (Dietz et al., 2003). Finally, a religious leader may also intervene. For example, in the rare cases when upstream farmers would not give up their water rights in Bali, the local priest brought the parties involved in the conflict to the water temple and reminded them that water is a gift from the Goddess, and should they fight over it, it will vanish (Lansing, 1987). In short, social norms, rituals, and religious beliefs not only prevent conflict from arising in the first place, they also increase the significance of the resolution process, which does not depend on authority. Although the role of norms in sustaining mediation/arbitration processes when conflicts arise is certainly important, our point is simply that particular institutions may be accomplishing even more behind the scenes by preventing the emergence of conflict in the first place. The alignment of values through socialization thus serves three purposes: The alignment may itself serve to curtail the emergence of conflicts in the first place; it can support norms that produce sanctions and thus act as a deterrent to conflict; and if conflict does indeed emerge, norms can legitimize local dispute resolution procedures without the need for recourse to an external legal system.

Implications for Organization Design

Unlike the Borg Collective, as humans we celebrate individual differences across implicit characteristics such as values and goals and explicit characteristics such as styles and behavioral patterns. These differences define our individuality and enable creative breakthroughs, yet make collaboration difficult, primarily due to the difficulty of managing conflicts arising from them. With large scale, collaboration either by the whole group or by a subgroup of individuals becomes increasingly challenging given such differences. The potential for conflict can grow with the sheer number of interactions or with the increased probability for any given interaction to result in a collaboration failure.

Therefore, our answer to the question of how to organize collaboration at scale without resorting to authority centers on the management of conflict. We distinguish two pathways to effective conflict management: preventing conflicts from arising in the first place and resolving conflicts once they arise. In reviewing a broad range of empirical studies of various less-hierarchical and nonhierarchical organizations, we identify two general mechanisms underpinning conflict prevention: modifying properties of actors or modifying properties of the interactions among them. Interaction properties can be modified by managing interdependencies and information flows through workflow design. Actor properties, which are at the core of organizing based on what Adler and Heckscher (2018) call "value rationality" or value alignment, can be tuned via sorting or socialization, or a combination of both (Koçak & Puranam, 2018; Schein, 2004). Both approaches – modifying the actors themselves or the interaction processes among them – seem to play an important role in reducing the potential for conflict, with shared norms built on common values also legitimizing third-party arbitration/mediation mechanisms when prevention fails and resolution becomes necessary.

Our findings and theorizing provide insights into the design of systems that support collaboration in the absence of authority. In aligning values, our examples of common-pool resource communities (predominantly via socialization) and online communities (predominantly via sorting) occupy the two extremes of a continuum. A traditional firm may find itself somewhere in between. In common-pool resource communities, individuals are born into a particular group in which deep socialization takes place. With a given set of actors, socialization through cultivating a shared belief through practice in local rituals and communal gatherings become the predominant means to create value alignment. Indeed, beliefs about what is moral and acceptable create powerful enforcement of norms even within modern hierarchical organizations (Chatman & O'Reilly, 2016; Schein, 2004). When deep socialization is not feasible (i.e., recruiting from childhood or lifetime employment is rare), another powerful means to promote value alignment is through sorting on common goals and values. Arguably, organizations like Valve Corporation and W. L. Gore publicize their nontraditional structures in part to attract the right kind of employees. The corollary is that hierarchical firms may find it difficult to transition to nonhierarchical structures with their existing set of employees. Such transitions may inevitably produce resistance and turnover.

We find that a suitable interaction structure – one that minimizes conflict – may arise through emergent rather than designed processes. The interaction structure embodied in the agricultural calendar adopted by Bali's water management system serves to ration a scarce resource (water) and control the risk of pests while minimizing the need for active coordination. It is a sophisticated solution that arose as a result of adaptation over time without design interventions (Lansing, 1991). But for company executives attempting to design an interaction structure that minimizes the possibility of conflict, long time frames may not be feasible. Nonetheless, emergent solutions can be a source of inspiration for designed solutions. For example, the way in which a common-pool resource community has come to organize itself without authority may inspire the design of a volunteer organization – by those with the authority to design it. But once the design has been put in place (e.g., through workflow restructuring and sorting processes), authority can then take a back seat. Similarly, the designers of "platforms" like Amazon and Uber have managed to solve the problem of authority-free organizing for a rather narrow form of dyadic collaboration involving transactions between buyers and sellers of goods or services. Extending that reasoning, one might imagine a platform for a large group of individuals to come together to create and run a business without an employment relationship or authority structure.

In recent years, the rise of digital technologies has presented new opportunities for collaborative organizing. Starting with conflict prevention, digital technologies introduce new ways to modify interaction structures among actors. For instance, in online communities, the nature of online interactions is such that it creates common knowledge and leaves a traceable record of past interactions as in, for example, GitHub. As more interactions in the economy are conducted online, the impact on preventing conflicts might be expected to increase. In addition, digitalization and the use of associated technologies (such as machine learning) may be a strong enabler of better sorting. By improving the match between individuals and organizations, value alignment can be boosted, possibly leading to stronger norms.

We do not argue that sorting will be fully equivalent to socialization in terms of the strength of norms created through underlying value alignment. However, the directional effect of enhanced sorting that digitalization can provide seems clear. Furthermore, even if online interactions are inferior to those in the real world for the creation of norms, there are features of online interaction that make norm enforcement easier (e.g., transgressions are widely and possibly permanently visible). Digitization also allows for mechanisms to create and broadcast reputation – a feature that online marketplaces such as Amazon and eBay exploit. Anonymity in providing information that is aggregated to construct reputation scores, comparable to the anonymous likes on YouTube rather than the traceable likes on Facebook, seems to be a desirable feature when creating reputation metrics within the organization.

In addition to prevention, digitization may offer advantages for the resolution of conflicts without recourse to formal authority. The involvement of many individuals is possible through crowdsourced dispute resolution. To the extent that norms emerging in online communities support and legitimize majority opinion as a form of dispute resolution, they should also make crowdsourced dispute resolution possible. Thus, one interesting prospect of digitization may be a reduced reliance on formal authority for conflict resolution.

Conclusion

Different types of organizations such as nonhierarchical firms, online communities, and common-pool natural resource communities are examples of the phenomenon *collaborative organizing*. The central idea of this chapter is that these diverse organizational forms share a commonality – they rely on conflict prevention to reduce the need for hierarchical conflict management. Conflict prevention can be achieved by modifying the properties of actors or the properties of their interactions. Such organization designs minimize the need for the exercise of authority – a "hidden hand" versus a "visible hand" approach to organizing. We hope that our ideas will inform organizational designs that enable and sustain large-scale collaboration without heavy reliance on authority.

Acknowledgments

The authors thank Shiko Ben-Menahem, J. Stephen Lansing, Mike Lee, Arianna Marchetti, and Kannan Srikanth for useful and timely feedback on early drafts of our chapter.

References

Adler, P. S. & Heckscher, C. 2018. Collaboration as an organization design for shared purpose. In L. Ringel, P. Hiller, and C. Zietsma (eds.), *Toward Permeable Boundaries of Organizations?* Research in the Sociology of Organizations, vol. 57: 81–112. Emerald Publishing Limited, Bingley, UK.

Aggarwal, V. A., Posen, H. E., & Workiewicz, M. 2017. Adaptive capacity to technological change: a microfoundational approach. *Strategic Management Journal* 38(6): 1212–1231.

Alchian, A. A. & Demsetz, H. 1972. Production, information costs, and economic organization. *American Economic Review* 62(5): 777–795.

Arazy, O., Ortega, F., Nov, O., Yeo, L., & Balila, A. 2015. Functional roles and career paths in Wikipedia. Proceedings of the 18th ACM Conference on Computer Supported Cooperative Work & Social Computing. Association for Computing Machinery, New York: 1092–1105.

Askin, N. & Petriglieri, G. 2016. Tony Hsieh at Zappos: structure, culture, and radical change. Harvard Business School Case IN1249-PDF-ENG.

Barnard, C. 1938. *The Functions of the Executive*. Harvard University Press, Cambridge, MA.

Brown, D. E. 1991. *Human Universals*. Mc-Graw-Hill, New York, NY.

Burton, R. M., Håkonsson, D. D., Nickerson, J., Puranam, P., Workiewicz, M., & Zenger, T. 2017. GitHub: exploring the space between boss-less and hierarchical forms of organizing. *Journal of Organization Design* 6(1): 1–19.

Camerer, C. F. & Knez, M. 1996. Coordination, organizational boundaries, and fads in business practices. *Industrial and Corporate Change* 5: 89–112.

Chandler, A. D. 1962. *Strategy and Structure: Chapters in the History of American Industrial Enterprise.* MIT Press, Cambridge, MA.

Chatman, J. A. & O'Reilly, C. A. 2016. Paradigm lost: reinvigorating the study of organizational culture. *Research in Organizational Behavior* 36: 199–224.

Coase, R. H. 1937. The nature of the firm. *Economica* 4(16): 386–405.

Cosmides, L. & Tooby, J. 1997. *Evolutionary Psychology: A Primer.* Center for Evolutionary Psychology, University of California, Santa Barbara, CA.

DeChurch, L. A., Mesmer-Magnus, J. R., & Doty, D. 2013. Moving beyond relationship and task conflict: toward a process-state perspective. *Journal of Applied Psychology* 98(4): 559–578.

Demsetz, H. 1988. The theory of the firm revisited. *Journal of Law, Economics, and Organization* 4(1): 141–161.

Dietz, T., Ostrom, E., & Stern, P. C. 2003. The struggle to govern the commons. *Science* 302(5652): 1907–1912.

Dunbar, R. 1992. Neocortex size as a constraint on group size in primates. *Journal of Human Evolution* 22(6): 469–493.

Faraj, S., & Johnson, S. L. 2011. Network exchange patterns in online communities. *Organization Science* 22(6): 1464–1480.

Faraj, S., von Krogh, G., Monteiro, E., & Lakhani, K. R. 2016. Special section introduction – online community as space for knowledge flows. *Information Systems Research* 27(4): 668–684.

Felin, T. 2015. Valve Corporation: strategy tipping points and thresholds. *Journal of Organization Design* 4(2): 10–11.

Fjeldstad, Ø. D., Snow, C. C., Miles, R. E., & Lettl, C. 2012. The architecture of collaboration. *Strategic Management Journal* 33(6): 734–750.

Forte, A., Larco, V., & Bruckman, A. 2009. Decentralization in Wikipedia governance. *Journal of Management Information Systems* 26(1): 49–72.

Foss, N. J. & Dobrajska, M. 2015. Valve's way: wayward, visionary, or voguish? *Journal of Organization Design* 4(2): 12–15.

Freeland, R. F. 1996. Governance, consent, and organizational change. *American Journal of Sociology* 102(2): 483–526.

Freeland, R. F. & Zuckerman, E. W. 2018. The problems and promises of hierarchy: voice rights and the firm. Unpublished manuscript, University of Wisconsin and MIT Sloan School of Management.

Gulati, R., Puranam, P., & Tushman, M. 2012. Meta-organization design: rethinking design in interorganizational and community contexts. *Strategic Management Journal* 33(6): 571–586.

He, F., Puranam, P., Shrestha, Y. R., & von Krogh, G. 2020. Resolving governance disputes in communities: a study of software license decisions. *Strategic Management Journal* 41(10): 1837–1868.

Heath, C. & Staudenmayer, N. 2000. Coordination neglect: how lay theories of organizing complicate coordination in organizations. *Research in Organizational Behavior* 22: 153–191.

Heckscher, C. & Adler, P. 2006. *The Firm as a Collaborative Community: Reconstructing Trust in the Knowledge Economy.* Oxford University Press, New York, NY.

Henrich, J. 2017. *The Secret of Our Success: How Culture Is Driving Human Evolution, Domesticating Our Species, and Making Us Smarter.* Princeton University Press, Princeton, NJ.

Jensen, C. & Scacchi, W. 2005. Collaboration, leadership, control, and conflict negotiation and the Netbeans.org open source software development community. Proceedings of the 38th Annual Hawaii International Conference, Honolulu, HI.

Jeppesen, L. B., & Lakhani, K. R. 2010. Marginality and problem-solving effectiveness in broadcast search. *Organization Science* 21(5): 1016–1033.

Kane, G. C., Johnson, J., & Majchrzak, A. 2012. Emergent life cycle: the tension between knowledge change and knowledge retention in open online co-production communities. *Management Science* 60(12): 3026–3048.

Kittur, A., Suh, B., Pendleton, B. A., & Chi, E. H. 2007. He says, she says: conflict and coordination in Wikipedia. Proceedings of the SIGCHI Conference on Human Factors in Computing Systems, San Jose, CA.

Klapper, H. & Reitzig, M. 2018. On the effects of authority on peer motivation: learning from Wikipedia. *Strategic Management Journal* 39(8): 2178–2203.

Koçak, Ö. & Puranam, P. 2018. Designing a culture of collaboration: when changing beliefs is (not) enough. In J. Joseph, O. Baumann, R. M. Burton, and K. Srikanth (eds.), *Organization Design, Advances in Strategic Management,* vol. 1: 27–52. Emerald Publishing, Bingley, UK.

Kogut, B. & Metiu, A. 2001. Open-source software development and distributed innovation. *Oxford Review of Economic Policy* 17(2): 248–264.

Kollock, P. 1998. Social dilemmas: the anatomy of cooperation. *Annual Review of Sociology* 24: 183–214.

Laloux, F. 2014. *Reinventing Organizations: A Guide to Creating Organizations Inspired by the Next Stage in Human Consciousness.* Parker Nelson Publishing, Millis, MA.

Langlois, R. N. & Garzarelli, G. 2008. Of hackers and hairdressers: modularity and the organizational economics of open-source collaboration. *Industry and Innovation* 15(2): 125–143.

Lansing, J. S. 1987. Balinese "water temples" and the management of irrigation. *American Anthropologist* 89(2): 326–341.

Lansing, J. S. 1991. *Priests and Programmers: Technologies of Power in the Engineered Landscape of Bali.* Princeton University Press, Princeton, NJ.

Lansing, J. S. & Kremer, J. N. 1993. Emergent properties of Balinese water temple networks: co-adaptation on a rugged fitness landscape. *American Anthropologist* 95(1): 97–114.

Lansing, J. S., Thurner, S., Chung, N. N. et al. 2017. Adaptive self-organization of Bali's ancient rice terraces. *Proceedings of the National Academy of Sciences* 114(25): 6504–6509.

Lawrence, P. R. & Lorsch, J. W. 1967. *Organization and Environment: Managing Differentiation and Integration*. Harvard University Press, Cambridge, MA.

Lee, G. K. & Cole, R. E. 2003. From a firm-based to a community-based model of knowledge creation: the case of the Linux kernel development. *Organization Science* 14(6): 633–649.

Lee, M. Y. & Edmondson, A. C. 2017. Self-managing organizations: exploring the limits of less-hierarchical organizing. *Research in Organizational Behavior* 37: 35–58.

MacCormack, A. D., Rusnak, J., & Baldwin, C. Y. 2006. Exploring the structure of complex software designs: an empirical study of open source and proprietary code. *Management Science* 52: 1015–1030.

Malone, T. W. 2004. *The Future of Work: How the New Order of Business Will Shape Your Organization, Your Management Style, and Your Life*. Harvard Business School Press, Boston, MA.

Malone, T. W. 2016. *Superminds: The Surprising Power of People and Computers Thinking Together*. Hachette Book Group, New York, NY.

March, J. G. & Simon, H. A. 1958. *Organizations*. Wiley, New York, NY.

Mintzberg, H. 1979. *The Structuring of Organizations: A Synthesis of the Research*. Prentice-Hall, Englewood Cliffs, NJ.

Morgan, J. 2012. *The Collaborative Organization: A Strategic Guide to Solving Your Internal Business Challenges Using Emerging Social and Collaborative Tools*. McGraw-Hill, New York, NY.

Mortensen, M. & Haas, M. R. 2018. Perspective – rethinking teams: from bounded membership to dynamic participation. *Organization Science* 29(2): 341–355.

Nicholson, N. 1997. Evolutionary psychology: toward a new view of human nature and organizational society. *Human Relations* 50(9): 1053–1078.

O'Reilly, C. A. & Chatman, J. A. 1996. Culture as social control: corporations, cults, and commitment. In B. M. Staw and L. L. Cummings (eds.), *Research in Organizational Behavior: An Annual Series of Analytical Essays and Critical Reviews*, Vol. 18: 157–200. Elsevier Science/JAI Press, Oxford.

Ostrom, E. 1990. *Governing the Commons: The Evolution of Institutions for Collective Action*. Cambridge University Press, Cambridge, UK.

Ostrom, E. 2005. *Understanding Institutional Diversity*. Princeton University Press, Princeton, NJ.

Ostrom, E., Gardner, R., Walker, J., & Walker, J. 1994. *Rules, Games, and Common-Pool Resources*. University of Michigan Press, Ann Arbor, MI.

Ouchi, W. G. 1980. Markets, bureaucracies, and clans. *Administrative Science Quarterly* 25(1): 129–141.

Piskorski, J. & Gorbatai, A. 2017. Testing Coleman's social-norm enforcement mechanism: evidence from Wikipedia. *American Journal of Sociology* 122(4): 1183–1222.

Piskorski, M. & Spadini, L. 2007. Procter & Gamble: Organization 2005. Harvard Business School Case 707402-PDF-ENG.

Pittman, T. S. & Zeigler, K. R. 2007. Basic human needs. In A. W. Kruglanski and E. T. Higgins (eds.), *Social Psychology: Handbook of Basic Principles*: 473–489. The Guilford Press, New York, NY.

Prendergast, C. 1999. The provision of incentives in firms. *Journal of Economic Literature* 37(1): 7–63.

Puranam, P. 2018. *The Microstructure of Organizations*. Oxford University Press, Oxford, UK.

Puranam, P. & Håkonsson, D. D. 2015. Valve's way. *Journal of Organization Design* 4(2): 2–4.

Puranam, P., Alexy, O., & Reitzig, M. 2014. What's "new" about new forms of organizing? *Academy of Management Review* 39(2): 162–180.

Puranam, P., Raveendran, M., & Knudsen, T. 2012. Organization design: the epistemic interdependence perspective. *Academy of Management Review* 37(3): 419–440.

Robertson, B. J. 2015. *Holacracy: The New Management System for a Rapidly Changing World*. Macmillan, New York, NY.

Ryan, R. M. & Deci, E. L. 2018. *Self-Determination Theory: Basic Psychological Needs in Motivation, Development and Wellness*. The Guilford Press, New York, NY.

Schein, E. H. 2004. *Organizational Culture and Leadership*. Wiley, New York, NY.

Simon, H. A. 1947. *Administrative Behavior*. Macmillan Press, New York, NY.

Smith, A. 1776. *An Inquiry into the Nature and Causes of the Wealth of Nations*. W. Strahan and T. Cadell, London, UK.

Stewart, K. J. & Gosain, S. 2006. The impact of ideology and effectiveness in open source software development teams. *MIS Quarterly* 30(2): 291–314.

Turco, C. 2016. *The Conversational Firm: Rethinking Bureaucracy in the Age of Social Media*. Columbia University Press, New York, NY.

Van Vugt, M. 2006. Evolutionary origins of leadership and followership. *Personality and Social Psychology Review* 10(4): 354–371.

Van Vugt, M. 2017. Evolutionary psychology: theoretical foundations for the study of organizations. *Journal of Organization Design* 6(9). https://doi.org/10.1186/s41469-017-0019-9.

Van Vugt, M. & Ahuja, A. 2011. *Naturally Selected: The Evolutionary Science of Leadership*. HarperCollins, New York, NY.

Wang, J., Shih, P. C., & Carroll, J. M. 2015. Revisiting Linus's Law: benefits and challenges of open source software peer review. *International Journal of Human-Computer Studies* 77: 52–65.

Weber, M. 1922. *Economy and Society*. University of California Press, Berkeley, CA.

Williamson, O. E. 1975. *Markets and Hierarchies: Analysis and Antitrust Implications*. Free Press, New York, NY.

Wilson, D. S., Ostrom, E., & Cox, M. E. 2013. Generalizing the core design principles for the efficacy of groups. *Journal of Economic Behavior & Organization* 90: 21–32.

Zenger, T. 2015. Valve Corporation: composing internal markets. *Journal of Organization Design* 4(2): 20–22.

5 | The Platform Organization

ANNABELLE GAWER, MICHAEL A. CUSUMANO,
AND DAVID B. YOFFIE

Organizational platforms have steadily grown in importance in recent years. We focus on digital platforms that, along with their associated ecosystems, are uniquely positioned to create and capture value in the digital economy. One type of digital platform, which we call *innovation platforms*, enables third-party firms such as software developers to build millions of applications that enhance the functionality of foundational products such as Microsoft Windows or Google's Android. Another type, which we call *transaction platforms*, includes companies such as Uber, Airbnb, Facebook, Alibaba, and Amazon Marketplace. These platforms link buyers and sellers and thereby reduce search and other transaction costs for millions and billions of customers and providers. Both types of platforms are an organizational form that extends beyond traditional firm and supply chain boundaries to encompass ecosystems of innovators and suppliers of various products and services.

In this chapter, we discuss the origins and characteristics of organizational platforms as well as the economics that underpin their operation. We then describe two basic types of platforms, innovation and transaction, and point out that some companies combine the two into hybrid platforms. We identify the four key steps that designers and entrepreneurs must take if they want to build a successful platform business. Finally, we discuss current societal and regulatory challenges associated with the increasing dominance of the most powerful platform companies.

Rise of Platforms

The Industrial Revolution brought us the modern corporation. As Alfred Chandler (1990) explained in *Scale and Scope: The Dynamics of Industrial Capitalism*, the modern corporation was born and evolved to take advantage of production techniques made available by the Industrial Revolution. The industrial firm, with its multidivisional managerial hierarchies, was able to create value and generate competitive advantage by harnessing the new technological infrastructures of the time, such as electricity and railroads, to operate efficient production processes. Firms obtained, controlled, and coordinated resources to create products through increasingly integrated and automated manufacturing systems.

If the Industrial Revolution enabled massive economies of scale and scope, the Digital Revolution dramatically lowered the costs of rapid scaling on a global basis. The emergence of personal computers (PCs), the Internet, mobile devices, and Cloud servers allowed digital platforms to form and grow, sometimes exponentially. Companies no longer need to do all their own innovation or own all the assets they provide to consumers. Digital technologies allow individuals to connect with other individuals and organizations with minimal friction. With many digital technologies, the cost to service an additional customer can be close to zero. The zero-marginal cost economics of digital technologies allowed Facebook to grow from a few million users to 2.4 billion in slightly over a decade. Such a growth pace would have been impossible before the Internet linked markets globally and instantly.

One profound difference in the digital world is the opportunity for companies to achieve demand-side scale and scope economies from positive feedback loops called network effects (Armstrong, 2006; Katz & Shapiro, 1985; Parker & Van Alstyne, 2005). A network effect exists when the value that a user obtains from a particular product or service grows as more users adopt the product or service. For example, an increase in the number of Uber drivers is valuable for Uber riders (shorter wait times), and as more riders sign up with Uber, drivers have access to a larger market. Developers creating apps for a mobile operating system represents a different type of network effect. The larger the number of iPhone users, the more attractive it is for developers to create apps for the AppStore (a larger market). iPhone users, in turn, benefit from an increased number of available apps (more things to do with their phones).

Today, included among the most valuable firms in the world, and the first to surpass the trillion-dollar mark in market value, are platform companies such as Apple, Microsoft, Amazon, Google, Alibaba, and Tencent. Platform companies make up between 60 percent and 70 percent of all "unicorns" – privately held companies with valuations exceeding $1 billion, including Ant Financial, Didi Chuxing, Byte Dance, and Airbnb. All these organizations take advantage of modern digital infrastructures such as the Internet, the Cloud, and global mobile connectivity. They also take advantage of the behavioral habits of billions of users who, by connecting daily to these platforms through their digital devices to consume digital services, continuously (and often unwittingly) generate data. This data-as-output, in turn, becomes a key resource that platform companies leverage to further enhance the digital services they offer or to develop new services.

Platforms as Organizational Forms

Platforms are used to organize economic activity within firms, across firms in industry supply chains, and in multi-industry ecosystems (see Figure 5.1). The notion of a platform as an organizing mechanism arose in firms that created "families" of products based on a common platform to which diverse modules could be fitted in order to tailor products to market niches (Wheelwright & Clark, 1992).

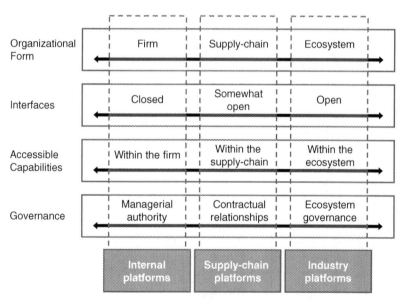

Figure 5.1 Types of organizational platforms
Adapted from Figure 1 in Gawer (2014). Published by Elsevier, www
.sciencedirect.com/science/article/pii/S0048733314000456

Early examples were observed in automobile manufacturing, stereo equipment, medical electronic equipment, and computers. For example, an automobile manufacturer could use one chassis to support multiple car models. The key to early platform architectures was standardizing the interfaces so that different modules could work together (Baldwin & Clark, 2000). Early platforms were company-specific and allowed product development processes to be controlled and coordinated in a way that dramatically accelerated the pace and quality of product development.

The use of platforms as an organizing mechanism also extended to industry supply chains. For example, the modular architecture of the IBM System/360 mainframe computer enabled other firms to create modules that could "plug-in" to IBM's systems. Several companies started offering compatible products including disk drives, terminals, printers, and memory devices (Baldwin & Clark, 2000). When IBM introduced its PC in 1981, it was built with off-the-shelf parts from an industry supply chain that included Intel and Microsoft. Supply chain platforms increased the diversity of product options available to customers and allowed platform owners to enjoy increased economies of scale in the supply of components. Virtually every global supply chain today can be viewed as a platform: A particular company acts as the platform leader, it designs processes and infrastructures that allow suppliers to provide their inputs in an efficient manner, and governance of the entire system is accomplished largely through contracts.

Moore (1993) suggested that some companies be viewed not as members of a single industry but as part of a business ecosystem that crosses a variety of industries. For example, he pointed out that Apple is the leader of an ecosystem that crosses at least four major industries: computers, consumer electronics, information, and communications. He also noted that the community of firms providing software and hardware for the Microsoft Windows operating system, and the Intel processor architecture on which it relied, was an example of organizing as a business ecosystem. A key characteristic of the Intel/Microsoft ecosystem was that suppliers of complementary components could utilize free, openly available interfaces to both the processors and the operating system for purposes of innovation, and they would independently supply components to users without having contractual relationships with either Microsoft or Intel, as would be the case in a supply chain. This organizational arrangement spurred intense innovation around the new technological platform at the center of a rapidly expanding ecosystem, in which the platform leader plays the central role (Gawer & Cusumano, 2002). As platform scope broadens from the firm to industry supply chain to multi-industry ecosystem, access to innovating agents and their diverse capabilities increases (Gawer, 2014).

The Economics of Platforms

Platforms that mediate economic exchange constitute private markets (Gawer & Cusumano, 2002). The company that owns the platform connects two or more distinct categories of economic actors (referred to as "sides" of a market) whose benefits from interacting through the common platform give rise to network effects (Rochet & Tirole, 2003). For example, the Uber platform connects drivers and riders. Both drivers and riders are users of Uber, but they belong to two different sides of the market – sellers of rides and buyers of rides. Benefits related to connecting users on different sides give rise to cross-side network effects (Parker & Van Alstyne, 2005). For example, eBay sellers attract eBay buyers, and more buyers attract more sellers. More Airbnb hosts attract more potential guests. Lots of users attract app developers or advertisers. When users benefit from connecting directly with similar others (Katz & Shapiro, 1985), we speak of same-side network effects. Same-side effects occur in social networks: Users join because they want to connect to other users; they bring in their friends, and friends of friends, and so on. Facebook, Twitter, Instagram, Snap, and Tik Tok are powerful examples. Strong network effects can lead to "winner-take-all" dynamics, where one firm takes a very large share of the market (Shapiro & Varian, 1998). Market dominance is likely to occur if there are few opportunities for competitors to differentiate, it is costly for users to engage in "multi-homing" (the ability of users to use more than one platform at the same time for the same purposes), and high barriers to entry exist (Cusumano, Gawer, & Yoffie, 2019; Eisenmann, Parker, & Van Alstyne, 2006; Parker, Van Alstyne, & Choudary, 2016).

Platform competition is centered around adoption by users, fueled by network effects. As the value of the platform stems principally from the access of "one side" to the "other side" of the platform, the question of platform adoption becomes "how to bring multiple sides on board" (Evans, 2003; Rochet & Tirole, 2006). Platform designers must figure out how to solve the chicken-and-egg problem (Caillaud & Jullien, 2003; Eisenmann et al., 2006) – that is, one side of the market (e.g., Uber drivers) may see little or no value in a platform without significant presence on the other side (Uber riders). So, when launching a platform, which side should come first, drivers (sellers) or riders (buyers)? Or should a platform try to bring both sides on board at the same time? This coordination problem can be solved by subsidizing the side of the platform that is most needed to attract the other side (Parker & Van Alstyne, 2005; Rochet & Tirole, 2003, 2006). A platform such as Upwork, for example, connects freelance labor with companies that need skilled workers. Upwork charges only the freelancer (approximately 10 percent of their pay), while companies get the service for free. In this case, the value that both users and the platform owner can capture increases with a growing user base in a virtuous cycle of network effects that reflect the interdependence of demand between user groups.

Platform leaders may own few assets and yet create high value. For example, Uber provides rides but owns no vehicles; Airbnb provides rooms to rent but owns and manages no rooms. Amazon provides millions of products to its customers through its marketplace, which links buyers and sellers. Amazon also buys and resells goods through its online store, which uses the same digital infrastructure as the marketplace for purchasing and billing. Both the marketplace and the store may also use the same physical infrastructure for the delivery of goods.

In platform organizations, data has become a raw material. In the digital economy, with billions of users connected through mobile online devices, and constantly engaging with other users, many platforms have added advertisers as one of their market sides. Companies such as Google, Facebook, and Amazon record and analyze enormous amounts of user-generated data, tracked via cookies and other means. This data has high economic value because it allows advertisers to target specific types of users and behaviors. Data is also invaluable in developing new products and services.

Innovation and Transaction Platforms

In our book *The Business of Platforms: Strategy in the Age of Digital Competition, Innovation, and Power* (Cusumano et al., 2019), we divided digital platforms into two basic types, depending on their

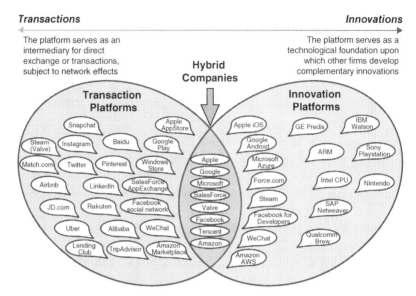

Figure 5.2 Innovation and transaction platform companies
From Cusumano et al. (2019). Used with permission of HarperCollins.

primary function (see Figure 5.2). We call the first type *innovation platforms*. These platforms usually consist of common technological building blocks that the owner and ecosystem partners can share in creating complementary products and services such as smartphone apps. By complementary, we mean that these innovations add functionality or access to assets that make the platform increasingly useful. The network effects come from the number and utility of the complements: The more complements there are, or the higher quality they are, the more attractive the platform becomes to users and complementors as well as other potential market actors such as advertisers and investors. Microsoft Windows is a classic innovation platform. Microsoft sold the Windows operating system to PC manufacturers and developed application programming interfaces (APIs), which allowed software developers to create applications. Billions of PCs were sold, attracting an army of independent developers who delivered millions of applications that ran on Windows. Developers were not suppliers to Microsoft, writing applications under contract; they were ecosystem participants. With the emergence of smartphones in 2007, Google Android and Apple iOS became new high-volume innovation platforms. In the last ten years, Amazon Web Services and Microsoft Azure have become the leading innovation platforms for the Cloud ecosystem, which became an innovation environment complete with development tools and app stores (Cusumano, 2019).

Ecosystems vastly expand the pool of innovation sources because those sources are not restricted to the focal firm or the focal firm's pool of suppliers as is the case in traditional supply chains. Instead, innovators can be anyone and may be found anywhere. The platform leader may not even be able to forecast who or where innovators may be. Steve Jobs initially wanted the iPhone to be a firm-level platform, where Apple would build or buy and bundle all the applications. Had Jobs stuck to his original strategy, the iPhone would have never delivered anything close to the more than two million apps on the platform in 2020. A feature of ecosystem platforms is that the platform leader does not need to know in advance who a complementary innovator might be to be able to capture value from the innovation. Open interfaces are crucial as facilitators of external complementary innovation (Gawer, 2014; West, 2003) – they enable specialization and mix-and-match innovation through recombination of modules (Garud & Kumaraswamy, 1995; Langlois, 2002; Parnas, 1972; Simon, 1962).

The second platform type is called *transaction platforms*. These organizations are intermediaries or online marketplaces that make it possible for people and companies to share information or to buy, sell, or access a variety of goods and services (Stabell & Fjeldstad, 1998). Classic examples are credit card companies and telecommunication services. In transaction services, the network effects come from the connections that can be made among users (North & Wallis, 1994). The more users a platform can connect, and the more content and functionality it makes available, the more useful the platform becomes. It is the digital technology and scale that make today's platforms unique and powerful. Google Search, Amazon Marketplace, Facebook Social Network, Twitter, and WeChat are examples of transaction platforms used by billions of people every day.

There are important differences between the two platform types. Innovation platforms create value by facilitating the development of complementary products and services, sometimes built by the platform owner but mostly by third-party firms. They capture value ("monetize the platform") by selling or licensing products. In cases where the platform is free (e.g., Google Android), it is monetized by selling advertising or other services. In contrast, transaction platforms create value by facilitating exchange and capture value through combinations of subscriptions, transaction fees, and advertising.

Some firms begin with one type of platform and then add the second type. We refer to companies that support both types as *hybrid platforms*. In the 1980s and 1990s, innovation and transaction platforms were distinct businesses. In recent years, a growing number of successful innovation platforms have integrated transaction platforms into their business models. An example is the Apple AppStore, which sells apps to iPhone users. Correspondingly, successful transaction platforms have created open interfaces to encourage third parties to develop complementary products and services. For example, Facebook opened its platform to external developers of games and other applications. Other prominent hybrid examples include Google's decision to launch the Android operating system, Amazon's decision to create multiple innovation platforms around Amazon Web Services and the Alexa "smart" speaker, and the decisions of Uber and Airbnb to allow developers to build services on top of their transaction platforms. We expect that competition will turn more and more platform firms into hybrids.

Strategic Choices for Companies That Want to Build a Platform Business

To create a sustainable platform business, designers and entrepreneurs should start with the value proposition they envision. If value will come mainly from enabling third parties to build their own products or services that utilize and enhance the platform, then they should develop an innovation platform. If value will come mainly from allowing different sides of a market to interact, rather than building or delivering a product or service directly, then they should develop a transaction platform. Successful platform companies tend to adopt a hybrid approach. Once the value proposition is clear, then platform designers need to proceed through four decision-making steps as shown in Figure 5.3.

The first step is to identify the various market sides managers and entrepreneurs want for their platform and how to create value through them – the role different actors (buyers, sellers, complementors) will play and who specifically will take on those roles. LinkedIn, for example, has users, application developers, advertisers, and recruiters. Over

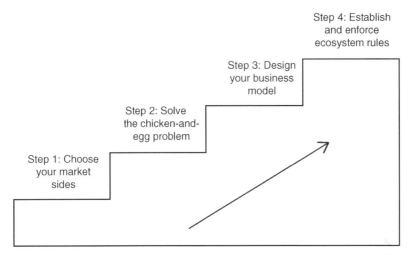

Step 4: Establish
and enforce
ecosystem rules

Step 3: Design
your business
model

Step 2: Solve
the chicken-and-
egg problem

Step 1: Choose
your market
sides

Figure 5.3 Four steps to build a sustainable business platform
From Cusumano et al. (2019). Used with permission of HarperCollins.

the years, the company has debated adding new sides such as consultants, experts, and company intranets. The potential problem for all platforms is that adding more sides may generate more revenue opportunities but also more conflicts among the sides.

The second step is to launch the platform, which requires solving the chicken-and-egg problem of how to get started and then how to attract increasing numbers of users and complementors to generate strong, persistent network effects. The question is: How do you make your platform sufficiently valuable to early users when there are no complementors or other users to connect with? Some innovation platform leaders, such as Apple, start by developing the initial complements to their platform – Apple developed the iPhone, its operating system, and an initial set of applications to make the phone useful for early buyers. Subsequently, Apple attracted independent app developers to their ecosystem. Correspondingly, a classic transaction platform strategy, referred to as penetration pricing, involves subsidizing initial users to reach a critical mass (Katz & Shapiro, 1994). Initially, Facebook offered its service for free and later monetized the platform by selling targeted advertising services and user data.

The third step is to design revenue mechanisms that will monetize network effects without depressing them. The monetization challenge involves deciding how long the subsidies required to launch the platform will need to be continued and identifying the sides that eventually will generate positive cash flow. Uber, for example, has yet to create a business model with positive cash flow. It built its business by subsidizing drivers with aggressive bonuses and lowering prices significantly below the price of a taxi for riders. As the company tries to satisfy its investors, it has been working to revise the business model by lowering subsidies to both sides. The jury is still out on whether this strategy will work.

Lastly, managers and entrepreneurs must establish an effective ecosystem governance regime. They need to decide what behaviors to encourage and discourage on the platform and how to enforce the rules. The challenge of platform governance has become one of the most difficult problems managers face at companies such as Facebook, Twitter, and YouTube. Governance mechanisms include elements such as property rights, interfaces and other standards, as well as rules related to platform membership and actor behavior (Jacobides, Cennamo, & Gawer, 2018).

Harnessing Platform Power

In a global economy where many resources can be digitized, and where such resources can be utilized even if they are geographically dispersed, platforms are positioned to facilitate the exchange of those resources as well as combine them in innovative ways (Yoo, Henfridsson, & Lyytinen, 2010). A platform is, by design, a central agent at the nexus of a network of value creators. A platform leader can capture a significant proportion of the value being created in the distributed network, and resources can be monitored, controlled, and used without owning them.

One ongoing challenge for both innovation and transaction platforms (as well as hybrids) is the potential centralization of power by companies whose platforms become highly successful. The Internet once promised to deliver a fairer world, bringing down old power structures, where distributed computing and communication networks provided equal access for all to digital information and economic opportunities (Benkler, 2006). While an open, democratic Internet is partly true, so is the opposite. Platform dynamics has led to the concentration of economic and social activity in a small number of large and powerful companies. In response, we see growing demands from both users and governments to regulate or break up some of the biggest platforms.

The huge platforms – Apple, Amazon, Google, Microsoft, Facebook – have become so large that they are wealthier and more influential than many countries. As a group, the top platform firms have garnered so much power that one observer labelled them the Frightful Five (Manjoo, 2017). These tech giants may have become too big to control. Google and Facebook dominate two-thirds of digital advertising, with Google controlling about 90 percent of internet search in most markets (except China) and about 80 percent of smartphone operating systems with the free Android operating system. Apple has captured 90 percent of the world's profits in smartphones and a large percentage of digital content sales with iTunes. Amazon presides over more than 40 percent of e-commerce in the United States and dominates e-books. Microsoft owns more than 90 percent of the world's PC operating systems. Intel provides some 80 percent of the microprocessors for PCs and more than 90 percent of the microprocessors for Internet servers. Facebook accounts for approximately two-thirds of social media activity. The most powerful platform companies have started to look like the big banks in the 2008–2009 financial crisis: Are they too big to fail? Consider as well how platforms enable the dissemination of fake news or Russian manipulation of social media and election tampering, and clearly, we have reached an inflection point. We now must view the most powerful platform companies as double-edged swords, capable of both good and evil.

A significant platform concern is: Who controls personal data? Control of personal data can lead to violation of privacy, exemplified by complaints against major social networks such as Facebook. A series of scandals, including that of Facebook and Cambridge Analytica, demonstrate how easy it can be for malevolent actors to take control of user data and to influence individuals through the information they see on social networks, influence national elections, and ultimately threaten democracy. The centrality of data extraction in platform business models (Srnicek, 2016) and the reliance on user monitoring for profit-making have raised the possibility that "surveillance capitalism" (Zuboff, 2015) may now be occurring. Facebook and Google capture data on users (and their friends) even when they are not on the website.

Managers and entrepreneurs need to understand what constitutes an abuse of market power and what conditions may lead to potentially illegal market actions. Sometimes the conditions for winner-take-all outcomes are met. In such cases, platform companies have many opportunities to abuse their market power – harm consumer welfare, hurt local or global competitors, and extract monopoly or quasi-monopoly rents. As a regulatory antidote, antitrust cases are costly and lengthy affairs that usually take many years to resolve. Platform companies would do themselves and society a considerable favor if they learned how not to violate the law and user trust, misuse their market positions to harm competitors, or garner excessive profits.

Managers in platform companies also need to be careful with how their organizations impact labor and labor regulations. One of the most attractive features of platforms for financial investors is that they can be "asset light." Uber does not own taxis or employ drivers directly. Airbnb does not own apartments or houses or employ the people who manage properties listed on its site. OpenTable does not own or manage restaurants. Microsoft, Google, Apple, and Facebook do not employ the millions of engineers that independently choose to write software applications for Windows, Android, iOS, and the Facebook APIs. While asset-light platforms potentially provide highly leveraged returns to investors, they create another challenge for human capital: How should platform owners manage a workforce largely composed of independent contractors (Jordan, 2017)? Unlike employees, independent contractors are due no benefits, guarantee of hours, or minimum wage, enabling the enterprises that employ them to keep labor costs low. There were 57 million freelancers in the United States in 2017; for one-third of those people, freelance activity was their main source of income (Pofeldt, 2017). One estimate suggested that, if current trends continue, freelancers could represent 50 percent of all US workers by 2027 (Pofeldt, 2017).

Platforms such as Uber, GrubHub, TaskRabbit, Upwork, Handy, and Deliveroo classify much of their workforce as independent contractors. The companies justify this practice because the workers tend to perform their jobs as a side activity, with significant flexibility in their hours. In reality, the classification is about keeping labor costs low. Industry executives have estimated that classifying workers as employees tends to cost 20–30 percent more than classifying them as contractors (Scheiber, 2018). Some analysts argue that the entire "gig economy" would collapse if start-ups were obliged by law to classify all their workers as employees (Kessler, 2015). Overall, the practice of classifying workers as independent contractors is becoming increasingly controversial. In the United States, the situation is particularly complex because laws that determine independent contractor and employee status vary from state to state and even city by city. Many regulations focus on how much control workers have over their work. Researchers are beginning to study "algorithmic labor" and the role that information asymmetries embedded in the algorithmic management of workers' tasks shape control and power relations (Rosenblat, 2018; Rosenblat & Stark, 2016). In Europe, regulators are also starting to pay attention to the labor practices of platform firms.

Until recently, the dominant mood in the business press (and in many business books on platform companies) was unbridled enthusiasm for the efficiency of platforms and awe at the speed at which they introduced both innovation and disruption. Parker, Van Alstyne, and Choudary (2016), Evans and Schmalensee (2016), and Cusumano, Gawer, and Yoffie (2019), among other publications, all have shown that platforms can create enormous value for users and investors – they can reduce search and transaction costs, and fundamentally restructure entire industries, within a few years. We have seen this phenomenon in computers, online marketplaces, lodging, financial services, and many other sectors. Nonetheless, it appears that the tide of public perception seems to have turned as media coverage of platforms has become increasingly negative. Calls to break up Google have appeared in major newspapers. The movement to delete Facebook from smartphone apps gained substantial traction among the public. Uber has faced internal turmoil from failing to properly vet drivers, abusing digital technology (e.g., the Greyball software that helped drivers evade law enforcement in markets where Uber was prohibited), and aggressively challenging local governments. This change in public sentiment reflects the fact that platforms regulate their ecosystems by developing and enforcing their own rules of platform access and interaction. Furthermore, platforms gain access to personal data and set the rules by which this data is extracted and used.

As platforms have gained so much power over their ecosystems, a major concern among government regulators is that it has become too easy for platform owners to erect long-term barriers to entry. Many government agencies and think tanks have been working on whether and how to regulate competition in digital markets (Furman, 2019). Calls for updating antitrust laws have become louder (Khan, 2017). In 2019, the European Commission issued new regulations for platform-to-business trading practices, aiming to create a fair, transparent, and predictable business environment for smaller businesses and traders when using online platforms (European Commission, 2019). A report for the European Commission titled Shaping Competition Policy in the Era of Digitisation (Crémer, de Montjoye, & Schweitzer, 2019), which is likely to be influential in shaping the European legislative and enforcement agenda in the longer term, states that digital markets require vigorous enforcement of competition policies and laws, arguing that large incumbent digital players are difficult to dislodge and may have strong incentives to engage in anticompetitive behavior. A key area of concern in the report is the hotly debated topic of "killer acquisitions," whereby dominant firms acquire small start-ups with quickly growing user bases that might otherwise have developed into strong rivals. The report concludes that adjustments are needed with respect to the application of competition law.

To be sustainable enterprises, and to be accepted as contributors to society, platform companies need to adopt values that are congruent with those of the societies in which they function. With growing sensitivity to issues of power and fairness, platforms that ignore those issues risk destroying their reputations. With increasing calls to reign in platform businesses, entrepreneurs, managers, and boards of directors at leading platform companies must take more responsibility for their social, political, and economic impact.

Conclusion

Platforms, by controlling standards, interfaces, and rules of membership and user interaction, organize an enormous amount of innovation, commercial exchange, and social interaction. Given the dramatic growth of platforms in the global economy and the increasing public concern with their market power, organizational researchers studying platforms need to expand their focus from describing the features and operation of platform companies to studying their contribution to society. We need a comprehensive understanding of platform ecosystems – how capabilities are developed and harnessed within them, the principles by which they are organized, and what constitutes good ecosystem performance.

References

Armstrong, M. 2006. Competition in two-sided markets. *RAND Journal of Economics* 37(3): 668–691.

Baldwin, C. Y. & Clark, K. B. 2000. *Design Rules: The Power of Modularity*, vol. 1. MIT Press, Cambridge, MA.

Benkler, Y. 2006. *The Wealth of Networks: How Social Production Transforms Markets and Freedom*. Yale University Press, New Haven, CT.

Caillaud, B. & Jullien, B. 2003. Chicken & egg: competition among intermediation service providers. *The RAND Journal of Economics* 34(2): 309–328.

Chandler, A. D. 1990. *Scale and Scope: The Dynamics of Industrial Capitalism*. The Belknap Press of Harvard University Press, Cambridge, MA.

Crémer, J., de Montjoye, Y.-A., & Schweitzer, H. 2019. Competition policy for the digital era. Report for the European Commission. https://ec.europa.eu/competition/publications/reports/kd0419345enn.pdf.

Cusumano, M. A. 2019. The cloud as an innovation platform for software development. *Communications of the ACM* 62(10): 20–22.

Cusumano, M. A., Gawer, A., & Yoffie, D. B. 2019. *The Business of Platforms: Strategy in the Age of Digital Competition, Innovation, and Power*. Harper Business, New York, NY.

Eisenmann, T., Parker, G., & Van Alstyne, M. W. 2006. Strategies for two-sided markets. *Harvard Business Review* 84(10): 92–101.

European Commission. 2019. Platform to business trading practices. https://digital-strategy.ec.europa.eu/en/policies/platform-business-trading-practices.

Evans, D. S. 2003. Some empirical aspects of multi-sided platform industries. *Review of Network Economics* 23(3): 191–209.

Evans, D. S. & Schmalensee, R. 2016. *Matchmakers: The New Economics of Multi-sided Platforms*. Harvard Business Review Press, Boston, MA.

Furman, J. 2019. *Unlocking Digital Competition: Report of the Digital Competition Expert Panel*. HM Treasury: London, UK. www.gov.uk/government/publications/unlocking-digital-competition-report-of-the-digital-competition-expert-panel.

Garud, R. & Kumaraswamy, A. 1995. Technological and organizational designs for realizing economies of substitution. *Strategic Management Journal* 16(S1): 93–109.

Gawer, A. 2014. Bridging differing perspectives on technological platforms: toward an integrative framework. *Research Policy* 43(7): 1239–1249.

Gawer, A. & Cusumano, M. A. 2002. *Platform Leadership: How Intel, Microsoft, and Cisco Drive Industry Innovation*. Harvard Business School Press, Boston, MA.

Jacobides, M. G., Cennamo, C., & Gawer, A. 2018. Towards a theory of ecosystems. *Strategic Management Journal* 39(8): 2255–2276.

Jordan, J. M. 2017. Challenges to large-scale digital organization: the case of Uber. *Journal of Organization Design* 6(1): 1–12.

Katz, M. L. & Shapiro, C. 1985. Network externalities, competition, and compatibility. *American Economic Review* 75(3): 424–440.

Katz, M. L. & Shapiro, C. 1994. Systems competition and network effects. *Journal of Economic Perspectives* 8(2): 93–115.

Kessler, S. 2015. The Gig economy won't last because it is being sued to death. *Fast Company*, February 17. www.fastcompany.com/3042248/the-gig-economy-wont-last-because-its-being-sued-to-death.

Khan, L. M. 2017. Amazon's antitrust paradox. *Yale Law Journal* 126(3): 710–805.

Langlois, R. N. 2002. Modularity in technology and organization. *Journal of Economic Behavior & Organization* 49(1): 19–37.

Manjoo, F. 2017. The Frightful Five want to rule entertainment. They are hitting limits. *New York Times*, October 11. www.nytimes.com/2017/10/11/technology/the-frightful-five-want-to-rule-entertainment-they-are-hitting-limits.html.

Moore, J. F. 1993. Predators and prey: a new ecology of competition. *Harvard Business Review* 71(3): 75–86.

North, D. C. & Wallis, J. J. 1994. Integrating institutional change and technical change in economic history: a transaction cost approach. *Journal of Institutional and Theoretical Economics (JITE)/Zeitschrift für die Gesamte Staatswissenschaft* 150(4): 609–624.

Parker, G. G. & Van Alstyne, M. W. 2005. Two-sided network effects: a theory of information product design. *Management Science* 51(10): 1494–1504.

Parker, G. G., Van Alstyne, M. W., & Choudary, S. P. 2016. *Platform Revolution: How Platform Markets Are Transforming the Economy and How to Make Them Work for You.* W. W. Norton, New York, NY.

Parnas, D. L. 1972. On the criteria to be used in decomposing systems into modules. *Communications of the ACM* 15(12): 1053–1058.

Pofeldt, E. 2017. Are we ready for a workforce that is 50% freelance? *Forbes*, October 17. www.forbes.com/sites/elainepofeldt/2017/10/17/are-we-ready-for-a-workforce-that-is-50-freelance/#7c4614613f82.

Rochet, J. C. & Tirole, J. 2003. Platform competition in two-sided markets. *Journal of the European Economic Association* 1(4): 990–1029.

Rochet, J. C. & Tirole, J. 2006. Two-sided markets: a progress report. *The RAND Journal of Economics* 37(3): 645–667.

Rosenblat, A. 2018. *Uberland: How Algorithms Are Rewriting the Rules of Work.* University of California Press, Berkeley, CA.

Rosenblat, A. & Stark, L. 2016. Algorithmic labor and information asymmetries: a case study of Uber's drivers. *International Journal of Communication* 10: 3758–3784.

Scheiber, N. 2018. Gig economy business model dealt a blow in California ruling. *New York Times*, April 30. www.nytimes.com/2018/04/30/business/economy/gig-economy-ruling.html.

Shapiro, C. & Varian, H. R. 1998. *Information Rules: A Strategic Guide to the Network Economy*. Harvard Business School Press, Boston, MA.

Simon, H. A. 1962. The architecture of complexity. *Proceedings of the American Philosophical Society* 106(6): 467–482.

Srnicek, N. 2016. *Platform Capitalism*. Polity Press, Cambridge, UK.

Stabell, C. B. & Fjeldstad, Ø. D. 1998. Configuring value for competitive advantage: on chains, shops, and networks. *Strategic Management Journal* 19(5): 413–437.

West, J. 2003. How open is open enough?: Melding proprietary and open source platform strategies. *Research Policy* 32(7): 1259–1285.

Wheelwright, S. C. & Clark, K. B. 1992. *Revolutionizing Product Development: Quantum Leaps in Speed, Efficiency, and Quality*. Free Press, New York, NY.

Yoo, Y., Henfridsson, O., & Lyytinen, K. 2010. The new organizing logic of digital innovation: an agenda for information systems research. *Information Systems Research* 21(4): 724–735.

Zuboff, S. 2015. Big other: surveillance capitalism and the prospects of an information civilization. *Journal of Information Technology* 30(1): 7589.

6 | *Circular Organizing*

JOHN A. MATHEWS

Consider the case where a group of firms – for example, textile-producing firms – join forces to share a common platform for providing energy and resources for their export-oriented activities. The critical resource is water, needed as a fresh supply by the firms for their dyeing operations and as a waste disposal issue if nearby lakes and rivers are not to be contaminated. The firms create a solution in the form of a water treatment plant that circulates 90 percent recycled water to all firms, supplying "gray water" (not potable but useful for all other activities) in place of the alternative of fresh "blue water." This saves all firms the costs of both water supply and wastewater disposal. But as it stands, the treatment plant generates sludge that needs to be disposed of after it has been separated from the recirculated water by physical and chemical means.

Consider further a situation where the water treatment plant incorporates a solar facility for drying the sludge and then links with a nearby cement plant to supply the powder-dry sludge as an input to the cement-making process. This additional feature has a dramatic effect, as it now means that the firms are jointly operating a zero-liquid discharge system where 90 percent of the water is recycled and the remaining 10 percent evaporates through solar means – and no wastewater is discharged to the environment. Moreover, an industrial cycle is established between the textile industry and the building materials (cement) industry, with the supply of sludge to the cement industry serving as a means of closing the loop between the two industries. The utilization of the dried textile waste sludge as an input to the cement industry provides a means for the cement industry to reduce its ecological footprint, having lower impact on the environment in that it needs fewer mined resources as inputs. At the same time, it also reduces the environmental impact of the textile industry, which no longer draws fresh water from the surrounding waterways and reduces its wastewater discharge to zero.

In this example, we see the power of firms coming together to turn outputs (wastes) from one process into inputs for another process. This switch from a linear flow of materials – mined at one end of the process and dumped at the other end – to a circular flow, where industrial loops are closed, is an instance of what is described generally as a *circular economy* (Winans, Kendall, & Deng, 2017). The firms involved have engaged in organization design, where the design concerns multifirm processes – that is, processes that span several firms in different industries. In this case, the firms have been shifting their operations in a green direction, in that they have jointly reduced their environmental impact and have utilized green (solar) power to do so.

The interesting aspect of this story is that the firms involved are not found in Silicon Valley or in some advanced industrial park where such cutting-edge circular economy initiatives might be expected. Instead, the firms are located in Africa, in an export-oriented industrial park in Addis Ababa, Ethiopia, in the Bole Lemi Industrial Park (Phase 2). The operation of this zero-waste discharge facility gives the textile firms a clear competitive advantage, in that their costs for freshwater supply and contaminated water disposal have been dramatically reduced. The firms' operations have become clean and green – as well as more profitable and sustainable. Similar zero-liquid discharge operations can be found in other Ethiopian export-oriented industrial parks. The firms have effectively leapfrogged from being latecomers and technological laggards to utilizing an advanced circular economy organizational design (Oqubay & Kefale, 2020).

A further twist to this story is that the water treatment plant, which knits together the operations of the firms into an efficient multifirm network, is operated by a public agency, the Industrial Parks Development Corporation. This wholly owned state agency is taking the entrepreneurial step of supplying essential shared infrastructure for the textile firms and introducing a circular economy ecosystem linking the textiles industry to the cement industry and reducing the environmental impact of both. The public agency thereby saves the private firms both resource and energy costs and generates a competitive advantage for them over competitors that do not have access to these shared resources.

This example of circular organizing motivates our discussion of the role played by organization design in the greening of industry – not just in developed countries and involving advanced firms but in newly industrializing countries where greening of energy and circular economy design issues can be expected to generate distinct competitive advantages. What role do organizational issues play in the greening of business, as sustainable business becomes a powerful trend worldwide? Some organizational architectures work better than others in shifting the balance between competition and collaboration and propagating sustainable business practices. Where firms are enabled to form self-defined clusters and develop platforms, through recognition of mutual benefits, sustainable business practices can be accelerated and diffused. In keeping with a strategic perspective on organizational clusters as being driven by choices and business models focused on their collective resources, activities, and routines, sustainable business platforms likewise follow these strategic categories. At the industry level, the focus is on integrating cycles of industrial activity to form closed loops in which residuals or wastes from one firm are used as resources by another firm. By providing financial and fiscal incentives, state actors play an important role in linking potentially related firms and leveraging their collective resources and activities (Mathews, Tan, & Hu, 2018). It is a matter of urgent interest to diffuse circular organizing practices – to alter global industrial dynamics and develop new, sustainable systems based on renewable energy and the recirculation of resources.

In this chapter, I describe the concept and process of circular organizing. "The circular economy is based on three principles, driven by design: Eliminate waste and pollution; Circulate products and materials at their highest value; and Regenerate nature. It is underpinned by a transition to renewable energy and materials" (ellenmacarthurfoundation.org). Circular organizing can be implemented within a single integrated firm or across firms in multiple industries. Successful examples of both are offered, with a focus on the way that platforms – infrastructures and processes that facilitate actor interactions and exchanges (Cusumano, Gawer, & Yoffie, 2019; Fjeldstad et al., 2012) – accelerate the process of transformation. We will examine three platform characteristics – practicability, replicability, and scalability. These platform features are the drivers of the global green shift, exerting far more power and influence than carbon taxes or carbon prices widely favored by mainstream economists and policymakers. As the need for sustainability becomes ever more urgent, circular organizing ideas and practices can lead the way.

Resource Flows, Industrial Loops, and the Evolution of Hypercycles

Organizations do not operate on their own but in relation to a host of other organizations – competitors, collaborators, and other actors of various kinds. As the green economy develops, firms engage in the development of industrial loops of varying size, density, and strength. Circular resource flows can evolve from linear industrial processes (Mathews, 2015). In Figure 6.1, the economy is depicted as consisting of firms in six unconnected industries. Each firm uses raw material inputs to produce finished goods. Each firm also produces waste as a by-product. Each of the resource flows could be eco-improved through a process known as "cleaner production" (which is company-specific). In Figure 6.2, links have been established between firms via their interconnected processes: Some firms in industries A, B, and C have been connected through by-product exchanges; firms in industries D and E are connected to each other but not to A, B, or C; and firms in industry F are not connected to any other industry. These various resource flows have potential for industrial symbiosis, which occurs between two or more firms, and typically within a single eco-industrial park. In Figure 6.3, links have proliferated to the point where industry F is now

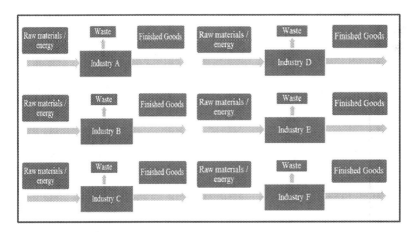

Figure 6.1 The economy depicted as six unconnected industries
From Mathews (2014). Used with permission of Stanford University Press; permission conveyed through Copyright Clearance Center, Inc. © 2014 by the Board of Trustees of the Leland Stanford Jr. University. All rights reserved.

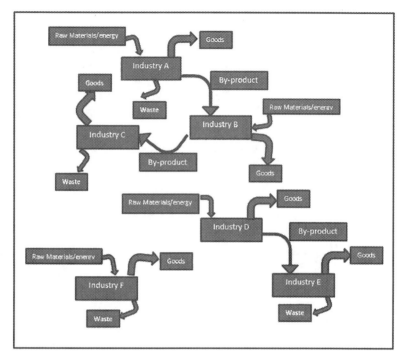

Figure 6.2 Early stage in the evolution of an industrial loop
From Mathews (2014). Used with permission of Stanford University Press; permission conveyed through Copyright Clearance Center, Inc. © 2014 by the Board of Trustees of the Leland Stanford Jr. University. All rights reserved.

connected to industry A, through by-product exchanges among some firms in each industry. This is the critical link that closes the loop – the starting point of one process is the result of another process, thereby joining all the industries in a closed industrial loop.

Perhaps the purest eco-example of a closed industrial loop is where renewable energy processes make use of recirculated resources, thereby generating sustainable pathways. Take the case of the manufacture of wind turbines, using steel. As the level of recycled steel builds up, circular steel reprocessing is advanced. Closing the loop in this case means substituting more and more recycled steel for "virgin" steel sourced by mining iron ore. To the extent that renewable sources of energy are utilized in manufacturing the wind turbines (for heating and other electrical power inputs), another circular process is set in motion – in effect, utilizing renewable power to generate renewable power.

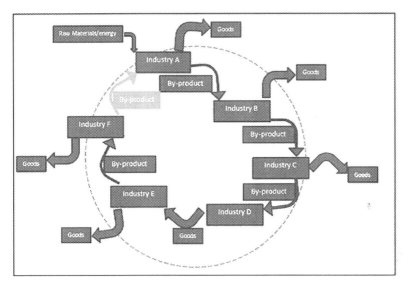

Figure 6.3 A closed industrial loop
From Mathews (2014). Used with permission of Stanford University Press; permission conveyed through Copyright Clearance Center, Inc. © 2014 by the Board of Trustees of the Leland Stanford Jr. University. All rights reserved.

All industrial recycling and resource recirculation processes can be described in this way. We can have plastics assembled at a collection point and utilized as input for the production of new plastics. We can have paper products assembled at a collection point and utilized as input for the production of new paper products. We can have metal products collected and assembled, then utilized as input for the production of new metal ingots (via a lengthy process of decontamination and purification). Or we can have firms sharing water treatment facilities that save on resource supply of fresh water and on costs of wastewater disposal, as in the Bole Lemi Industrial Park described earlier. Each of these processes follows the organizational architecture of the circular economy – using Commodity A for the production of Commodity A.

The organizational aspect of this industrial process lies in bringing firms to the point where they recognize their common interests in participating in an industrial loop, where one firm takes an initiative in supplying some material to another firm for a profit, and so a chain of such transactions builds up with the ultimate step being the supply of the commodity that began the chain. How firms recognize and act on those common interests is the key organizational issue. Typically, it takes a supra-organization with responsibility for the value chain as a whole to take the initiative. This is how industrial parks can evolve into eco-industrial parks, where one of the park entities takes responsibility for identifying and acting on the industrial symbiosis opportunities revealed. In China, industrial parks generally come equipped with an administrative organization that controls entry of firms to the park as well as their exit. Such an organization can take the further step of identifying profitable opportunities where a gap in a value chain can be filled by making the appropriate investments (Mathews et al., 2018).

Successful establishment of circular systems stands to benefit the participating firms in two ways. First, environmentally conscious consumers have demonstrated a preference for buying products and services from sustainable firms. Second, waste to resource generation can lead to greater efficiency, profitability, and sustainability for the firms that are part of the industrial loop. To the extent that either or both of these mechanisms make firms participating in circular systems successful, other firms will be incentivized to adopt circular practices. This can lead to a replication of the circularity principles within the population of firms and hence make the formation of new circular systems quicker and more viable. Furthermore, increased experience with waste to resource generation, and with how the process is organized, makes it easier for firms to successfully apply circularity principles in new areas. This phenomenon is the industrial counterpart to what the German evolutionary biologists Eigen and Schuster (1977) meant by a hypercycle – an autocatalytic, self-replicating cycle. Transposing the hypercycle concept to the industrial domain, we may propose that the ultimate goal of industrial ecology is to ensure zero waste from industrial processes. Circular organizing involves identifying potential industrial loops in practice and then promoting investments in the critical platforms and processes that close the loops.

Circular Business Platforms

A growing category of multifirm structures exists in the form of platforms, which bring firms together in collaborative relationships that support further economic activity (Cusumano et al., 2019). Once the potential of the platform is identified and the firms involved take the step of setting up the platform, circular industrial activities can be accelerated and diffused. In the case of well-known platforms such as Google's Android platform or Facebook's YouTube platform, these collective entities provide the basis for many other firms to utilize the platform as their operating system. The platform acts as a catalyst to facilitate further rounds of industrial activity. We are concerned here with the kinds of platforms that accelerate the greening of business and industry – and which can best be described as green platforms. Green platforms emerge as a means of allowing groups of firms to recognize their common interests in promoting green activities (e.g., through a collective response to collection and disposal of waste or the generation and distribution of renewable power) and accelerating what would otherwise be a slow and painful process (Mathews, 2020). Let us examine several existing cases before drawing some general conclusions about green platforms.

Nanjing Chemical Industrial Park

The Nanjing Chemical Industrial Park was purpose-built as an eco-industrial park in China, opening in 2001. It now accommodates the operations of more than 100 chemical and petrochemical companies, including many of the world's top multinationals. A complex series of intersecting value chains have been established, making for multiple symbiotic links and eliminating many toxic wastes that have been redirected to become inputs into related chemical processes. The park's goal is to achieve a 90 percent reutilization rate for toxic solid waste. Retreatment processes now enable polycarbonate manufacturers in the park to reutilize upstream wastes such as benzene and propylene, turning them into phenol and acetone that are fed to the polycarbonate producers, thereby turning toxic outputs into valuable inputs. Other value chains in the industrial park involve carbon, taking sources such as waste carbon dioxide and turning them into inputs to related industrial processes such as beverage production and cement production. The firms within the park secure competitive advantages by sharing resource inputs, eliminating wastes, and building new industries around newly created value chains (Mathews et al., 2018).

Tesla, Inc.

American entrepreneur and industrialist Elon Musk built a green energy and transport platform, Tesla, that is focused on electrical vehicle (EV) and photovoltaic (PV) power generation businesses. The EV business, producing successive car models, is the manufacturing core, supplemented by battery manufacture. Manufacturing extends to energy storage systems (batteries, the Tesla Powerwall system) and to solar panel production. Tesla's SolarCity business offers solar power systems to homeowners, providing its own fabricated PV systems that are compatible with Tesla's EV units and Powerwall energy storage. This green platform can be extended to encompass power production, through solar PVs, and energy storage, through Tesla's Powerwall domestic batteries and through aggregation of Tesla's EVs. Thus, Tesla is growing businesses in EV transport, EV charging infrastructure, PV roofing tiles, and energy storage, with cross-subsidies and synergies that derive from the platform character of the Tesla business model. (The research literature is beginning to refer to an electric mobility ecosystem, encompassing EV builders, EV sales systems, EV charging infrastructure, and the value chains associated with these activities – see, e.g., Gharib, Duwe, & Weber, 2018.)

Green Food Platforms

Many food companies are now breaking with the global food production behemoths, with its waste of land and water and its ruinous runoffs from overuse of fertilizers, herbicides, and pesticides. The world is on the cusp of a fifth food production revolution – the first being the invention of agriculture, where soil is prepared by digging, seed is sown, water is irrigated, and plants are harvested; the second involving mechanization of these activities; the third involving intensive use of herbicides, pesticides, and fertilizers; and the fourth involving IT-enhanced (digital) "smart farming." The fifth and latest stage transforms food production by utilizing enclosed spaces (greenhouses) with multiple stories; controlled inputs with water recycling; controlled light using either sunlight or LEDs; and the use of renewables as the energy source (Mathews, 2018a). The advantages of such a green food platform are clear: drastic reduction in land requirements for the same level of food production, drastic reduction in the use of water and recycling of water, very low (or zero) use of herbicides and pesticides, and advantages such as year-round production of fresh food and proximity to markets in the world's cities. Fifth-generation, closed-loop agricultural platforms will substantially raise the sustainability profile of global food production.

Plenty, an indoor vertical farming company based in California, is an exemplary case in that it is building a platform that can be replicated and scaled adjacent to cities around the world. Plenty is perfecting the optimal inputs for a range of vegetable and fruit outputs, all produced by computer-controlled robots. The company is focused on perfecting its enclosed farming platform before expanding to produce food at new locations (Peters, 2019). Another model is Sundrop Farms in South Australia. Started a decade ago by Sunridge Partners, it is a world-first food production platform for closed-environment culture of fresh tomatoes using solar power and desalinated seawater to provide all needed inputs for hydroponically grown vegetables (Dulaney, 2017). After a decade of ownership by Sunridge, the business was sold as a going concern to an Australian investment firm in 2019.

Industrial Symbiosis

A particular kind of green platform consists of firms linked to each other through industrial symbiosis (Chertow, 2000). Industrial symbiosis brings companies together in innovative collaborations where the waste materials of one firm become the inputs to another firm, creating a closed industrial loop. This is the circular economy in action, exemplified in cases in Kalundborg, Denmark, Yokohama, Japan, and elsewhere such as the Bole Lemi Industrial Park in Ethiopia discussed earlier. As outlined in case studies of Kalundborg and its origins (Ehrenfeld & Chertow, 2002; Jacobsen, 2006), the green platform that evolved in this Danish industrial town is the first full realization of industrial symbiosis. It involves resource flows among an oil refinery, a power plant, a biotech company, a soil remediation company, a plasterboard company, and an associated fish farm that utilizes warm wastewater. While the details of the Kalundborg case do not concern us here, the point is that Kalundborg pioneered the creation of a green industrial symbiosis platform that could then be scaled up and emulated around the world – as it has been, particularly in China (Mathews & Tan, 2011).

Suzhou Industrial Park

China has vast industrial parks where hundreds and thousands of firms are co-located in order to achieve aggregation economies, economies of scale, and synergies flowing from enhanced specialization. Several of those industrial parks are making the transition to eco-industrial parks where energy and resource flows are shared and former industrial outputs (wastes, pollution) are turned into industrial inputs, thereby closing industrial loops. A particularly good example is found in the Suzhou Industrial Park where a range of electronic and IT products are produced by world-leading firms such as Samsung, Sony, and Matsushita. The core product that is involved is the printed circuit board (PCB) with its copper printing to create electronic circuits, and where the copper is regenerated from waste and discarded electronic products. In place of virgin copper produced from copper ore, the copper is regenerated from electronic products in a process called "urban mining." The PCB footprint is thereby reduced with each iteration of the circular flow of the copper through the PCB products, thus achieving increased levels of resource security and saving China from the burden of having to rely on copper imported from unstable parts of the world (Mathews & Tan, 2016).

All of the green business initiatives discussed here involve aspects of circular organizing. Each initiative's organizational mechanisms and the competitive advantages they afford are summarized in Table 6.1.

Propagation Dynamics: Platforms That Are Practicable, Replicable, and Scalable

The key to the green transition in different industrial sectors is that platforms facilitate – indeed accelerate – the pace of diffusion through their own propagation. This is a general feature of platforms, as discussed most commonly in the case of digital platforms (Kenney & Zysman, 2016; Kenney et al., 2019). By providing a base on which other firms may build and develop their own business models, platforms play a role analogous to catalysts in the biological world. They do so through their practicability (cost effectiveness), replicability (via standardization), and scalability (due to minimal geopolitical barriers). This trio of factors governs the pace at which platforms propagate.

Table 6.1 *Green business initiatives involving circular organizing*

Green business initiative	Circular context	Organizing mechanisms	Competitive advantages
Nanjing Chemical Industrial Park	Chemical and petrochemical company linkages	Identification and selection of firms with potential complementarities; coordination across multiple value chains	Reduced costs; reduced environmental impact; new business development
Suzhou Industrial Park	Urban copper mining – extraction of raw material inputs from recycled products	Promotion of cross-firm linkages by industrial park administrator; joint ventures with multinational firms; network governance; interrelated online platforms	Reduced costs; reduced environmental impact; new business development
Industrial Symbiosis (Kalundborg, Denmark)	Shared resources and waste disposal	Colocation of firms; shared resource infrastructure; sharing of personnel, equipment, and information	Reduced costs; reduced environmental impact; new business development
Bole Lemi Industrial Park (Addis Ababa, Ethiopia)	Water retreatment plant shared by textile and cement-producing firms	Colocation of firms; shared resource infrastructure; state agency sponsor and coordinator	Reduced costs; reduced environmental impact
Clean food platforms	Closed-environment agriculture	Integrated facilities; within-firm coordination	Increased food safety; lower cost of distribution
Tesla, Inc.	Within-corporation circular resource flows among electric vehicle, power production, and power storage businesses	Corporate provision and operation of a common platform	Corporate internalization of product complementarities

Source: Author original

Practicability

Platforms have to be practicable, in the sense that they will need to depend on available technologies that are accessible and feasible. The paramount issue of practicability is costs – whether they are low and below those of existing energy and resource systems and whether they are declining. The common feature of all the green platforms taken as exemplary is that they are designed around manufacturing and benefit from cost reductions associated with increased manufacturing volume, a process known as the learning curve (Wright, 1936) or experience curve (Henderson, 1974). Practicability is evident in platforms involving energy devices that utilize renewable sources of energy and resource devices that make use of recirculated flows – all of which are products of manufacturing. In this respect, they stand in marked contrast to energy sources and resources that are products of mining or drilling, and where costs are contingent on geological and geographical features that vary with geopolitical conditions.

The requirement for practicability rules out accepting speculative developments or inventions that are not yet out of the laboratory, thereby ensuring that the technology utilized by the green platform is already tested and available. While in some cases this might be a restriction, it ensures that discussions and decisions remain close to business and industrial realities.

Replicability

All the green platforms are replicable in that they consist of standardized elements that can be independently produced in mass production fashion, particularly when they have a modular structure. Modularity means that the platform can be extended simply by adding new modules, such as a new enclosed food production module, or a new PV/EV module, or a new water/steam/electric power module at Kalundborg and its emulators around the world. It is the replicability of standardized manufactured systems and subsystems that enable them to be propagated in the fastest and most efficient way.

The opposite of replicability is one-off production or customized production, where no economies of scale are to be captured. Just about all prior versions of "brown production" are characterized by one-off features, even where large size generates economies of scale.

Scalability

Green platforms are most easily scalable when there are no barriers standing in the way of their expansion. Insofar as they are able to make use of recycled materials, they do not encounter resource barriers. Insofar as they rely on renewable power, they are able to access replenishable energy sources including solar and wind power. These features may be contrasted with the barriers encountered in operations relying on fossil fuels for energy and virgin resources for material flows.

Once a platform is established (e.g., for the sharing of water recirculation or energy sourcing from waste), it does not have to be reinvented. The platform acts as a permanent accelerator of industrial transformation – in the same way as a catalyst operates in accelerating biochemical reaction pathways. This focus on industrial dynamics, as opposed to one-off choices shaped by changes in price linked to carbon taxes and other "green" charges, is what gives credibility to the account of greening framed as a Schumpeterian process of creative destruction (Mathews, 2018b).

Conclusion

No economy has actually reached a state where it can be described as fully circular – 100 percent renewable energy and 100 percent recirculated resources flowing through closed industrial loops. Economies green as they move closer to renewable energy flows and recirculation of resources. We are witnessing a trend that takes business-as-usual pathways, with their dependence on fossil fuels, virgin resources, and attendant geopolitical risks, in a new, sustainable direction. The greening of an economy depends on firms interacting in a circular fashion. Circular organizing is increasingly demonstrating that it can be efficient, profitable, and sustainable.

References

Chertow, M. 2000. Industrial symbiosis: literature and taxonomy. *Annual Review of Energy and the Environment* 25(1): 313–337.

Cusumano, M. A., Gawer, A., & Yoffie, D. B. 2019. *The Business of Platforms: Strategy in the Age of Digital Competition, Innovation, and Power*. HarperCollins, New York, NY.

Dulaney, M. 2017. Waiting for the sun: Port Augusta's search for a post-coal identity. *Griffith Review* 55: 22–23.

Ehrenfeld, J. R. & Chertow, M. R. 2002. Industrial symbiosis: the legacy of Kalundborg. In R. U. Ayres and L. W. Ayres (eds.), *A Handbook of Industrial Ecology*: 334–348. Edward Elgar, Cheltenham, UK.

Eigen, M. & Schuster, P. 1977. The hypercycle: a principle of natural self-organization. Part A: emergence of the hypercycle. *Die Naturwissenschaften* 64: 541–565. https://ellenmacarthurfoundation.org/topics/circular-economy-introduction/overview.

Fjeldstad, Ø. D., Snow, C. C., Miles, R. E., & Lettl, C. 2012. The architecture of collaboration. *Strategic Management Journal* 33: 734–750.

Gharib, R., Duwe, D., & Weber, P. 2018. Establishing an electric mobility ecosystem. *2018 IEEE International Conference on Engineering, Technology and Innovation (ICE/ITMC)*: 1–5. DOI: 10.1109/ICE.2018.8436305.

Henderson, B. D. 1974. *The Experience Curve – Reviewed (Part 1)*. Boston Consulting Group, Boston, MA.

Jacobsen, N. B. 2006. Industrial symbiosis in Kalundborg, Denmark: a quantitative assessment of economic and environmental aspects. *Journal of Industrial Ecology* 10(1–2): 239–255.

Kenney, M. & Zysman, J. 2016. The rise of the platform economy. *Issues in Science and Technology* 32(3): 61–69.

Kenney, M., Rouvinen, P., Seppälä, T., & Zysman, J. 2019. Platforms and industrial change. *Industry and Innovation* 26(8): 871–879.

Mathews, J. A. 2015. *Greening of Capitalism: How Asia Is Driving the Next Great Transformation*. Stanford University Press, Stanford, CA.

Mathews J. A. 2017. *Global Green Shift: When Ceres Meets Gaia*. Anthem Press, London, UK.

Mathews, J. A. 2018a. "New wave" revolution in city-focused, closed environment food production. *CABI Reviews. CABI International*. DOI: 10.1079/PAVSNNR201813006.

Mathews, J. A. 2018b. Schumpeter in the twenty-first century: creative destruction and the global green shift. In L. Burlamaqui and R. Kattel (eds.), *Schumpeter's Capitalism, Socialism and Democracy: A Twenty-First Century Agenda*: 233–254. Routledge, Abingdon-on-Thames, UK.

Mathews, J. A. 2020. Schumpeterian economic dynamics of greening: propagation of green eco-platforms. In A. Pyka and K. Lee (eds), *Innovation, Catch-up and Sustainable Development: A Schumpeterian Perspective*: 339–361. Springer International Publishing, Cham, Switzerland.

Mathews, J. A. & Tan, H. 2011. Progress towards a circular economy in China: drivers (and inhibitors) of eco-industrial initiatives. *Journal of Industrial Ecology* 15(3): 435–457.

Mathews, J. A. & Tan, H. 2016. Circular economy: lessons from China. *Nature* 531(24 March): 440–442. https://doi.org/10.1038/531440a

Mathews, J. A., Tan, H., & Hu, M. C. 2018. Moving to a circular economy in China: transforming industrial parks into eco-industrial parks. *California Management Review* 60(3): 157–181.

McIntyre, D. P. & Srinivasan, A. 2017. Networks, platforms, and strategy: emerging views and next steps. *Strategic Management Journal* 38: 141–160.

Oqubay, A. & Kefale, D. M. 2020. A strategic approach to industrial hubs: learnings in Ethiopia. In A. Oqubay and J. Y. Lin (eds.), *The Oxford Handbook of Industrial Hubs and Economic Development*: 876–913. Oxford University Press, Oxford, UK.

Peters, A. 2019. Robots are already farming crops inside this Silicon Valley warehouse. Fast Company, June 20. www.fastcompany.com/90365627/robots-are-already-farming-crops-inside-this-silicon-valley-warehouse

Winans, K., Kendall, A., & Deng, H. 2017. The history and current applications of the circular economy concept. *Renewable and Sustainable Energy Reviews* 68: 825–833.

Wright, T. P. 1936. Factors affecting the cost of airplanes. *Journal of Aeronautical Sciences* 3(4): 122–128.

7 | *Organizing Intelligent Digital Actors*

VEGARD KOLBJØRNSRUD

Artificial intelligence (AI) is the study of *digital agents* that perceive their environment and take actions in pursuit of goals. Organizations are increasingly incorporating digital agents – machines that use computer algorithms to make decisions and act – into their operations to be better able to solve problems and adapt faster and more effectively to changes in their environment. Banks, insurance companies, government agencies, and many other organizations use "chatbots" – communicative software robots – to hold conversations with customers. Amazon uses physical robots in its warehouses to assemble customer orders. Tesla uses "cobots" – collaborative robots – to work alongside human workers to manufacture electric vehicles. Software firms develop machine learning algorithms to be used in a wide variety of situations, including diagnosing illnesses and detecting fraudulent behavior. The Swedish venture capital firm EQT Ventures uses AI to identify and assess little-known companies with large investment potential (Byrne, 2018).

AI is a broad academic discipline combining computer science, robotics, and neuroscience, and the goal of AI research is to develop increasingly intelligent machines. Early applications of AI required human specification of the knowledge that the computer would use. With recent advancements in sensors, communications, cloud computing, and machine learning, AI enables knowledge-based coproduction by humans and machines, and AI's influence on how activities and resources are organized continues to grow (Brynjolfsson & McAfee, 2014; Shrestha, Ben-Menahem, & von Krogh, 2019; von Krogh, 2018).

This chapter examines how AI is incorporated into the design of organizations. The first section discusses the two main ways intelligent machines are being used in organizations: *substituting* for human actors on routine tasks and *augmenting* human actors' ability in complex situations to search, comprehend problems, generate and evaluate alternative solutions, and make choices. The second section discusses means of integrating the efforts of human and digital actors. These include digital infrastructures and tools, actor capabilities, and shared representations of the task environment. The last section describes how the collective intelligence of human and digital actors is activated by increasing situation awareness, trust, and accountability in the human–machine relationship.

Impact of Artificial Intelligence on Organizations

Although the term "artificial intelligence" was coined in 1956, its roots go back to the late 1940s at the dawn of electronic computing. In subsequent decades, the field of AI made halting progress, and it was not until the late 1990s that research progress in AI began to accelerate. The current wave of progress began around 2010, driven by three inter-related factors: (1) the availability of big data from various sources, (2) improved machine learning approaches and algorithms, and (3) more powerful computers (Executive Office of the President, 2016).

AI enables computer-guided machines to exhibit intelligent behavior, which involves sensing, comprehending, acting, and learning in complex environments (Kolbjørnsrud, Amico, & Thomas, 2017; Nilsson, 1998; Simon & Newell, 1958; Winston, 1992). A computer's behavior is determined by algorithms – step-by-step procedures for solving problems – and thus the machine's capabilities result from its algorithms. Although some core algorithms are programmed into a computer's software, machine learning is a class of algorithms that enable a computer to develop new algorithms from captured data, which, in turn, can be used in decision-making and problem-solving. Machine learning algorithms vary both in form and function – that is, their sequence of computational steps and the kind of output they produce. *Supervised* machine learning identifies statistical relationships between independent and dependent variables (e.g., correlations). The term "supervised" means that the variables are labeled by an external actor. For example, supervised machine learning has been used to train a computer to recognize cancer by feeding the algorithm tens of thousands of images from lung scans that have been labelled with diagnostic information provided by expert medical professionals. *Unsupervised* machine learning means that groupings or patterns in data are identified without human input. Unsupervised machine learning is used, for example, to segment markets and power recommendation engines, such as Netflix creating customer profiles and making content recommendations based on them. *Imitation* learning involves machines mimicking human behavior in the performance of a given task. The learning algorithms create a mapping between observations and actions. The resulting models predict appropriate actions in various situations (Hussein et al., 2017). Imitation learning is used in training various types of robots, including self-driving cars (Goldberg, 2019). *Reinforcement* learning involves experimentation and learning from feedback. Neural networks, a computing technology that mimics the neuron-synapse structure of the human brain, is an important alternative to statistics-based algorithms. Neural networks are particularly valuable in identifying patterns in large-volume, complex data.

Google's AlphaGo program illustrates the use of AI not only in solving complex problems but in learning *how* to solve them as well (Silver et al., 2017). Go is an ancient two-player Chinese board game. Each player has a set of black or white stones that they take turns placing, and the goal is to surround more territory than the opposing player. Because of its large board, Go contains more alternative move sequences than chess and therefore is more difficult to master. AlphaGo plays an opponent by using Monte Carlo simulation (repeated random sampling) to draw moves and countermoves from probability distributions and assess the payoff of alternative moves. The large number of unique alternative move–countermove sequences is too large for the computer to exhaustively generate and assess while playing. Therefore, AlphaGo relies on two types of heuristics to select its moves. First, it uses policy heuristics to choose the moves that it will investigate and, second, it uses valuation heuristics to assess the attractiveness of the endpoints of the generated sequences. In this way, AlphaGo mimics how humans solve problems (Tversky & Kahneman, 1974). Monte Carlo-based search is a commonly used AI problem-solving technique, and the search algorithms have been programmed into AlphaGo. On the other hand, the policy and value heuristics are the result of machine learning. A combination of neural network-based supervised imitation and reinforcement machine learning was used to learn from expert human players.

Following this initial training, AlphaGo played many games against itself and learned from the successes and failures of its own choices. This reinforcement learning process was used to refine the policy and valuation heuristics. Eventually, it achieved a level of capability sufficient to beat any expert human Go player (Moyer, 2016). The fact that AlphaGo can outperform human experts by relying on learned heuristics rather than exhaustive generation and search of all possible move–countermove sequences is the real accomplishment of Google's AI endeavor. Overall, the AlphaGo example illustrates how AI involves machines both *learning* and *doing* – that is, becoming increasingly intelligent while performing tasks.

During the last decade, AI has made dramatic inroads into the operations of organizations and is becoming mainstream organizational technology (Daugherty & Wilson, 2018). Specifically, AI expands organizational capabilities by *substituting* digital actors for human actors and *augmenting* organizational problem-solving and decision-making – drawing on the capabilities and overcoming the constraints of each actor type. See Table 7.1 for a comparison of distinctive characteristics of human and digital actors.

Substituting Digital Agents for Human Actors

Automation is the substitution of machines that follow prespecified rules in performing repetitive tasks for human actors. Increasingly, machines are controlled by algorithms that allow them to intelligently take action in pursuit of goals (Glikson & Woolley, 2020). Using recent AI solutions, machines can now match or exceed human intelligence in a wide range of sophisticated, specialized domains such as route planning and predictive maintenance in transportation networks (Bast et al., 2016; Hodson, 2014), energy use optimization (Evans & Gao, 2016), factory assembly of products (Sharma, Zanotti, & Musunur, 2019), warehouse operations and logistics (Woschank, Rauch, & Zsifkovits, 2020), predicting market potential in different geographies (Andersen et al., 2018), and the automation of administrative tasks (Tambe, Cappelli, & Yakubovich, 2019). The main benefits of intelligent automation include cost efficiency, continuous operation, and increased speed and quality (Goldberg, 2012; Parasuraman, Sheridan, & Wickens, 2000). Based on the current state of AI technology, digital agents are well suited for the performance of cognitive and physical tasks that exhibit high degrees of regularity. Regularity refers to tasks where the cognitive component – perceiving, matching, predicting, and planning – can be executed by relying on patterns learned from large datasets. Many such tasks, which involve choosing among

Table 7.1 *Comparison of problem-solving capabilities and constraints of human actors and digital agents*

	Human actors	Digital agents
Specificity of problems	Human actors can accommodate ambiguous problems.	Digital agents require highly specified problems.
Data volume	They can learn from few examples.	They require many examples to learn from.
	Their data processing capacity has constraints.	They can process large volumes of data.
Speed	They are comparatively slow.	They are comparatively fast.
	There is a high trade-off between speed and accuracy.	There is limited trade-off between speed and accuracy.
Noise and replicability	Noise – random error in judgments – can be a significant problem. Replicability is vulnerable to inter- and intra-individual factors such as differences in experience, attention, context, and emotional state of the problem solver.	No noise from data processing but noisy data can affect outcomes. Problem-solving process and outcomes are highly replicable due to standard computational procedure.
Bias	Bias – systematic error in judgments – can be a significant problem. It can arise from cognitive constraints, heuristics, and predispositions of the problem solver.	Bias can be a significant problem. It can arise from inaccurate, incomplete, and unrepresentative data as well the predispositions of human programmers.
Explainability	Solutions and decisions are explainable and interpretable, though vulnerable to retrospective sensemaking.	Complexity of the functional forms can make it difficult to interpret the problem-solving process and outcomes.

Source: Adapted from Shrestha et al. (2019: 68).

alternatives with probabilistic outcomes (Simon, 1993), are found in manufacturing, transportation, and financial services. A recent study estimates that over 70 percent of tasks in these and other sectors are automatable (Muro, Maxim, & Whiton, 2019).

Rather than displacing human labor, the automation of tasks often leads to the creation of new tasks in which human labor has a comparative advantage (Acemoglu & Restrepo, 2019). The automation by Associated Press (AP) of a major segment of its financial news reporting exemplifies what can happen when tasks are automated. The news agency expanded its quarterly earnings reporting from approximately 300 to 4,400 news stories by using AI-powered software robots to write articles (Colford, 2014). In doing so, technology freed up AP's journalists to conduct more investigative and interpretive reporting. Through its new human–machine division of labor, AP increased both the volume and quality of its publications.

Increasingly, organizations use digital agents to perform administrative tasks such as directing, evaluating, and rewarding workers (Kellogg, Valentine, & Christin, 2019). For example, Uber uses algorithms to assign drivers to rides and plan efficient routes. Centralized algorithmic planning allows Uber to be timely in its response to customer requests and efficient in the service it provides (Liu, Brynjolfsson, & Dowlatabadi, 2021). eBay uses algorithms to promote particular sellers based on buyer evaluations (Curchod et al., 2020). IBM uses algorithms to recommend training to employees based on the experiences of other IBM employees (Tambe et al., 2019).

In summary, algorithms are used to substitute for human actors in a variety of operational and administrative tasks. Substitution, however, may carry hidden costs associated with biased decision-making (Cowgill, 2019). Knowledge acquired through machine learning is biased by the data on which the machine was trained. If the data sample is not representative of factors that explain variation in outcomes, biases are inevitable and may result in undesirable decisions. For example, Google's advertisement settings were found to display fewer advertisements of high-paying jobs to females than males (Raj & Seamans, 2019). Furthermore, many facial recognition systems have been found to be less accurate for people with darker skin and for women, which is problematic when used in criminal justice or healthcare (Buolamwini & Gebru, 2018; Khalil et al., 2020; Najibi, 2020). Therefore, when using algorithms to substitute for humans, it is important to keep "humans in the loop" to ensure that the algorithms perform according to the organization's requirements and can be adapted as needed (Grønsund & Aanestad, 2020). The key to keeping human actors actively in the loop is to design the system such that human actors maintain supervisory control over digital agents. This requires that human actors understand the actions of their digital teammates as well as the reasons why the actions are taken (Endsley, 2017; Major & Shah, 2020).

Augmenting Organizational Problem-Solving

Compared to tasks that can be standardized, tasks that require complex problem-solving, creativity, or emotional intelligence are less amenable to automation. For those types of tasks, digital agents are used to augment human problem-solving and decision-making. According to Engelbart (1962: 1) augmentation can improve problem comprehension and decision-making by a mixture of the following: gaining comprehension more quickly; gaining better comprehension; gaining a useful degree of comprehension where previously the situation was too complex; producing solutions more quickly; producing better solutions; and finding solutions where previously humans could find none. Digital augmentation of human problem-solving is becoming increasingly common as evidenced in medical diagnosis, drug discovery, product design, fraud detection, investment opportunity identification, and sales recommendations (Esteva et al., 2017; Kwun, 2018; Linsell, 2018; Ngai et al., 2011; Zhang et al., 2017). AI research and applications have made substantial contributions to organizational problem-solving activities, specifically in the form of algorithms that improve organizational comprehension, option generation, and organizational choice.

Improving organizational comprehension. Comprehension refers to actors' ability to understand their external and internal environments. Comprehension is challenging when operating in complex, dynamic environments characterized by a large number of constantly changing, interacting elements. The increased availability of data captured from a variety of sources makes it possible to use algorithms to improve organizational comprehension (Schmidt, 2017). By filtering, integrating, and highlighting information, algorithms can improve organizational actors' understanding of an evolving situation, including the prediction of its future states (Endsley, 2017). For example, Delta Air Lines uses Airbus' Skywise platform to collect and analyze data about aircraft and ground operations. Modern aircrafts supply data on more than 14,000 variables, which are fed into the analytics platform. The Skywise algorithms identify aircraft parts that need to be serviced or replaced before they fail. Such predictive maintenance has allowed Delta to reduce maintenance-related flight cancellations from more than 5,600 in 2010 to 55 in 2018 and lower the overall cost of repairs (Delta, 2019).

Improving option generation. The generation of possible courses of action occurs through a combination of search for existing solutions and the development of customized solutions (Simon, 1993). Organizations search their internal and external environments for technologies, suppliers, collaborators, and other resources. Modern business ecosystems include vast amounts of resources – information, software, development toolkits, and physical assets – all available through Application Programming Interfaces (APIs). Making use of those resources would not be possible without intelligent search engines. A foundational finding in organization science is that humans are constrained by bounded rationality (Simon, 1957) – individuals and firms seek to behave rationally but are constrained by their perceptual and computational capacities. Modern search engines use AI to scan, filter, and prioritize vast amounts of data "so that search can discover the important items" (Simon, 2002: 615). For search engines to intelligently deliver information, they need to understand both their users and the material that they are searching (Hu et al., 2018; Lin et al., 2014). Machine learning is used to improve search agents' ability to recognize the material being searched, such as Google's continuous scanning of the Internet to obtain and learn from captured information. Machine learning is also used to continually refine search agents' ability to profile their users. The Swedish venture capital firm EQT Ventures uses its Motherbrain system to search for little-known companies with high investment potential. This system collects a variety of data, such as financial information, social network activity, and app and web ranking data, and uses both supervised and unsupervised machine learning to develop profiles of companies as prospective investment opportunities. Thus, Motherbrain greatly expands the available set of investment opportunities. In addition, EQT's investment professionals continually add their assessments of companies to train the system to focus on the right opportunities. Overall, the Motherbrain system supports the full investment decision process from lead identification to evaluation and final decision, and it helps EQT's investment professionals prioritize their time by focusing on leads with the highest potential and the right maturity.

In addition to searching the environment, generating options involves problem-solving activities that seek to develop customized courses of action (Simon, 1993). Algorithms are used in a variety of contexts, such as in architecture or product design, to expand the number of alternative solutions and evaluate their feasibility and attractiveness (Amabile, 2020). Promising solutions are often presented to human actors as part of a joint human–machine decision process. For example, the design phase of large construction projects involves many interdependent choices. Traditionally, design teams develop and evaluate only a few alternative solutions, making some choices based on personal experience and rules of thumb. In its Forma suite (formerly Spacemaker), Autodesk offers software that allows architects, property developers, and urban planners to generate and explore a large set of site proposals for a construction project, identify the best ones, and examine detailed analyses of each alternative (O'Hear, 2019). The software enables the design team to optimize such things as space, light, and noise and to speed up the planning process (Kolbjørnsrud & Sannes, 2021).

Improving organizational choice. Choice is the process of (1) predicting the consequences of each of the options, (2) comparatively evaluating consequences across the option set, and (3) selecting and implementing a course of action (Simon, 1947, 1993). Machine learning is used to predict consequences of options based on regularities in large datasets. For example, because of ambiguities in the US tax law about how to report certain kinds of corporate income, algorithms are used to identify patterns in prior cases and rulings in order to provide firms with predictions of their tax liability related to specific transactions (Agrawal, Gans, & Goldfarb, 2019). When choice criteria are well defined, digital agents can also evaluate consequences and recommend best courses of action. Marketing recommender systems, for example, use information about consumers and competitors to help managers choose content for online marketing (Overgoor et al., 2019).

In the absence of well-defined choice criteria, however, human judgment is required (Agrawal et al., 2019; Tichy & Bennis, 2007). Drawing on principles from what is called *swarm intelligence* (Bonabeau &

Théraulaz, 2000), machine learning can be used to improve the collective judgment and choices of a group of human actors (Metcalf, Askay, & Rosenberg, 2019). The company Unanimous AI offers a technology that helps a group of decision makers converge on a choice through an interactive process in which group members indicate their preferences for a set of options. The system continuously computes and feeds back the group's preferences for and confidence in the options; in turn, the actors alter their preferences. Actor confidence is inferred by a machine learning algorithm using data about the actors' choices and the speed with which they make them. This process has been shown to improve the diagnosis of pneumonia based on radiographic images and the assessment of online demand for fashion clothing designed by a US company (Metcalf et al., 2019; Patel et al., 2019).

In summary, dividing labor between human and digital actors can occur in a variety of ways, ranging from full substitution to different forms of augmentation (Abbass, 2019; Daugherty & Wilson, 2018; Endsley, 2017; Parasuraman et al., 2000).

Integrating Human and Digital Actors

Artificial intelligence has introduced a novel type of organization member, digital agents. As human actors, we are faced with the question of how to work with our new intelligent partners (Major & Shah, 2020). The design challenge is to create organizational environments in which human actors and intelligent digital agents can collaborate effectively. Integration can be achieved by using elements of actor-oriented organizing, specifically, digital infrastructures and tools, actor capabilities, and shared situation awareness (Fjeldstad et al., 2012).

Digital Infrastructures and Tools

Organizing entails dividing labor among actors and controlling and coordinating their performance of activities and use of resources. Communication is essential to organizing – human and digital actors must have the ability to communicate with and understand each other. Human actors are increasingly communicating with each other through digital media such as Slack, Workplace from Facebook, and Microsoft Teams. The availability of collaborative software platforms enables both direct and indirect communications among collaborating human and digital actors. For example, users can add so-called Power Virtual Agents to Microsoft Teams and make interactions with them available to teammates. The pervasive digitization of modern organizations allows intelligent digital agents to seamlessly communicate and share situation awareness with their human collaborators as well as with each other. In EQT Ventures, human and digital actors collaborate via a digital infrastructure. The company has integrated the calendars of its investment professionals with the Motherbrain system. Motherbrain recognizes leads-related meetings and directly after such a meeting sends a push notification in Slack asking how the meeting went and provides the professionals with a link where they can give their assessment with a few touches on their phones. Their inputs are used in assessing the focal company as well as for training the algorithm to improve future recommendations.

So far, human–machine interaction has occurred mostly on machine terms. New human–machine interfaces are increasing machines' capabilities to interact on human terms through spoken and written natural language, gestures, and in the future perhaps even direct brain–computer interfaces (Nicolas-Alonso & Gomez-Gil, 2012; Wilson & Bataller, 2015).

Actor Capabilities

Once actors are connected, effective communication requires both a shared language and collaborative capabilities (Blomqvist & Levy, 2006). Intelligent agents trained by machine learning have historically suffered from a lack of transparency (Pasquale, 2015). That is, a digital agent may be good at identifying patterns and matching them to actions but not necessarily good at explaining how it arrived at its conclusions. In response, considerable research and resources have been directed at developing "explainable" AI. Explainable AI is important in all human–machine interactions but especially so in medical, military, and legal applications where decisions carry significant consequences and where human actors, and the organizations they belong to, are accountable for those decisions regardless of how they were made (Gunning & Aha, 2019). The European Union's General Data Protection Regulation, for example, requires that decisions be explained to those that they affect even if they were made by a machine (Goodman & Flaxman, 2017).

A digital agent using a machine learning-generated model to make decisions will need additional algorithms if it is to explain its reasoning. Explanations can take various forms – an account of the factors that were most important in making the decision, a presentation of proto-typical versions, visualizations, or canonical examples of objects or situations that the model relies on (Samek & Müller, 2019). Explaining is an important collaborative capability. A collaborating human actor needs to understand whether and in what situations it can rely on its digital collaborators and take appropriate action, such as correcting or not accepting actions because the models that digital agents use are imperfect. A machine-generated model may reflect extraneous data from the context or noise in the training dataset and therefore make erroneous predictions when applied outside of the context in which it was trained. For example, a model trained to recognize a sailboat from pictures may incorrectly include the presence of water if the pictures on which it was trained did not include boats stored on land (Samek & Müller, 2019). For a human actor to discover such problems of "overfitting," the digital agent must be able to reveal the knowledge that it uses.

A digital collaborator must be able to express itself in ways that human actors can understand. Both types of actors need to have a mental model of the other, including what the other is capable of and trying to accomplish as well as expected actions and results (Major & Shah, 2020; Selkowitz, Lakhmani, & Chen, 2017). Digital agents that can explain how they think can acquire new knowledge in an area and then use that knowledge to train human actors. For example, one study showed how powerful human–machine collaboration can be (Pawlowicz & Downum, 2021). The researchers chose four experienced archaeologists to classify images of pottery sherds (called Tusayan White Ware) found in northeastern Arizona. They also trained a neural network to sort photographs of Tusayan White Ware fragments. The neural network sorted thousands of photographs in a few minutes whereas it took the archaeologists three to four months. Moreover, the neural network matched two of the archaeologists for accuracy and outperformed the other two. But, most importantly, the algorithm presented a sorting observation that was new to the archaeologists, one that deepened their knowledge of Tusayan White Ware and promised to be useful in future research.

Explainable AI not only improves collaboration among human and digital actors, it increases trust that humans have in machines. If

human actors do not trust digital agents, they forgo the potential benefits that intelligent machines can provide. Managers need to understand how an intelligent system works, that it is able to explain its
logic, and that it has a track record for accuracy in order for them to
be willing to trust the advice emanating from the system (Kolbjørnsrud
et al., 2017). Trust in digital counterparts needs to be calibrated both
to the capabilities that digital agents possess and to the potential
harmful biases that they may harbor (Parasuraman & Riley, 1997).
Trust between human and digital actors develops over time through
experience, and it has both cognitive and emotional components.
Transparent, reliable, and predictable machine behaviors foster cognitive trust, whereas digital agents that exhibit human-like traits affect
emotional trust (Glikson & Woolley, 2020). The thoughtful design of
the human–machine relationship increases trust and is critical to effective collaboration.

Shared Situation Awareness

In addition to being able to communicate with and understand each
other, human and digital actors need a means of coordinating their
respective activities. A shared representation of the task environment
is key to effective collaboration between human and digital actors. A
task environment representation provides a specific context for direct
communication between the actors. For example, many firms use chatbots – digital agents that communicate using natural language – in
customer service. Chatbots usually work in teams that include human
service representatives. Whereas chatbots can typically handle a large
portion of questions without assistance, sometimes a human actor
must intervene to resolve or respond to a customer request. When this
occurs, there is a handoff from the chatbot to the human. Handoffs
can be triggered by the customer specifically requesting a human representative or by the chatbot concluding that a human is needed either
because it is unable to resolve the customer's issue itself or because
it infers that the customer would prefer to interact with a human. In
such cases, the chatbot signals a handoff to a specific human actor
or to a task assignment system and refers to the dialogue so far. The
message typically includes information about the customer's problem
as well as inferences that the chatbot has made from the interaction,
such as what the customer is trying to accomplish or the customer's

knowledge of the situation. Having access to this context enables human representatives to comprehend the situation and resume the conversation with the customer more quickly (Microsoft, 2020). In some cases, the conversation may be handed back to the digital agent once the aspects that required human intervention have been resolved (Uliyar, 2017). In other situations, the main communication with customers is conducted by a human representative with a digital agent serving as a "virtual wingman." Clients of wealth management firms, for example, prefer communicating with human representatives, and firms such as Morgan Stanley use a recommender system to make suggestions that financial advisors can raise in their conversations with clients (Davenport, 2020). In both of these examples, the division of labor between the digital and human actors is dynamic and results from collaboration.

To be useful, the shared representation of the task environment must be accurate and up to date. Autodesk Forma allows property developers and architects to rapidly create virtual representations of a site (the "problem") and alternative building structures (the "solution") around which human–machine collaboration takes place. Users import relevant data about the site from public records, including information about terrain, surrounding buildings, infrastructures, noise conditions, and regulatory constraints. The software creates a virtual representation of the site that is used for machine generation and evaluation of thousands of alternative solutions, reduced to a feasible set. Users can add drawings and modify solutions. Machine and human inputs are used iteratively throughout the process (Kolbjørnsrud & Sannes, 2021).

The need for accurate and up-to-date representations is true not only for virtual agents (software) but also for physical agents (robots). For example, the Danish firm Mobile Industrial Robots (MiR) makes autonomous mobile robots (AMRs) that are used in factories and hospitals to automate the in-house transportation of goods. The robots use laser scanners to create their own maps of the facilities in which they work and then use those maps to navigate efficiently when picking up and delivering cargo. The AMRs use data from cameras and other types of sensors to detect their surroundings. When encountering obstacles, they choose a safe alternative route to maneuver around them. Moreover, the AMRs can integrate with customers' enterprise resource planning systems so that when a sales representative issues a new order, the mobile robots will receive a list of deliveries to be made and will execute their tasks autonomously. AMRs enable warehouses, factories, and hospitals to operate 24/7 (MiR, 2021).

Implications for Design

Digital agents can assist human actors, they can perform certain tasks autonomously, and they can learn and even teach humans based on the knowledge they acquire. To take full advantage of the benefits that digital agents can provide, two conditions must be met. One is shared digital task environment representations that digital agents draw on and update in the performance of their activities. The other is digital messaging systems for direct communication between actors. Organizations are increasingly meeting these conditions as an inherent part of their ongoing digitization of work processes. Beyond being able to technically incorporate digital agents into the organization, designs need to accommodate situation awareness, trust, and accountability in the human–machine relationship (Kolbjørnsrud et al., 2017; Ziemke, Schaefer, & Endsley, 2017).

Effective collaboration between human and digital actors requires shared situation awareness (Ziemke et al., 2017). To make sound decisions and take appropriate actions, both types of actors need to be aware of the current task environment. Human disengagement from the situation can be a problem in automated environments. Endsley (2017) recommends that collaborative human–machine systems be designed such that the human actors remain cognitively engaged in situations where the digital agents perform a large portion of the task. Continuous engagement is necessary for human actors to take corrective actions when needed. For humans to remain engaged, digital agents must work transparently and be able to explain their recommendations and actions.

Trust allows autonomous actors to work together. Both human and digital actors must feel assured that the other can carry out a given task and will do so dependably. Users may trust machines too much or too little. Too much trust is exemplified by airplane accidents caused by pilots not overriding the autopilot when they should have (Lee & See, 2004). Too little trust is exemplified by users rejecting useful technology because they do not understand how it works (Zuboff, 1988). Digital agents also need to have informed trust vis-à-vis human actors. For example, when the safety system of a car brakes to avoid a collision, it is because it does not trust the driver to respond appropriately to an obstacle in its path. As digital agents learn autonomously, their capabilities and implicit intentions may change. Systems must be designed to keep "humans in the loop" in order to assess the trustworthiness of the capabilities and intentions of digital agents (Abbass, 2019).

In a digital world, accountability is apportioned across both human and digital actors (Parker & Grote, 2020). Currently, organizations are struggling with accountability issues as humans and machines make decisions together. Incorporating algorithmic rationality into decision-making raises important organizational, legal, and societal concerns (Lindebaum, Vesa, & Den Hond, 2020). First, who is responsible for algorithms doing what they are intended to do? As discussed earlier, algorithms are subject to biases introduced by programmers or by the data on which the algorithms have been trained. Leaving decision-making and monitoring to algorithms eliminates human discretion in extraordinary situations, those not anticipated by programmers or reflected in training data. Human actors must direct their attention not only to the development of algorithms but also to the auditing and assessment of algorithms to intervene when necessary. Digital agents can also be part of the solution to bias as algorithms can detect and mitigate bias in both machine and human behaviors (Guo & Caliskan, 2021; Kleinberg et al., 2020; Lohia et al., 2019). Second, whose interests do algorithms represent? Algorithmic decision-making begs the question of ensuring that decisions are being made in the best interests of relevant stakeholders (König & Wenzelburger, 2021; Lepri et al., 2018; Mason, 1969; Newlands, 2021). Responsible human actors must identify those stakeholders who are affected by algorithmic decisions, they need to understand the interests of those stakeholders, and they must devise means of transparency and dialogue around the decision-making process. Third, how can organizations and society ensure that decisions made algorithmically comply with continuously changing laws and regulations? The European Union's proposed Artificial Intelligence Act stipulates that humans, including the providers of AI and the organizations using it, will ultimately be held accountable for decisions made by machines. In furtherance of holding humans accountable, the proposed Act requires transparency in the data used for training machines, the ability of machines to explain the decisions they make, and automatic logging of events to enable traceability (European Commission, 2021).

Conclusion

Artificial intelligence continues to make advances, and managers will increasingly incorporate AI into their organizations, judiciously blending the substitution and augmentation of human actors with digital agents. The current wave of AI is being driven by machine learning, which increasingly takes place autonomously by way of unsupervised reinforcement learning. To be effective moving forward, organizations will need to master AI as a strategic resource. Organizational designers and managers must learn and diffuse practices that are conducive to collaboration in organizations composed of both human and digital actors. Ultimately, the success of their efforts rests on having human actors who have the knowledge and skills to work effectively with their digital colleagues as well as the processes and infrastructures that allow them to communicate and collaborate.

References

Abbass, H. A. 2019. Social integration of artificial intelligence: functions, automation allocation logic and human-autonomy trust. *Cognitive Computation* 11(2): 159–171.

Acemoglu, D. & Restrepo, P. 2019. Automation and new tasks: how technology displaces and reinstates labor. *Journal of Economic Perspectives* 33(2): 3–30.

Agrawal, A., Gans, J., & Goldfarb, A. 2019. Economic policy for artificial intelligence. *Innovation Policy and the Economy* 19(1): 139–159.

Amabile, T. 2020. Guidepost: creativity, artificial intelligence, and a world of surprises. *Academy of Management Discoveries* 6(3): 351–354.

Andersen, E., Johnson, J. C., Kolbjørnsrud, V., & Sannes, R. 2018. The data-driven organization: intelligence at SCALE. In A. Sasson (ed.), *At the Forefront, Looking Ahead*: 23–42. Universitetsforlaget, Oslo, Norway.

Bast, H., Delling, D., Goldberg, A. et al. 2016. Route planning in transportation networks. In L. Kliemann and P. Sanders (eds.), *Algorithm Engineering*: 19–80. Springer, Berlin, Germany.

Blomqvist, K. & Levy, J. 2006. Collaboration capability – a focal concept in knowledge creation and collaborative innovation in networks. *International Journal of Management Concepts and Philosophy* 2(1): 31–48.

Bonabeau, E. & Théraulaz, G. 2000. Swarm smarts. *Scientific American* 282(3): 72–79.

Brynjolfsson, E. & McAfee, A. 2014. *The Second Machine Age: Work, Progress, and Prosperity in a Time of Brilliant Technologies*. W. W. Norton & Company, New York, NY.

Buolamwini, J. & Gebru, T. 2018. Gender shades: intersectional accuracy disparities in commercial gender classification. ACM Conference on Fairness, Accountability and Transparency, New York, NY, 77–91.

Byrne, C. 2018. This AI helps find great startups before the world discovers them [Online]. *Fast Company*. www.fastcompany.com/40588028/ this-ai-helps-find-great-startups-before-the-world-discovers-them.

Colford, P. 2014. A leap forward in quarterly earnings stories [Online]. Associated Press. https://blog.ap.org/announcements/a-leap-forward-in-quarterly-earnings-stories.

Cowgill, B. 2019. Bias and productivity in humans and machines. *Columbia Business School, Research Paper*. https://dx.doi.org/10.2139/ssrn.3584916

Curchod, C., Patriotta, G., Cohen, L., & Neysen, N. 2020. Working for an algorithm: power asymmetries and agency in online work settings. *Administrative Science Quarterly* 65(3): 644–676.

Daugherty, P. R. & Wilson, H. J. 2018. *Human + Machine: Reimagining Work in the Age of AI*. Harvard Business Review Press, Boston, MA.

Davenport, T. 2020. The future of work now: Morgan Stanley's financial advisors and the next best action system [Online]. *Forbes*. www.forbes.com/sites/tomdavenport/2020/05/16/the-future-of-work-now-morgan-stanleys-financial-advisors-and-the-next-best-offer-system/?sh=32bcba837027.

Delta. 2019. Delta TechOps expanding predictive maintenance capabilities with new Airbus partnership [Online]. Delta Air Lines. https://news.delta.com/delta-techops-expanding-predictive-maintenance-capabilities-new-airbus-partnership.

Endsley, M. R. 2017. From here to autonomy: lessons learned from human–automation research. *Human Factors* 59(1): 5–27.

Engelbart, D. C. 1962. *Augmenting Human Intellect: A Conceptual Framework*. Stanford Research Institute, Menlo Park, CA.

Esteva, A., Kuprel, B., Novoa, R. A. et al. 2017. Dermatologist-level classification of skin cancer with deep neural networks. *Nature* 542(7639): 115–118.

European Commission. 2021. Proposal for a regulation of the European Parliament and of the Council: laying down harmonised rules on artificial intelligence (Artificial Intelligence Act) and amending certain union legislative acts. Brussels, Belgium. https://eur-lex.europa.eu/resource.html?uri=cellar:e0649735-a372-11eb-9585-01aa75ed71a1.0001.02/DOC_1&format=PDF

Evans, R. & Gao, J. 2016. DeepMind AI reduces Google data centre cooling bill by 40% [Online]. Deep Mind. https://deepmind.com/blog/deepmind-ai-reduces-google-datacentre-cooling-bill-40/.

Executive Office of the President. 2016. *Artificial Intelligence, Automation, and the Economy*. Executive Office of the President, United States of America, Washington, DC.

Fjeldstad, Ø. D., Snow, C. C., Miles, R. E., & Lettl, C. 2012. The architecture of collaboration. *Strategic Management Journal* 33(6): 734–750.

Glikson, E. & Woolley, A. W. 2020. Human trust in artificial intelligence: review of empirical research. *Academy of Management Annals* 14(2): 627–660.

Goldberg, K. 2012. What is automation? *IEEE Transactions on Automation Science and Engineering* 9(1): 1–2.

Goldberg, K. 2019. Robots and the return to collaborative intelligence. *Nature Machine Intelligence* 1(1): 2.

Goodman, B. & Flaxman, S. 2017. European Union regulations on algorithmic decision-making and a "right to explanation." *AI Magazine* 38(3): 50–57.

Grønsund, T. & Aanestad, M. 2020. Augmenting the algorithm: emerging human-in-the-loop work configurations. *The Journal of Strategic Information Systems* 29(2): 1–16.

Gunning, D. & Aha, D. 2019. DARPA's explainable artificial intelligence (XAI) program. *AI Magazine* 40(2): 44–58.

Guo, W. & Caliskan, A. 2021. Detecting emergent intersectional biases: contextualized word embeddings contain a distribution of human-like biases. The 2021 AAAI/ACM Conference on AI, Ethics, and Society: 122–133.

Hodson, H. 2014. The AI boss that deploys Hong Kong's subway engineers [Online]. *New Scientist*. www.newscientist.com/article/mg22329764-000-the-ai-boss-that-deploys-hong-kongs-subway-engineers/.

Hu, Y., Da, Q., Zeng, A., Yu, Y., & Xu, Y. 2018. Reinforcement learning to rank in e-commerce search engine: formalization, analysis, and application. Proceedings of the 24th ACM SIGKDD International Conference on Knowledge Discovery & Data Mining 2018: 368–377.

Hussein, A., Gaber, M. M., Elyan, E., & Jayne, C. 2017. Imitation learning: a survey of learning methods. *ACM Computing Surveys* 50(2): 1–35.

Kellogg, K., Valentine, M., & Christin, A. 2019. Algorithms at work: the new contested terrain of control. *Academy of Management Annals* 14(1): 366–410.

Khalil, A., Ahmed, S. G., Khattak, A. M., & Al-Qirim, N. 2020. Investigating bias in facial analysis systems: a systematic review. IEEE Access 8130751-130761.

Kleinberg, J., Ludwig, J., Mullainathan, S., & Sunstein, C. R. 2020. Algorithms as discrimination detectors. *Proceedings of the National Academy of Sciences* 117(48): 30096–30100.

Kolbjørnsrud, V. & Sannes, R. 2021. Augmented intelligence: the case of AI in early-stage property development. Strategic Management Society Annual Meeting, Toronto, Canada.

Kolbjørnsrud, V., Amico, R., & Thomas, R. J. 2017. Partnering with AI: how organizations can win over skeptical managers. *Strategy & Leadership* 45(1): 37–43.

König, P. D. & Wenzelburger, G. 2021. The legitimacy gap of algorithmic decision-making in the public sector: why it arises and how to address it. *Technology in Society* 67(101688): 1–10.

Kwun, A. 2018. These chairs were designed by an AI bot, and they're surprisingly good [Online]. *Fast Company*. www.fastcompany.com/90228357/these-chairs-were-designed-by-an-ai-bot-and-theyre-surprisingly-good.

Lee, J. D. & See, K. A. 2004. Trust in automation: designing for appropriate reliance. *Human Factors* 46(1): 50–80.

Lepri, B., Oliver, N., Letouzé, E., Pentland, A., & Vinck, P. 2018. Fair, transparent, and accountable algorithmic decision-making processes. *Philosophy & Technology* 31(4): 611–627.

Lin, T., Maire, M., Belongie, S. et al. 2014. Microsoft COCO: common objects in context. In D. Fleet, T. Pajdla, B. Schiele, and T. Tuytelaars (eds.), *Computer Vision – ECCV 2014. ECCV 2014. Lecture Notes in Computer Science, vol 8693*: 740–755. Springer, Cham, Switzerland.

Lindebaum, D., Vesa, M., & Den Hond, F. 2020. Insights from "the machine stops" to better understand rational assumptions in algorithmic decision making and its implications for organizations. *Academy of Management Review* 45(1): 247–263.

Linsell, K. 2018. Meet the robot who knows how to trade bonds better than you do [Online]. Bloomberg. www.bloomberg.com/news/articles/2018-11-12/meet-the-robot-who-knows-how-to-trade-bonds-better-than-you-do.

Liu, M., Brynjolfsson, E., & Dowlatabadi, J. 2021. Do digital platforms reduce moral hazard? The case of Uber and taxis. *Management Science* 67(8): 4665–4685.

Lohia, P. K., Ramamurthy, K. N., Bhide, M., Saha, D., Varshney, K. R., & Puri, R. 2019. Bias mitigation post-processing for individual and group fairness. IEEE International Conference on Acoustics, Speech and Signal Processing (ICASSP): 2847–2851.

Major, L. & Shah, J. 2020. *What to Expect When You're Expecting Robots: The Future of Human-Robot Collaboration*. Basic Books, New York, NY.

Mason, R. O. 1969. A dialectical approach to strategic planning. *Management Science* 15(8): B-403–B-414.

Metcalf, L., Askay, D. A., & Rosenberg, L. B. 2019. Keeping humans in the loop: pooling knowledge through artificial swarm intelligence to improve business decision making. *California Management Review* 61(4): 84–109.

Microsoft. 2020. Trigger hand-off to a live agent [Online]. Microsoft, Seattle, WA. https://docs.microsoft.com/en-us/power-virtual-agents/advanced-hand-off.

MiR. 2021. MiR launches two powerful autonomous mobile robots to optimize all logistics [Online]. Mobile Industrial Robots, Odense, Denmark. www.mobile-industrial-robots.com/en/about-mir/news/mir-launches-two-powerful-autonomous-mobile-robots-to-optimize-all-logistics/.

Moyer, C. 2016. How Google's AlphaGo beat a Go world champion [Online]. *The Atlantic.* www.theatlantic.com/technology/archive/2016/03/the-invisible-opponent/475611.

Muro, M., Maxim, R., & Whiton, J. 2019. Automation and artificial intelligence: how machines are affecting people and places. Brookings Institution, Metropolitan Policy Program, Washington, DC.

Najibi, A. 2020. Racial discrimination in face recognition technology [Online]. Harvard University, The Graduate School of Arts and Sciences. https://sitn.hms.harvard.edu/flash/2020/racial-discrimination-in-face-recognition-technology/.

Newlands, G. 2021. Algorithmic surveillance in the gig economy: the organization of work through Lefebvrian conceived space. *Organization Studies* 42(5): 719–737.

Ngai, E. W. T., Hu, Y., Wong, Y. H., Chen, Y., & Sun, X. 2011. The application of data mining techniques in financial fraud detection: a classification framework and an academic review of literature. *Decision Support Systems* 50(3): 559–569.

Nicolas-Alonso, L. F. & Gomez-Gil, J. 2012. Brain computer interfaces, a review. *Sensors* 12(2): 1211–1279.

Nilsson, N. J. 1998. *Artificial Intelligence: A New Synthesis.* Morgan Kaufmann Publishers, San Francisco, CA.

O'Hear, S. 2019. Spacemaker scores $25M Series A to let property developers use AI [Online]. TechCrunch. https://techcrunch.com/2019/06/09/spacemaker/.

Overgoor, G., Chica, M., Rand, W., & Weishampel, A. 2019. Letting the computers take over: using AI to solve marketing problems. *California Management Review* 61(4): 156–185.

Parasuraman, R. & Riley, V. 1997. Humans and automation: use, misuse, disuse, abuse. *Human Factors* 39(2): 230–253.

Parasuraman, R., Sheridan, T. B., & Wickens, C. D. 2000. A model for types and levels of human interaction with automation. *IEEE Transactions on Systems, Man, and Cybernetics-Part A: Systems and Humans* 30(3): 286–297.

Parker, S. K. & Grote, G. 2020. Automation, algorithms, and beyond: why work design matters more than ever in a digital world. *Applied Psychology* 71(4): 1–45.

Pasquale, F. 2015. *The Black Box Society: The Secret Algorithms That Control Money and Information.* Harvard University Press, Cambridge, MA.

Patel, B. N., Rosenberg, L., Willcox, G. et al. 2019. Human–machine partnership with artificial intelligence for chest radiograph diagnosis. *NPJ Digital Medicine* 2(111): 1–10.

Pawlowicz, L. M. & Downum, C. E. 2021. Applications of deep learning to decorated ceramic typology and classification: a case study using Tusayan White Ware from Northeast Arizona. *Journal of Archaeological Science* 130(105375): 1–14.

Raj, M. & Seamans, R. 2019. Primer on artificial intelligence and robotics. *Journal of Organization Design* 8(1): 1–14.

Samek, W. & Müller, K.-R. 2019. Towards explainable artificial intelligence. In W. Samek, G. Montavon, A. Vedaldi et al., *Explainable AI: Interpreting, Explaining and Visualizing Deep Learning*: 5–22. Springer, Cham, Switzerland.

Schmidt, A. 2017. Augmenting human intellect and amplifying perception and cognition. *IEEE Pervasive Computing* 16(1): 6–10.

Selkowitz, A. R., Lakhmani, S. G., & Chen, J. Y. 2017. Using agent transparency to support situation awareness of the Autonomous Squad Member. *Cognitive Systems Research* 46: 4613–4625.

Sharma, A., Zanotti, P., & Musunur, L. P. 2019. Enabling the electric future of mobility: robotic automation for electric vehicle battery assembly. *IEEE Access* 7: 7170961–170991.

Shrestha, Y. R., Ben-Menahem, S. M., & von Krogh, G. 2019. Organizational decision-making structures in the age of artificial intelligence. *California Management Review* 61(4): 66–83.

Silver, D., Schrittwieser, J., Simonyan, K. et al. 2017. Mastering the game of Go without human knowledge. *Nature* 550(7676): 354–359.

Simon, H. A. 1947. *Administrative Behavior: A Study of Decision-Making Processes in Administrative Organization.* Macmillan, New York, NY.

Simon, H. A. 1957. *Models of Man: Social and Rational; Mathematical Essays on Rational Human Behavior in a Social Setting.* Wiley, New York, NY.

Simon, H. A. 1993. Strategy and organizational evolution. *Strategic Management Journal* 14(S2): 131–142.

Simon, H. A. 2002. Organizing and coordinating talk and silence in organizations. *Industrial and Corporate Change* 11(3): 611–618.

Simon, H. A. & Newell, A. 1958. Heuristic problem solving: the next advance in operations research. *Operations Research* 6(1): 1–10.

Tambe, P., Cappelli, P., & Yakubovich, V. 2019. Artificial intelligence in human resources management: challenges and a path forward. *California Management Review* 61(4): 15–42.

Tichy, N. M. & Bennis, W. G. 2007. *Judgment: How Winning Leaders Make Great Calls*. Penguin, New York, NY.

Tversky, A. & Kahneman, D. 1974. Judgment under uncertainty: heuristics and biases. *Science* 185(4157): 1124–1131.

Uliyar, S. 2017. A primer: Oracle intelligent bots – powered by artificial intelligence, white paper. Oracle, Redwood Shores, CA.

von Krogh, G. 2018. Artificial intelligence in organizations: new opportunities for phenomenon-based theorizing. *Academy of Management Discoveries* 4(4): 404–409.

Wilson, H. J. & Bataller, C. 2015. How people will use AI to do their jobs better. *Harvard Business Review*: 1–6. https://hbr.org/2015/05/how-people-will-use-ai-to-do-their-jobs-better

Winston, P. H. 1992. *Artificial Intelligence*, 3rd ed. Addison-Wesley Longman, Reading, MA.

Woschank, M., Rauch, E., & Zsifkovits, H. 2020. A review of further directions for artificial intelligence, machine learning, and deep learning in smart logistics. *Sustainability* 12(3760): 1–23.

Zhang, L., Tan, J., Han, D., & Zhu, H. 2017. From machine learning to deep learning: progress in machine intelligence for rational drug discovery. *Drug Discovery Today* 22(11): 1680–1685.

Ziemke, T., Schaefer, K. E., & Endsley, M. 2017. Situation awareness in human-machine interactive systems. *Cognitive Systems Research* 46(1): 1–2.

Zuboff, S. 1988. *In the Age of the Smart Machine: The Future of Work and Power*. Basic Books, New York, NY.

8 | *Agile Organizing*

STÉPHANE J. G. GIROD

Highly dynamic environments require organizations to be agile – able to promptly correct organizational misalignments and respond rapidly to new opportunities (Doz & Kosonen, 2010; Girod & Králik, 2021). Agility is a capability that organizations create and enhance in response to pressures from global competition, increased digitization, and the quest for environmental sustainability (Gothelf, 2014; Ivory & Brooks, 2018). Traditional organizational designs, which optimize for risk management in a predictable world, are unlikely to offer the necessary solutions to these adaptive challenges (Teece, Peteraf, & Leih, 2016). An organization that adopts agile principles and practices increases problem-solving iteration and coordination by feedback. Agile practices reduce friction in organizational processes so that the organization can act faster and more effectively. In an agile organization, empowered customer-focused teams experiment, learn, and make decisions in self-organized ways. A successful transformation from bureaucratic to agile practices enables organizations to respond effectively to adaptive pressures in volatile, uncertain, complex, and ambiguous environments (Davis, Eisenhardt, & Bingham, 2009).

This chapter discusses what it means for an organization to be agile and the process of transformation from a hierarchical, bureaucratic design to an agile design. It draws on extensive research on organizational agility, including interviews with senior executives from leading global firms as well secondary sources (Girod et al., 2018). The first section presents a brief history of agile principles and practices as well as the benefits of organizational agility. The second section describes how agility has been achieved in the Dutch bank ING and the Chinese manufacturing company Haier. ING has more than 350 agile teams that operate within a flat hierarchical structure. Haier changed from a highly bureaucratic organization to the use of organizing mechanisms that enable more than 4,000 microenterprises to self-organize customer-focused, entrepreneurial efforts. Each case represents a different path to agility. The third section discusses implications for organization design.

Agility: Concepts, Processes, and Benefits

Interest in agility originated in software development as programmers sought better ways to meet the needs and demands of users. In February 2001, a small group of like-minded software developers met in Snowbird, Utah, to ski, relax, and share their experiences. From that gathering emanated The Agile Manifesto, which emphasizes people over tools and processes; minimum viable products over excessive documentation; close collaboration with end users over contract negotiation; and responding to change via quick feedback loops over following a plan (Beck et al., 2001). Over time, a set of agile methods and practices has emerged that reflect the principles articulated in The Agile Manifesto. The most widely adopted agile framework is *Scrum*, a term used to describe how rugby teams quickly pass the ball among themselves as they advance up the field. In product and software development, scrums are small, cross-functional teams that, in an iterative process, combine bursts of activity called "sprints" with feedback from users (Prange & Heracleous, 2018; Takeuchi & Nonaka, 1986). The Scrum framework captures the essence of agile development.

The use of agile principles and practices in large development efforts (referred to as large-scale agile) creates a need for interteam coordination (Dikert, Paasivaara, & Lassenius, 2016; Dybå, Dingsøyr, & Moe, 2014). The Swedish music streaming company Spotify pioneered an approach to organizing multiteam efforts that has served as a design template for many large organizations adopting agile principles and methods. The aim of the design is to "promote innovation, collaboration and teamwork and enable bottom-up governance and autonomy" (Smite et al., 2019: 51). Spotify's architecture includes a language for describing organizational entities and roles: *Squads* are self-organized, cross-functional development teams aligned with specific customer missions. *Chapters* are groups of developers or engineers that report to the same manager (called a chapter lead). Chapter members share knowledge and discuss common challenges. *Tribes* are groupings of squads with connected customer missions, led by experienced leaders. *Guilds* are communities of interests whose participants share knowledge, tools, and code (Smite et al., 2020).

Agile practices share properties with Design Thinking's and lean start-up's creative problem-solving and innovation approaches (Liedtka, 2018; Ries, 2011; Simon, 1969). In a complex world where cause and effect are often obscured, agile practices enable probing and sensing before action (Ackoff, 1999; Rigby, Sutherland, & Takeuchi, 2016). The use of agile practices in software development has yielded benefits such as increased success rates in product development; improved quality and speed to market; and empowered teams who act as originators and "pull" work toward themselves instead of having it "pushed" their way (Rigby, Elk, & Berez, 2020). Currently, agile practices are applied to a wide variety of problems beyond product development, including marketing, manufacturing, organization-wide transformation, human resource management, and even finance (Cappelli & Tavis, 2018; Gunasekaran, 1999; Kalaignanam et al., 2021).

Organizational agility entails continuous adaptation to changing environmental conditions. The traditional, periodic approach to adaptation is costly, time-consuming organizational restructuring (Lamont, Williams, & Hoffman, 1994). In turbulent environments, restructuring is likely to compromise rather than improve performance, and such environments favor small, continuous reconfigurations (Brown & Eisenhardt, 1997; Girod & Whittington, 2017). Accordingly, agility is an organizational capability that enables firms to continuously adapt without creating disorder (Girod & Karim, 2017). The major design trade-offs to resolve in an existing organization to create greater agility are shown in Figure 8.1.

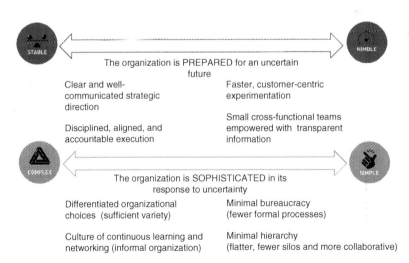

Figure 8.1 Agile tensions
From Girod and Králik (2021). Reproduced by permission of Kogan Page Ltd.

Agile Management: The Cases of ING and Haier

ING and Haier are both highly agile organizations (Birkinshaw, 2018; Fischer, Lago, & Liu, 2013; Hamel & Zanini, 2020). These companies represent two distinct pathways in the quest for organizational agility. ING's path combined agile principles and practices with a dramatic flattening of its hierarchy to increase the nimbleness of service development. Haier's path, on the other hand, was a radical transformation of organizing processes and mechanisms to achieve rapid mobilization of resources around entrepreneurial opportunities.

ING's Agile Design Choices

Established in 1991 through a merger of the Dutch insurer Nationale-Nederlanden and the postal bank NMB, ING is one of the world's largest banking and financial services companies. Its businesses include retail banking, direct banking, commercial banking, investment banking, wholesale banking, private banking, asset management, and insurance services. It has a workforce of more than 55,000 people. In response to advances in digital financial technologies, ING in 2014 launched its Think Forward strategy. This strategy emphasized omnichannel convenience, efficiency, and cost leadership, while passing along cost savings to customers. With the idea of "customer takes center stage" firmly in place, the focus shifted to organization design. The new design had to embody the philosophy of customer focus and empowerment, particularly in developing new products. After visiting digital exemplars such as Google, Netflix, and Spotify, ING set up a structure in its product development organization rooted in agile methods.

In the product development organization, ING formed 350 autonomous squads of approximately 9 employees each, representing a variety of backgrounds and disciplines. These teams formed the backbone of ING's agile organization. Each squad held end-to-end responsibility for achieving its particular customer mission. All squads used Scrum to develop new products, and they relied heavily on lean start-up concepts such as minimum viable products. This fostered an intimate understanding of customer needs and pain points along with speedy experimentation with new solutions. As a result, product modifications could be performed in a fast and self-organizing manner instead of following top-down instructions. Subsequently, ING added *chapter leads* and *agile coaches* to support and develop the squads. Chapter leads are responsible for growing competence and awareness in a particular discipline (how things are done), and coaches are responsible for introducing new ways of working and leading.

ING believed that each squad could be effective only if it understood the overall goals of the bank. Careful alignment and disciplined accountability were required to prevent inefficiency. Squads that worked on interconnected missions were grouped into one of thirteen tribes (e.g., Securities and Private Banking, Mortgage Services, Customer Experience Business Banking), with a tribe leader who represented one of the two hierarchical layers between the front line and the C-suite (the second one was chapter leads), to ensure greater coordination, discipline, and alignment. In addition to tribe roles and responsibilities, ING adapted the Quarterly Business Review (QBR) from Netflix to provide the organization with strategic alignment as well as fluid resource allocation. In keeping with tribe-focused QBR principles, squad members reviewed their accomplishments in the previous quarter and laid out their objectives for the next quarter in support of the bank's overall strategy. These reviews were then discussed in a larger meeting of all tribe leaders (and a few other relevant leaders) to align priorities, thus enhancing transparency and situation awareness. QBR became an essential tool that management used to allocate budgets in a flexible fashion. Short, memorable strategy statements were used to keep accountability in focus quarter after quarter.

As much as ING wanted to simplify and speed up operations, it recognized that agile practices were not appropriate for all areas of the bank. Management decided that scrums, squads, and tribes would not work in its customer-facing retail branches and call centers. In those areas, working toward agility meant creating customer circles to frequently capture customers' evolving concerns and passing that information on to the product development squads. Simultaneously, the bank gave high priority to the formation of learning networks open to the external world. Chapter leads orchestrated learning development in their respective disciplines, such as data analytics, mortgage customer journeys, and product management processes. Chapter leads were thus in charge of continuous learning and expertise development – what ING called the craftsmanship of its professionals. They were in charge of squad members' annual performance appraisal.

To use our agility framework, ING's transformation made great strides in reconciling the tensions of stable versus nimble and simple versus complex to get in tune with an uncertain environment. What made the revamped organization nimble was its emphasis on customer-centric experimentation, fueled by a close-knit and empowered network of cross-functional teams. Nimble attributes were balanced – that is, infused with a degree of stability – thanks to the predefined components of the Think Forward strategy and the universal QBR dashboard. As such, nimbleness was in concert with disciplined execution, fluid budget allocation, and goal alignment. On the simple versus complex continuum, the changes that ING had set in motion naturally resulted in fewer silos and reduced bureaucracy. ING believed that its organizational design was the key to improved customer-centricity. This simplification also led to greater sophistication when responding to a changing environment. Finally, the customer-centric structures and processes ensured greater information transparency and a culture of learning.

Haier's Approach to Agility

Established in 1984, Haier is a Chinese multinational home appliance and consumer electronics company that designs, develops, manufactures, and sells products such as refrigerators, air conditioners, washing machines, microwave ovens, mobile phones, computers, and televisions. Haier is the number one global brand in major home appliances. The company's organizational model, called Rendanheyi, takes advantage of the growing opportunities made possible by the Internet of Things (IoT) – buildings, airplanes, automobiles, mobile devices, home appliances, and so on connected to the Internet, thus generating and capturing massive amounts of data and often acting on it automatically.

Haier has become increasingly agile over the last couple of decades. Its transformation began when CEO Zhang Ruimin decided that Haier needed to radically reinvent itself in order to succeed in the digital age (Haier, 2014). He started by breaking up the hierarchical organization and removing all mid-level departments. Today, Haier's 80,000-plus employees are organized into more than 4,000 *microenterprises*, most consisting of 10–15 people. Of these, 200 are customer-facing units that identify and develop market opportunities, and 50 are incubators that help launch new microenterprises (Fischer et al., 2013; Hamel & Zanini, 2018; Reeves, Haanaes, & Sinha, 2015). The remaining microenterprises act as nodes in this huge network, providing components, services, and expertise through a process of templated and facilitated but otherwise open bidding.

In 2012, Haier implemented its Network Strategy, an organizational design in which all microenterprises are empowered to make their own business and operating decisions. Microenterprises are grouped around approximately twenty platforms, which allow them to connect and collaborate. New microenterprises are typically created by entrepreneurs who pitch the concept to internal or external investors. Customer-facing microenterprises scan the market for promising opportunities and use the platform to contract with other microenterprises that supply design, marketing, engineering, manufacturing, and other types of services. The resulting temporary network remains operational for as long as there is demand for products and services. Often, entrepreneurs pitch their business idea to an incubating microenterprise that can help them with financing. Kanter and Dai (2018) provide an example of how Haier's model of organizing works. Thunderobot, one of the earliest microenterprises, used customer complaints on e-commerce sites to identify an opportunity to provide specialized gaming computers. It pitched its idea to the owner of the Intelligent Interconnection Platform. That platform enabled Thunderobot to connect with other microenterprises that could provide supply chain, logistics, and after-sales services. As Thunderobot grew, it also obtained funding from external investors. Eventually, it built an ecosystem of partners who created ongoing value for users. Having more than sixteen million users enabled Thunderobot to incubate additional microenterprises in the gaming ecosystem.

The introduction of Network Strategy shaped Haier's microenterprise structure in which customer-facing and other types of microenterprises constantly innovate with customers. This organizational design creates room for experimentation and for open and parallel innovation projects. It also requires precise measures of success. Microenterprises can go bankrupt, and employees can fire their boss if the microenterprise underperforms. Thus, Haier replaced its steep hierarchy with an open, entrepreneurial ecosystem where no more than two layers separate front-line workers from CEOs. In effect, the entire organization is a network of empowered entrepreneurs who regularly tap into external sources of ideas and business acumen from end users, suppliers, road show participants, and other partners (Hamel & Zanini, 2018).

Following our agility framework, Haier's actions come across as very nimble: Customer-facing microenterprises simply would not survive unless they involve the customer in everything they do. Proposed microenterprise projects must include customer collaboration in order to obtain central funding, and a microenterprise's share of profits depends on its use of customer feedback to guide innovation. Any microenterprise that does not stay at the top of its game will eventually run out of orders and die. Although Haier does not run scrums, all stakeholders come together at the outset of defining a product and then work in parallel (including with external partners) to stimulate creative problem-solving. Microenterprise employees see their businesses as networks of collaboration, not linear production processes.

Where does Haier find the sources of stability to mitigate and anchor this freewheeling organizational ethos? To date, the company has largely equated stability with retaining high-performing employees. It has instituted an intricate system of individual and team rewards, for example, employee investment accounts and profit-sharing arrangements. Strategy has been another source of stability, giving microenterprises the freedom to pursue what – in their own estimation – works and discard what does not, thus organically channeling resources in productive directions.

In resolving the tension between simplicity and complexity, Haier's approach has been to reduce bureaucracy and hierarchy to a minimum. To that end, the company has put forward standardized tools that (1) facilitate strategy (microenterprises set their own direction and priorities, forming internal and external partnerships); (2) enable people interactions (hiring and firing, defining work relationships, aligning individuals with jobs and roles, etc.); (3) set rewards (pay rates and bonuses); and (4) support internal negotiations (mostly related to performance standards and profit sharing).

Implications for Organization Design

Agile transformation enables a firm to embrace uncertainty through flexibility and adaptability. Both ING and Haier are close to customers, attuned to market trends, and adept at reconfiguring their internal resources as needed. Organizations having such capabilities can (1) strengthen adaptability and resilience to unexpected changes; (2) enhance employee engagement; (3) heighten the accuracy and speed of innovation; (4) lower costs; and (5) stimulate collaboration by reducing bureaucratic hurdles. The key to designing for agility is to optimize for nimbleness *and* stability on the one hand and simplicity *and* complexity on the other.

Traditionally, large companies have optimized for stability through exploitation of their core businesses and by focusing on predictability and efficiency. To satisfy stakeholders, firms must deliver on their current strategy with discipline and accountability. In an uncertain environment, however, nimbleness – the ability to experiment and adapt to unexpected change – is essential (March, 1991; O'Reilly & Tushman, 2013). In many large firms, the complexity of the current global business environment is reflected in high internal complexity and associated high control and coordination costs. Therefore, achieving agility also requires large, differentiated firms to simplify their organizational models as much as possible. As Nick Jue, Chairman of ING Netherlands, commented: "I want to remain an elephant because I want to keep the power of the elephant. But I also want to be fast and flexible."

ING and Haier have thoughtfully resolved the tensions between nimbleness and stability and between simplicity and complexity. Each company has a rich mix of organizational structures and processes that allow it to obtain the benefits of agility. Across the two cases, we also observe three particular factors that underpin agility and make it work. The first is decision rights. It is not enough to simply group employees into squads and tribes; teams must be empowered with meaningful decision-making authority and accountability. The second factor is the ability to work with customers. Agility requires timely feedback from customers regarding ongoing operations as well as inputs to the development of new products and services. Lastly, both companies revamped their reward systems to incentivize and compensate teams/microenterprises for their entrepreneurial efforts.

ING and Haier have made bold choices – in strategy, structure, process, and culture – to support and sustain their revamped organizations. ING chose to flatten its hierarchical structure by introducing agile processes and structures such as squads and tribes. Haier flattened its hierarchy by creating a dynamic system of self-organizing microenterprises. Along the way, each firm articulated and implemented new ways of working and leading as well as capturing and utilizing knowledge. Most importantly, both firms viewed their transformation as a means to an end – that is, achieving adaptability in response to external volatility and complexity. We can summarize the lessons from ING's and Haier's distinct but equifinal agile transformation processes in four guidelines:

- Drive agile transformation from the top. Agile transformation is not a bottom-up rebellion against the hierarchy; it is the hierarchy changing itself.
- Set clear strategic objectives. Agile transformation is a means to an end.
- Make consistent design choices that align structures, processes, and incentives. Focus on the organizational areas that are most conducive to agile organizing.
- Be agile in the transformation to agile. Experiment before scaling and scale rapidly.

Conclusion

Firms are increasingly operating in complex and dynamic environments, increasing pressure to be more flexible and adaptive. In response, firms are adopting agile principles, practices, and organizational designs. Large established firms depend on their reputation, scale, and scope for their success. Therefore, they need to find solutions that enable them to solve problems quickly and pursue new opportunities while preserving their established competitive advantages. Agile transformation includes making and executing design choices that enable the organization to balance tensions. These choices relate to all aspects of the enterprise – strategy, structure, process, people, and technology. Foremost, agile is a mindset that puts the customer first and values people and collaboration over bureaucracy and responsiveness to change over long-term plans.

References

Ackoff, R. L. 1999. *Re-creating the Corporation: A Design of Organizations for the Twenty-First Century.* Oxford University Press, New York, NY.

Beck, K., Beedle, M., Van Bennekum, A. et al. 2001. The agile manifesto. www.agilealliance.org/wp-content/uploads/2019/09/agile-manifesto-download-2019.pdf

Birkinshaw, J. 2018. What to expect from agile. *MIT Sloan Management Review, Special Collection: Redesigning Work*: 39–42.

Brown, S. L. & Eisenhardt, K. M. 1997. The art of continuous change: linking complexity theory and time-paced evolution in relentlessly shifting organizations. *Administrative Science Quarterly* 42(1): 1–34.

Cappelli, P. & Tavis, A. 2018. HR goes agile. *Harvard Business Review* 96(2): 46–52.

Davis, J. P., Eisenhardt, K. M., & Bingham, C. B. 2009. Optimal structure, market dynamism, and the strategy of simple rules. *Administrative Science Quarterly* 54(3): 413–452.

Dikert, K., Paasivaara, M., & Lassenius, C. 2016. Challenges and success factors for large-scale agile transformations: a systematic literature review. *Journal of Systems and Software* 119: 87–108.

Doz, Y. & Kosonen, M. 2010. Embedding strategic agility: a leadership agenda for accelerating business model renewal. *Long Range Planning* 43(2–3): 370–382.

Dybå, T., Dingsøyr, T. & Moe, N. B. 2014. Agile project management. In G. Ruhe and C. Wohlin (eds.), *Software Project Management in a Changing World*: 277–300. Springer, Berlin, Heidelberg.

Fischer, B., Lago, U., & Liu, F. 2013. *Reinventing Giants: How Chinese Global Competitor Haier Has Changed the Way Big Companies Transform.* Wiley, New York, NY.

Girod, S. J. G. & Karim, S. 2017. Restructure or reconfigure. *Harvard Business Review* 95(2): 128–132.

Girod, S. J. G. & Králik, M. 2021. *Resetting Management: Thrive with Agility in the Age of Uncertainty.* Kogan Page, London, UK.

Girod, S. J. G. & Whittington, R. 2017. Reconfiguration, restructuring and firm performance: dynamic capabilities and environmental dynamism. *Strategic Management Journal* 38(5): 1121–1133.

Girod, S. J. G., Philadelpho Fernandes de Pina, E., Tanfour, M., & Svedjedal, S. 2018. ING: An agile organization in a disruptive environment. IMD Case IMD-7-1852.

Gothelf, J. 2014. Bring agile to the whole organization. *Harvard Business Review*, November 14. https://hbr.org/2014/11/bring-agile-to-the-whole-organization

Gunasekaran, A. 1999. Agile manufacturing: a framework for research and development. *International Journal of Production Economics* 62(1–2): 87–105.

Haier.net. 2014. China's Philosopher-CEO Zhang Ruimin. www.haier.net/en/about_haier/news/201411/t20141114_252267.shtml.

Hamel, G. & Zanini, M. 2018. The end of bureaucracy. *Harvard Business Review* 96(6): 50–59.

Hamel, G. & Zanini, M. 2020. *Humanocracy: Creating Organizations as Amazing as the People inside Them.* Harvard Business Review Press, Boston, MA.

Ivory, S. B. & Brooks, S. B. 2018. Managing corporate sustainability with a paradoxical lens: lessons from strategic agility. *Journal of Business Ethics* 148: 347–361.

Kalaignanam, K., Tuli, K. R., Kushwaha, T., Lee, L., & Gal, D. 2021. Marketing agility: the concept, antecedents, and a research agenda. *Journal of Marketing* 85(1): 35–58.

Kanter, R. M. & Dai, H. N. 2018. Haier: incubating entrepreneurs in a Chinese giant. Harvard Business School Case 9-318-104. Rev: May 25, 2018.

Lamont, B. T., Williams, R. J., & Hoffman, J. J. 1994. Performance during "M-Form" reorganization and recovery time: the effects of prior strategy and implementation speed. *Academy of Management Journal* 37(1): 153–166.

Liedtka, J. 2018. Why design thinking works. *Harvard Business Review* 96(5): 72–79.

March, J. G. 1991. Exploration and exploitation in organizational learning. *Organization Science* 2(1): 71–87.

O'Reilly III, C. A. & Tushman, M. L. 2013. Organizational ambidexterity: past, present, and future. *Academy of Management Perspectives* 27(4): 324–338.

Prange, C. & Heracleous, L. (eds.). 2018. *Agility.X: How Organizations Thrive in Unpredictable Times*. Cambridge University Press, Cambridge, UK.

Reeves, M., Haanaes, K., & Sinha, J. 2015. *Your Strategy Needs a Strategy: How to Choose and Execute the Right Approach*. Harvard Business Review Press, Boston, MA.

Ries, E. 2011. *The Lean Startup: How Today's Entrepreneurs Use Continuous Innovation to Create Radically Successful Businesses*. Crown Publishing Group, New York, NY.

Rigby, D. K., Elk, S., & Berez, S. 2020. The agile C-suite: a new approach to leadership for the team at the top. *Harvard Business Review* 98(3): 64–73.

Rigby, D. K., Sutherland, J., & Takeuchi, H. 2016. Embracing agile. *Harvard Business Review* 94(5): 40–50.

Simon, H. A. 1969. *The Sciences of the Artificial*. MIT Press, Cambridge, MA.

Smite, D., Moe, N. B., Floryan, M., Levinta, G., & Chatzipetrou, P. 2020. Spotify guilds. *Communications of the ACM* 63(3): 56–61.

Smite, D., Moe, N. B., Levinta, G., & Floryan, M. 2019. Spotify guilds: how to succeed with knowledge sharing in large-scale agile organizations. *IEEE Software* 36(2): 51–57.

Takeuchi, H. & Nonaka, I. 1986. The new new product development game. *Harvard Business Review* 64(1): 137–146.

Teece, D., Peteraf, M., & Leih, S. 2016. Dynamic capabilities and organizational agility: risk, uncertainty, and strategy in the innovation economy. *California Management Review* 58(4): 13–35.

9 | *The Global Organization*

AMY KATES AND GREG KESLER

In the 1980s, Bartlett and Ghoshal (1989) laid out the fundamental dilemma facing multinational firms: how to achieve global scale while simultaneously being locally responsive. PepsiCo, a major company in the global food and beverage industry, illustrates this classic tension. While the PepsiCo brand is global, products in the company's expansive portfolio are closely adapted to local markets. Ingredients, flavor profiles, packaging, consumer marketing, and retail relationships must all be tailored to local tastes and practices. Product leaders have the authority to compete aggressively in this dynamic, tight-margins business. At the same time, PepsiCo gains scale advantages over local players by leveraging its expertise in food science research and the collection and analysis of global consumer data. Support functions, such as human resource and financial systems, are centralized at the enterprise level. Thus, PepsiCo resolves its global–local dilemma through coordination of certain activities at the enterprise level while empowering business and regional leaders to be entrepreneurial in product development and marketing execution.

While the challenge is not new, we are now witnessing trends that make resolution of the global–local dilemma more difficult than ever before.

- Innovative business models. Firms are adopting more consumer-oriented, digitally enabled business models that involve greater convergence across industries (e.g., media content and distribution).
- Integrated customer solutions. Firms are bundling products, services, and software into integrated customer solutions.
- Digital technologies and artificial intelligence. Firms are incorporating digital technologies and artificial intelligence into the enterprise infrastructure, strengthening the entire value stream from strategy to product development, marketing and selling, and production and supply chain operations.

- Ecosystem management. Firms are extending the depth and breadth of their offerings to include external partners in the development and distribution of products and services that span organizational, geographic, and cultural boundaries, often with both cooperation and competition among the partners.

The traditional solution to organizing the global corporation has been a multidimensional global matrix (Galbraith, 2000). The matrix organization design, originally developed in the US aerospace industry in the 1950s and 1960s (Davis & Lawrence, 1977; Mee, 1964), enables coordination across key organizational dimensions such as products/services, business functions, customers, and geographic regions (Galbraith, 2009). As the number of dimensions increases, the matrix structure becomes ever more complex and cumbersome, prompting calls for designs that are "reconfigurable" (Galbraith, 2010). The power of the reconfigurable organization is that leaders can move work to where talent, capabilities, and capacity are, regardless of where those resources are in the world. Based on our experience working with numerous multinational companies, we believe the current interest in global organization design centers on scale, agility, and networks (Kates, Kesler, & Dimartino, 2021). By focusing on these factors, a modern matrix design can enable a large multinational firm to minimize global–local tension; coordinate across products, functions, customers, and geographies; and obtain the twin benefits of scale and agility via lateral mechanisms such as formal organizational networks.

Our chapter presents a comprehensive model of the global organization. The first section discusses scale, agility, and networks, illustrating their role in the present-day global business environment. The second section discusses global operating models and the organization models that support them. A global operating model specifies the domains the multinational firm intends to operate in, and the organization model shows how resources will be utilized within those domains. The final section describes five "activators" that drive the growth and effectiveness of modern global firms.

Scale, Agility, and Networks

There is a simple reality in microeconomics that eventually comes to bear on even the most creative start-up organization. As entities grow, economies of scale can provide competitive advantages by reducing per-unit costs. But beyond unit cost reductions, there are compelling innovation- and growth-oriented benefits of scale and integration. VF Corporation is a global apparel company with familiar brands such as Timberland, Vans, and The North Face. For many of VF's brands, each region in the world created its own marketing stories, developed its own products, and created its own retail experience for consumers. At the same time, it was apparent that VF's quirky but powerful Vans footwear and apparel brand worked in a much more transnational manner, and with a stronger growth trajectory. Its Southern California skateboarding culture had transplanted to China surprisingly well.

When brand stories and ethos (what the brand stands for) can be harmonized across geographies and cultures, the result is a more powerful "customer promise" that can command higher sales, prices, and loyalty. Globally consistent products can deliver enormous productivity gains across the firm's value streams. Apple and Nike are cases in point – their scale is less about cost reduction and more about value creation. In VF Corporation, the Vans organization had already moved to a more global organization model than the other VF brands, and it served as an exemplar for the growing company. The collaborative processes and forums already at work inside this popular brand served as inspiration for realigning the other brand and regional commercial units across VF. Investments in product and brand innovation became more international, focused on fewer, bigger ideas.

Agility needs to be developed in tandem with scale. Agile methodology, originally focused on software product development, is a well-defined discipline and set of practices for managing complex programs. It relies on small teams led by product managers who connect the work of development teams to users, translating technical requirements and specifications into project plans. It features short bursts of iteration with quick releases of product coupled with immediate user feedback. Teams are empowered to set their own plans and schedules within broad limits. Essentially, Agile is a rigorous way to run cross-functional work teams. The prevalence of technology companies and the need for almost every company to develop some software internally have diffused Agile and related practices widely. At Siemens, Netflix, Amazon, and other leading firms, agile teams have long been used to define the customer experience and develop new products and services. PepsiCo and other more conventional companies are actively experimenting with their functional teams, using Agile to innovate human resources and other business functions.

Increasingly, companies are seeking to scale agile teams across the entire organization. Companies like ING and Bosch in Europe, Haier in China, and Home Depot in the United States have built on the organizational thinking pioneered at Spotify that connects scores or even hundreds of agile teams into networks and *teams of teams* to rethink the roles of their top leadership teams and incorporate agile thinking into their organizational models. However, large multinational companies with multidimensional strategies and lines of business will not find that merely adopting agile team methods makes the organization more effective. When you have multiple products delivered to multiple client segments around the world, you need to find a way to leverage your resources and move fast. *Organizational agility* means being able to easily form a team-of-teams across a global network. Such agility comes only through the thoughtful design of both vertical and horizontal structures, governance processes, and clear decision rights. The ability to set and communicate strategy (choosing what to do and not do) and priorities (setting a sequence of activities) requires a high degree of coordination among leaders. It is a team process, and one that must be originated at senior levels in the company.

In the current business environment, it is not an option to choose between agility and scale. Effective designs include both – the ability to scale up (or down) and the agility required to do so quickly. Actors and resources are linked through formal networks that become the means of moving assets, ideas, and talent across borders and boundaries. When we use the term "network," we distinguish between an informal, relationship-based network and a formal organization network. Informal networks connect individuals. High-trust work relationships are the foundation of organizations. Trust, and the social capital that comes from it, is the glue that binds the organizational parts together. While strong relationships and trust are necessary for cross-boundary work, they are not sufficient. Organizations cannot be run solely on relationships, goodwill, and favors.

Formal networks are an *organizational* property – they are woven into the fabric of the organization. When networks are well designed, local and global interests are met through the normal course of management and business processes, not by following the dictates of a top-down hierarchy. Reward systems and metrics must make it rational – part of everyday work – to collaborate and for senior leaders to invest the time to create conditions that facilitate collaboration. Business and management processes must align work, making it easier for teams to come together. People should be selected into teams considering their soft skills as well as their technical skills. There must be decision-making forums built to manage the trade-offs that inevitably arise between the total enterprise and its various parts. There will be network leaders, but those leaders must see themselves as integrators and facilitators rather than managers of a distinct organizational dimension.

Designing the Global Enterprise

A global operating model is how a firm delivers value to its customers or clients. It is the basic organizational architecture that makes it possible to execute strategies at the enterprise, business unit, and functional levels of the firm and is intended to encompass interactions among the networks that will build and utilize needed organizational capabilities (Kesler & Kates, 2016). Global operating models are typically composed of three elements:

- Geographic market units (regions, countries, or country clusters)
- Global business units (products/services, brands, categories, or customer segments)
- Global business and support functions (R&D, supply chain logistics, marketing, IT, HR, finance, etc.).

The design of the global operating model starts with aligning the main components of the enterprise's business portfolio – how closely they connect to gain the advantages of scale and how loosely they connect to foster local responsiveness. Four enterprise archetypes encompass most multinational corporations, as represented in Figure 9.1. The far-left column represents a single integrated global business, and the far-right column represents a holding company. Between these two extremes are closely and loosely related business portfolios. These four archetypes each need a particular form of integration across its portfolio of businesses. Companies in column 1 tend to have a single business model and a structure built around business functions. Functional leaders in marketing, sales, engineering, and operations work as a single team to run the business. Diversity in the single-business global

	1	2	3	4
	Fully Integrated Single Business	**Closely Related Portfolio**	**Loosely Related Portfolio**	**Holding Company or Conglomerate**
Strategy and Customer Value	Single strategy guides all P&L units with minor variations.	Complementary business portfolio and core strategies with synergies.	Diverse, relatively autonomous businesses set strategies, with limited synergies across units.	Buying and selling separate assets. Structuring financial deals.
Governance	Strategy and execution oversight comes from organizational center. All processes and practices are common. Homogeneous corporate culture.	Business units drive strategy and varying degrees of execution, often with shared resources (in a matrix). Seeks benefits of scale in core technologies, product and commercial platforms, and back-end operations.	Business units drive nearly full execution of results with limited matrix operations. Cross-business unit scale is limited (e.g., government relations, technology transfer, back-end shared services). Some effort to harmonize corporate culture.	Focused on appointing leaders. Business units return some profits to parent. Few or no common processes. Multiple corporate cultures.
Role of the Center	Drives functional policies, staffing, and standards to build a consistent function presence across the company. Functional costs managed centrally.	Orchestrates and owns a common strategic agenda and most processes. Collaborates closely with divisions to support execution. Manages company-wide talent management process and shared services. Influences functional cost structure.	Builds skills, tools, and talent practices necessary to strengthen a few functional capabilities. Priorities are guided mostly in divisions. May be a few selective shared services. Costs managed primarily within the business units.	Limited company-wide policies and practices mostly focused on risk and fiduciary matters.
Company Examples	Apple Heineken Coca-Cola	P&G Medtronic Deere & Co. PepsiCo	Aditya Birla Group Unilever United Technologies	Berkshire Hathaway Virgin Group

Figure 9.1 The business configuration framework
From Kates et al. (2021). Reproduced with permission of Kogan Page Limited through PLSclear.

firm tends to be geographic, or perhaps in vertical markets or channels. The business functions drive strategy decisions, and there is often a good deal of commonality in corporate policies and management practices across geographies. Companies that operate in column 4 are holding companies or conglomerates. They are simple organizations at the enterprise level, with a small corporate center focused on talent acquisition and management as well as financial decisions. Typically, the center is not involved with operational control or coordination of the business units.

The most complex operating models exist in the closely and loosely related corporate portfolios. In these cases, executives and designers want to allow some degree of business unit autonomy while obtaining the benefits of resource leverage (scale) that come with shared functions and processes. Business units in columns 2 and 3 are often arranged by product-service offering or customer type. In the closely related portfolio (column 2), business units are not fully independent, and they do not contain all the functions necessary to conduct the business. Here, business units focus mainly on the product-service offering, marketing, and product creation. In the loosely related portfolio (column 3), business units are much more autonomous, with most or all functional resources contained and largely controlled within the business units. Although those business units may share elements of sales or operations, they are usually full-fledged profit centers.

The decision on which of the four enterprise contexts best fits the business should be based on many factors. Nevertheless, there is usually a "best fit" option among the four, given a company's history and ambitions. Some company examples highlight the choice of operating model according to the four enterprise profiles shown in Figure 9.1. Apple exemplifies the single-business operating model (column 1). The company uses a tightly controlled, center-led governance process in which products, services, functions, and the entire ecosystem are well served, even with increasing diversity of its offerings. Apple's operating system and culture have produced one of the most valuable brands in the world. The holding company (column 4) is a declining segment of American and European business. Most holding companies today are based in Asia, and many are family-held. In the United States, investors have shunned conglomerates, and many have broken up or divested significant assets in recent years, notably General Electric, Honeywell, United Technologies, and Dupont/Dow. Investors have rewarded focus – they want the predictability of stock performance that a focused portfolio provides. As a result, an ongoing trend is that some holding companies are seeking ways to partially integrate their business units to achieve scale advantages. Even Berkshire Hathaway, famous for the independence of its various business units, has started to cross-leverage some of its assets. Top executives from the businesses meet to share strategies and best practices on subjects as diverse as purchasing, sustainability, cybersecurity, hiring practices, and healthcare costs (Friedman, 2019).

Procter & Gamble (P&G) and Unilever compete in similar consumer goods categories, and both companies are extensively international. Despite some adjustments back and forth, P&G has chosen to maintain a center-led global approach to managing its brands and innovation processes (column 2, closely related). P&G has largely exited the food business to focus on personal and homecare categories. Unilever, on the other hand, has always used a regionally focused operating model, reflecting the view that consumer differences across countries and regions require localized approaches (column 3, loosely related). It also has a more diverse set of products across foods and other consumer goods. Thus, the product/service portfolio clearly influences the choice of operating model, but it is not the only factor. Unilever's top leadership has for decades disliked center-led governance (outside of a few core capabilities) and encourages leaders in its regional and country-based units to stay close to local tastes and choices in the way they adapt products and marketing messages. Increasingly, Unilever seeks operational efficiencies to increase scale, but the company's global–local balance has always favored the local dimension.

As these examples illustrate, an operating model provides the overall architecture for how the businesses will be run. The careful design of enterprise roles lays out accountabilities for all the major units, and the relevant enterprise archetype suggests which capabilities should be centralized at the enterprise level and which should be held by business and geographic units. Thus, a multinational company's operating model provides the basic solution to its global–local dilemma. And clarity on where integration creates value sets the foundation for the design of the vertical and horizontal organizations.

The Vertical Organization

Perhaps there is no greater shibboleth in organization design than the idea of hierarchy. Hierarchy is often viewed as rigidity. The term suggests an organization in which information only moves up and down through a strict chain of command. An organization where variation and innovation are stifled at the front line. An organization of silos where people cannot work across unit lines without permission from above. But is hierarchy necessarily or always a bad thing?

It is useful to think of hierarchy as a way of differentiating thought and focus. In a well-designed hierarchy of leadership, each leader does not just perform a bigger version of the work of leaders below. At each layer there should be a different time horizon and scope of problems to solve (Simon, 1947). The notion of a hierarchy of thought and focus implies that each layer makes a unique contribution to the work of the organization. When we think of how work at the top of the organization empowers work at the lower levels of the organization, we can begin to build the backbone of an organization

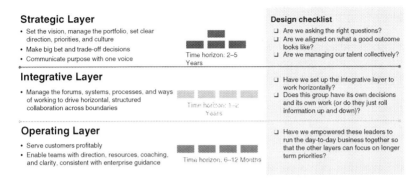

Strategic Layer
- Set the vision, manage the portfolio, set clear direction, priorities, and culture
- Make big bet and trade-off decisions
- Communicate purpose with one voice

Time horizon: 2–5 Years

Design checklist
- ❏ Are we asking the right questions?
- ❏ Are we aligned on what a good outcome looks like?
- ❏ Are we managing our talent collectively?

Integrative Layer
- Manage the forums, systems, processes, and ways of working to drive horizontal, structured collaboration across boundaries

Time horizon: 1–2 Years

- ❏ Have we set up the integrative layer to work horizontally?
- ❏ Does this group have its own decisions and its own work (or do they just roll information up and down)?

Operating Layer
- Serve customers profitably
- Enable teams with direction, resources, coaching, and clarity, consistent with enterprise guidance

Time horizon: 6–12 Months

- ❏ Have we empowered these leaders to run the day-to-day business together so that the other layers can focus on longer term priorities?

Figure 9.2 Layers of leadership
From Kates et al. (2021). Reproduced with permission of Kogan Page Limited through PLSclear.

that is agile and adaptive as well as coordinated and integrated. We use the term *vertical organization* to avoid confusion with the usual perception of hierarchy and the negative connotations associated with that word.

The design of the vertical organization is essentially the design of roles, decision rights, and management and reward systems to create the right mix of authority, accountability, and responsibility not just in individuals but also in entire layers of leadership. In many organizations, the layers of leadership are used primarily as a cascade mechanism for information to be transmitted from the top rather than each layer owning its own unique work. The result is that hierarchical relationships often become a source of unhealthy tension and ambiguity. It is difficult, of course, to fully divorce reporting relationships from a discussion of the vertical organization. However, by focusing on the work of each layer and then identifying the right roles and perspectives for conversations within and across layers, one can create a logic that reflects the work rather than individual status or power. Figure 9.2 shows the three core layers of leadership in a global organization.

Thoughtful role design is an essential step in creating the vertical organization. As part of our organization design work, we typically focus on those roles that are pivotal to new strategies, are crucial for connecting actors across organizational boundaries, or are new and not well understood. We help managers create role descriptions that highlight the contribution of the role, measures of success, decision authority, time horizons and time allocation, and the high-trust vertical and lateral relationships that will need to be built. We find that role descriptions (in contrast to conventional job descriptions) help to communicate expectations and match motivation and competencies to the work. Using this approach, one can ensure that roles stacked in a job family at the global (strategic), regional (integrative), and market (operational) layers are differentiated appropriately. Once roles are clarified at each leadership layer, one can look horizontally and start to build the forums that will foster the right kinds of conversations across job families at each layer.

The Horizontal Organization

The horizontal organization is a path to both agility and scale. Agility requires the timely assembly of resources, regardless of where they are produced or located, to meet unique customer needs. Scale is achieved by bridging services, platforms, and processes across business units. These lateral processes and mechanisms are what we call the *horizontal organization*. Well-designed horizontal organizations not only allow but encourage people to join cross-boundary teams and networks and to take responsibility for results they cannot deliver on their own. Horizontal mechanisms must be designed to foster discretionary responsibility, not merely impose accountability. Removing barriers to collaboration is hard work. It is certainly more than standing up cross-functional teams. Our identities tend to be connected to our most proximate team – the product line we work in, our location, or our functional group. Collaboration at scale – across teams – must be designed into the structure of the organization. We have a strong natural desire as humans for collaboration within our home team but often need to be helped to collaborate across team boundaries.

Our experience with helping companies develop their horizontal organizations yields several observations regarding what leads to success.

Shared purpose. Networks of individuals and teams must create a shared purpose that will guide priorities and activities associated with the business strategy. Network members usually have their own jobs with their own objectives. However, when the network is activated around the right collective ideas, the members can work together on activities driven by shared interests. At VF's North Face apparel business unit, for example, the brand is positioned the same in China as it is in Europe and North America. Team members share a vision. A new product idea can come from anywhere, and ideas in the network are quickly shared. Members of the network in any region have an opportunity to join in building a business case for a new product. If the idea gains traction across regions it becomes scalable, and those are the projects that will get priority funding. Members of the network will be more likely to opt in when the design idea has "forward-compatible" characteristics, meaning that local developers can build on the idea to make it more relevant to customers without duplicating investments.

Leadership. The role of leaders in horizontal networks is very different from leaders who run self-contained operating units. Networks are powerful development experiences for future general managers and senior executives. The essential talents and skills required to obtain results without well-defined authority include creating a compelling vision that ties team membership to a greater purpose. Such leaders enjoy building community processes, engaging diverse perspectives, and watching others get credit for successful outcomes.

Leaders need to be supported to work effectively in the horizontal organization, especially if they have been promoted and rewarded largely for leading their own units. Many leaders do not see the value in collaborating with peers or do not know how to lead without formal authority and reporting lines. Especially when power dynamics are not clearly spelled out and leaders are left to figure it out on their own, the rational response is to resort to old habits that worked in the past. Therefore, at the key network nodes where value is going to be created, leaders and their teams need to be empowered and provided with the enabling mechanisms that allow them to make decisions together so that they are motivated to take responsibility for enterprise-related outcomes. Underneath the mechanics is an organizational investment in trust-building across boundaries, modelled by senior leaders.

Lateral operating mechanisms. For networks to be able to deliver business results, they must have a clear presence in the company's operating model. They will be measured on overall business results, but they are also well served by metrics that reflect the unique, horizontal contribution they make to the business, tied directly to the uptake and consumption of solutions. Further, decision rights and decision-making forums should be developed within the network as well as the connections of the network to other business and management processes.

Activation. The design of the horizontal organization is not a once-and-done activity. The horizontal organization is always in tension with the vertical organization to some extent. Often leaders are sitting in both constructs, sometimes wearing multiple hats in the same meeting. Each organization requires an acceptable balance between vertical and horizontal tension for the overall relationship to be healthy and productive. Building effective formal networks requires learning; each cycle of decision-making must be reflected upon and improvements made where appropriate. Continuous assessment and adjustment are at the heart of successful horizontal organizations. (We will discuss specific activating mechanisms later in the chapter.)

Organization Models

An organization model sets the activity system that will fulfil the goals and requirements of the company's operating model. Large multinational corporations embody a huge amount of complexity in their far-flung operations, and global organization designs must embrace that complexity if they are to be effective. An example from P&G illustrates the magnitude of the challenge (Galbraith, 2010). One of P&G's biggest customers, Walmart, accounts for approximately one-third of P&G's total revenues. Walmart operates more than 10,500 stores and clubs under 48 banners in 24 countries and on e-commerce websites. To supply Walmart with the many P&G products it sells creates enormous logistical, inventory, and other problems for both companies. P&G has a team of about 250 people who are responsible for the Walmart account, and this team works across P&G's product categories, support functions, and geographic regions where Walmart has retail operations.

The generic organization design that best fits complex global operating models is the multidimensional, reconfigurable matrix (Galbraith, 2010, 2014; Kates et al., 2021). It remains the most used approach to integrate a multinational company's product/service lines, business functions, geographic regions, and key customers into an effective system (Galbraith, 2009). Matrix designs have evolved from the initial two-dimensional matrix of products and functions to a three-dimensional design that includes countries and regions to a four-dimensional design that incorporates key customers in planning and decision-making processes.

The notion of *reconfigurable* helps large, complex companies become more agile – to be able to regularly reorganize around opportunities as they arise (Galbraith, 2010). The reconfigurable organization consists of both stable and dynamic parts, and it configures and reconfigures itself around opportunities (Galbraith, 2010). The stable portion of the matrix consists of the basic structure and shared business processes. As people move from one team assignment to another, they engage with certain processes that remain the same: financial, new product development, customer relationship management, performance management, and so on. There are process "owners" who continually work to improve them, but business processes are stable and common throughout the organization. The variable parts of the organization are the teams that form and reform and the management decision-making groups that allocate resources and determine priorities. Teams are formed by gathering people from functional areas across the company. For example, teams may design and launch a new product or solution, generate a customer proposal, enter a new market or country, build a new distribution channel, implement a solution, and so on. Such teams are continuously reconfigured to address the set of opportunities facing the company. Teams also prepare business plans for their product line, customer segment, and country. Those plans are channeled into the planning and budgeting process to be reconciled and to produce an aligned set of goals for all the matrix dimensions. Agile teams can be part of this mix. Some teams may be temporary, and others may be continuous, owning a product, service, or process end-to-end across the stable structure of the matrix.

A multidimensional, reconfigurable matrix is not easy to install or operate. Most observers have concluded that large multinational corporations inevitably find themselves using some form of a matrix organization and that reported matrix failures are due to improper execution and not the organizational form itself. To work properly, the matrix structure must be accompanied by appropriate business and decision-making processes, shared infrastructure, reward systems, and human resource management practices (Galbraith, 2009).

Activating Global Operating Models

Continuing complexity in global strategy and organization, and all the challenges associated with it, is driven by the need for new sources of growth in diverse geographic markets across multiproduct companies whose demanding customers have lots of technology at their fingertips (Galbraith, 2014). In response to this complexity, most large multinational companies continually work to refine and improve their operating model. Our experience in working with companies that are not achieving the results they desire suggests that the fundamental design of their operating models is not the main problem – most models, in fact, appear to be quite logical and compelling. The challenge is ineffective or incomplete *activation* (Kates et al., 2021). Despite large-scale, well-funded change initiatives, sophisticated communications programs, and countless worldwide leadership summits, the hard work of bringing these complex operating models to life often lacks focus or is not sustained over the two or more years that it typically takes to fully embed new ways of working. We see common symptoms that indicate incomplete or ineffective activation:

- Excess hierarchical layers and duplicated work make the organization slow and internally focused.
- Global product teams and functions are overlaid on the existing regional (commercial) organizations without adjustments to legacy profit and loss structures, creating debilitating friction.
- Authority issues remain unresolved across global business units, regional teams, and functional units.
- Global functions are designed to do yesterday's work, often only loosely connected to the needs of the business.
- Leaders do not know how and are not motivated to work in a matrix – metrics and reward systems do not reinforce enterprise thinking.
- The corporate executive committee continues to act as a group of individual leaders, each focused on their own business versus the needs of the enterprise.

Our work and research reveal five activators for improving and accelerating business results in a global operating model (Kates & Kesler, 2015; Kesler & Kates, 2016). These activators are what differentiate companies that obtain sustainable results from their global operating model from those that do not. The activators are sorted

A. Right Connections

B. Right Conversations

C. The Right Leaders

1. **Value adding vertical layers:**
   Design leadership layers "fit for purpose" – move the work to where the talent sits

2. **Formal innovation and execution networks:**
   Start with a center-led perspective – where do we need networks?

3. **The business handshake:**
   Align accountability and metrics with the operating model

4. **Power, governance, and decision-making processes:**
   Design needed governance forums and use the right decision tools

5. **Matrix ready leaders:**
   Design leadership roles to fit the operating model and enable leaders to work in the new environment

Figure 9.3 Activation

against three outcomes: the right connections, the right conversations, and the right know-how. See Figure 9.3.

Activator #1: Value-Adding Vertical Layers

As discussed earlier, designers of the vertical organization must make sure that hierarchical layers do not overlap in responsibility and create unnecessary complexity. The Coca-Cola Company is an example of the need to adhere to the principle of unique, value-adding layers. In late 2014, senior leaders announced a company-wide initiative to establish an anchor layer of management in its international markets. Large clusters of countries, known as divisions, became the anchor operating-unit layer. The company eliminated its regional-group layer to create a direct connection between field divisions and global brand and category teams. The organization had become a complex web where big ideas, driven from the center, had to be negotiated with each region, and often country-level general managers, before they could be executed. By having the center-based marketers interact directly with countries or small clusters of countries, brand building and product expansion ideas could be driven more quickly around the world.

The anchor layer is where authority is located to make short- and long-term trade-offs. By removing the regional layer, Coca-Cola placed the anchor layer close to the consumer. Now the center marketers provide global direction but only after interaction with local marketers who are in close contact with consumer tastes and trends. In this instance, a regional marketing layer did not add value.

Activator #2: Formal Innovation and Execution Networks

A second valuable activator of a global operating model is the creation of formal networks of global and local capability with guidance from the center of the organization. Formal networks are useful in many ways:

- Ideas move not just from the center to the operating units but also across business units and geographies to generate innovation.
- The enterprise can provide strong, coordinated leadership from the center without relying on reporting relationships, for greater agility in the regions.
- Investments in people and systems are leveraged for the good of the entire company.
- Execution for initiatives is owned by the network, creating better accountability for results.

Over the last decade or so, many leading multinational firms have concluded that "marketing" should not be a discrete organizational entity but rather should be extended throughout the organization, tapping virtually every function (de Swaan Arons, van den Driest, & Weed, 2014). Today's marketing capability can be fully realized only by engaging the entire organization in pursuing the brand's purpose, integrating marketing with other functions, and ensuring that global, regional, and local marketing teams work interdependently. The same idea can be extended to the management of initiatives like innovation or key account management. To leverage innovation investments – to make them "go-forward compatible" and be relevant to customers in more than one region – companies like Nike, Medtronic, and Deere & Co. engage product developers from several regions to work with each other, often facilitated by a corporate team, against a shared agenda and targets. Common goals, methods, and tools are the integrator, the centripetal force that allows the work to be center-led, not centralized.

The center has an important role in the network, but it is not the dominant role. Leadership is often rotated in robust global networks. For example, PepsiCo connects global category managers with regional commercial and marketing managers from developed and developing markets. Any operating unit in the network might be designated as the lead for creating the content for a given innovation initiative. An operating unit or function in the network often assumes the lead when it has a major stake in the outcome, has the talent to lead the work, and is willing to invest resources. Some businesses or regions within the network may commit to launch the new product or brand idea early in the process and share in the funding. Other units may serve as a test market for the new idea. While some operating units in the network may completely opt out of a given initiative, other units may pick up the content once it is developed and adapt it locally. These "coalitions of the willing" are built on trust and a culture of mutual interdependence. There is no chief marketing officer at PepsiCo.

Activator #3: The Business Handshake

In one sense, an organization is made up of a series of requests and promises among actors (Sull & Spinosa, 2007). The most important of these are what we call the *business handshake*, which can be characterized as follows:

- It is the agreement across organizational boundaries on what results will be delivered and how.
- Goals are shared completely. The actors co-own the business customer and/or the consumer, they codevelop strategy, and they co-own the results.
- An integrated planning process connects strategic plans, including operating targets and budgets, and – in the handshake – it connects the partners across business lines, geographies, and functions.

Once interlocking targets and resource plans are set, the principals in the handshake own the execution of those plans. They will need to (1) align rewards and metrics, (2) develop a performance-management cadence that pulls the players together to manage results at the right level of detail and with the right frequency, and (3) create access to the same data for all partners, ensuring a single source of information and knowledge to enable smart trade-offs.

Activator #4: Power, Governance, and Decision-Making Processes

Decision-making is the essence of management, and one key to activating the global operating model is to allocate power for purpose. Once the handshake is set with interlocked plans and a shared business dashboard, operating governance forums and practices enable both agility and scale. This is seldom accomplished solely by using

RACI decision-making charts (responsible, accountable, consulted, informed). Decision-making should take place in a culture that supports the right balance of global, local, and functional influence, and it must value empowerment of cross-boundary teams. Decision-making in companies that have fully activated their operating models has the following characteristics:

- Governance forums for decision-making (executive committees, operating committees, policy councils, and the like) provide clear strategic direction and guidance to operating leaders.
- Simple, co-owned decision rights are focused on the highest-value decisions in the handshake, and they line up closely with accountabilities.
- Partners in the handshake work together with a regular cadence, transparency, and action focus.
- The power to decide and act is delegated to the accountable managers, and top executives intervene only on an exceptional basis.

Before using decision-making tools such as RACI charts, it is important to define clearly what the governance forums in the enterprise will be and what role each will play. Examples of governance forums include executive committees, operating committees, and councils focused on specific topics such as growth strategy, innovation project portfolio, pricing, marketing policy, or IT standards. Most multinational companies have a variety of these forums in place, but often their remit is unclear, they may overlap in some decision areas, and they may leave gaps in others. Corporate executive committees can empower and anchor business units by creating clarity for business decisions, such as stating the new-product investment priorities. This center-led, integrative executive work creates the framework in which managers close to the ground can be free to act. It provides them the context in which to make good decisions and judgments. It reduces the need for approval levels and controls around each transaction. Clear direction on priorities and boundaries from the top layer is required for true empowerment for the layers of leaders below.

Activator #5: Matrix-Ready Leaders

The characteristics of the global, boundary-spanning leader have been examined in-depth over the past decade or more (Ernst &

Chrobot-Mason, 2010). In companies that fully activate their global operating model, a pipeline of matrix-ready leadership is the sum of embedded selection and development practices, clearly defined behavioral criteria, and deep commitment to talent development at the top of the hierarchy. No number of formal processes, aligned objectives, or decision rights documents will bring the global operating model to life without the right leadership behaviors and relationships. In companies that make their operating model work:

- Global leaders constructively manage conflicts between global and local business (and functional) objectives across the matrix.
- Relationships and social capital – which are the foundation for effective leadership in all organizations – are strengthened and valued.
- Collaboration and working across all types of boundaries become the cultural norm for leaders.

The matrix organization that underlies a global operating model requires strong leaders that can manage multiple teams, influence peers without authority, and proactively align competing agendas. The success of a global operating model depends largely on competent leaders who are willing and able to navigate the power dynamics inherent in a complex organization. Building a global talent pipeline is a core capability for companies that want to activate a global operating model. Clear talent objectives drive the right talent-development focus. P&G provides a good example. Senior-level talent is needed in three broad areas: (1) global business units, (2) market development regions, and (3) functions and services. Talent depth is measured in each area, and strategies are devised to close projected gaps.

The best global leadership systems develop people and the organization simultaneously (Tichy et al., 1992). No other business process has more impact on shaping culture than company-wide talent development. Calibration and development councils can become the control center for activating the global operating model if used well. As an executive team at the top do the work of getting to know the company's talent by evaluating individuals with a common yardstick and vocabulary, they begin to calibrate a shared set of expectations about what global leadership looks like in their company. As senior executives plan moves among promotable candidates, they learn to trust, and they play more of an enterprise leadership role, often becoming a more collaborative leadership team. For many companies, these talent review discussions help to shift the role of each senior executive from being focused on the performance of his or her own unit to committing a portion of his or her attention to shared leadership of the enterprise.

Conclusion

Managing global business strategies across a diverse set of products and markets is challenging in a rapidly changing environment. The set of foundational concepts discussed in this chapter remain the best way to create a clear operating model and align leadership teams in order to balance the tensions of scaling platforms, brands, and distribution channels while remaining agile, local, and differentiated where it makes the most difference for the customer. It is of utmost importance to establish the relationship between the center and the business portfolio – where integration creates value and where it does not. Then one can design the vertical and horizontal organizations. The vertical organization – layers of leadership and key roles – allows for strong lateral connections across organizational boundaries. Those connections are the pathways for the right conversations and decisions involved in executing global strategies. In this way, the organization is designed to find opportunities for scale – not just for cost effectiveness but for innovation and speed to market as well.

References

Bartlett, C. A. & Ghoshal, S. 1989. *Managing across Borders: The Transnational Solution*. Harvard Business Review Press, Boston, MA.

Davis, S. M. & Lawrence, P. R. 1977. *Matrix*. Addison-Wesley, Reading, MA.

de Swaan Arons, M., van den Driest, F., & Weed, K. 2014. The ultimate marketing machine. *Harvard Business Review* 92(7–8): 54–63. hbr.org/2014/07/the-ultimate-marketing-machine

Ernst, C. & Chrobot-Mason, D. 2010. *Boundary-Spanning Leadership: Six Practices for Solving Problems, Driving Innovations, and Transforming Organizations*. McGraw-Hill, New York, NY.

Friedman, N. 2019. The Berkshire Empire Is Quietly Collaborating More than Ever. *Wall Street Journal*. April 4. www.wsj.com/articles/the-berk shire-empire-is-quietly-collaborating-more-than-ever-11554370201

Galbraith, J. R. 2000. *Designing the Global Corporation*. Jossey-Bass, San Francisco, CA.

Galbraith, J. R. 2009. *Designing Matrix Organizations That Actually Work*. Jossey-Bass, San Francisco, CA.

Galbraith, J. R. 2010. The multi-dimensional and reconfigurable organization. *Organizational Dynamics* 39(2): 115–125.

Galbraith, J. R. 2014. *Designing Organizations: Strategy, Structure, and Process at the Business Unit and Enterprise Levels*. 3rd ed. Jossey-Bass, San Francisco, CA.

Kates, A. & Kesler, G. 2015. Activating global operating models: the bridge from organization design to performance. *Journal of Organization Design* 4(2): 38–47.

Kates, A., Kesler, G., & Dimartino, M. 2021. *Networked, Scaled, and Agile: A Design Strategy for Complex Organizations*. Kogan Page, New York, NY.

Kesler, G. & Kates, A. 2016. *Bridging Organization Design and Performance: Five Ways to Activate a Global Operating Model*. Wiley, New York, NY.

Mee, J. F. 1964. Matrix organization. *Business Horizons* 7(2): 70–72.

Simon, H. A. 1947. *Administrative Behavior: A Study of Decision Making Processes in Administrative Organization*. Macmillan, New York, NY.

Sull, D. N. & Spinosa, C. 2007. Promise-based management: the essence of execution. *Harvard Business Review* 85(4): 78–86.

Tichy, N. M., Brimm, M. I., Charan, R., & Takeuchi, H. 1992. Leadership development as a lever for global transformation. In V. Pucik, N. M. Tichy, and C. K. Barnett (eds.), *Globalizing Management: Creating and Leading the Competitive Organization*: 47–60. Wiley, New York, NY.

10 | *Performance-Focused Organizing*

SCOTT A. SNELL AND KENNETH J. CARRIG

Organizations devise, implement, and execute strategies in pursuit of their mission and goals. They set short- and long-term goals, execute strategies intended to achieve goals, monitor the performance of activities, and take corrective actions if necessary. Steering an organization along its intended course requires having the necessary capabilities and the agility to deploy them quickly and efficiently in response to changing circumstances. Strategy per se does not differentiate how firms perform – it is how strategies are executed that makes the difference. Despite its importance, many organizations struggle with execution, in part because they are not designed for high performance. This chapter provides a framework for the design of effective strategic execution and performance management. The first section describes the elements of a performance management system and how they function. A well-designed performance management system provides a valid and accurate assessment of how well existing strategies are working, and it alerts the organization to where corrective actions may be needed. The second section discusses strategic execution, which is how the organization performs its tasks. Our approach to improving execution, called the 4A Framework (Carrig & Snell, 2019), discusses organizational alignment, architecture, ability, and agility. By integrating these four factors into a unified whole, organizational performance can be strong and sustainable.

Managing Organizational Performance

Organizational performance management draws on principles of cybernetics, the science of control and communication (Ashby, 1956; Wiener, 1948). Performance management processes align actors around goals and provides them with metrics to assess progress and results. They use both feedback and feedforward to guide organizational decision-making and actions. Consider an example from electric

176

vehicle manufacturing (Hawkins, 2021). In early 2021, the COVID-19 pandemic disrupted the operations of microprocessor manufacturers, drastically reducing the global supply of computer chips available to electric car manufacturers. Daimler and BMW, unable to obtain chips from their suppliers, shut down assembly lines and reduced output by tens of thousands of vehicles. By contrast, Tesla avoided disruption of its operations by taking anticipatory action. The company substituted alternative microprocessors and wrote new firmware such that those microprocessors could be used in Tesla's cars. Tesla's handling of this situation illustrates the use of feedforward – taking action based on projected rather than actual future states.

Organizations typically search for alternatives when performance falls short of expectations (Cyert & March, 1992) – they develop corrective actions based on feedback about their current situation. Organizational survival, however, depends on the ability to take anticipatory action, acting before things go wrong. In rapidly changing environments, feedback alone is not sufficient for high performance; it needs to be combined with feedforward so that the organization avoids problems rather than correcting them after they have occurred.

The 4A Framework

Effective execution of existing activities and new initiatives is difficult because it involves so many factors, some of them intangible and therefore difficult to manage directly. Moreover, execution is not a "once and done" phenomenon – it manifests from a series of iterative decisions, investments, and actions taken over time. Execution is a continuous, unending process undergirded by a performance management system. Our approach to strategic execution, called the 4A Framework, seeks to leverage the firm's resources to energize performance (Carrig & Snell, 2019). As shown in Figure 10.1, the framework juxtaposes two types of resources (human and organizational capital) and two types of energy (potential and kinetic) to highlight four organizational factors where purposeful design can enhance execution capability. These factors are alignment, architecture, ability, and agility. Where companies have performance problems, usually these are the most troublesome areas. When companies achieve performance breakthroughs, these are the variables that largely account for it.

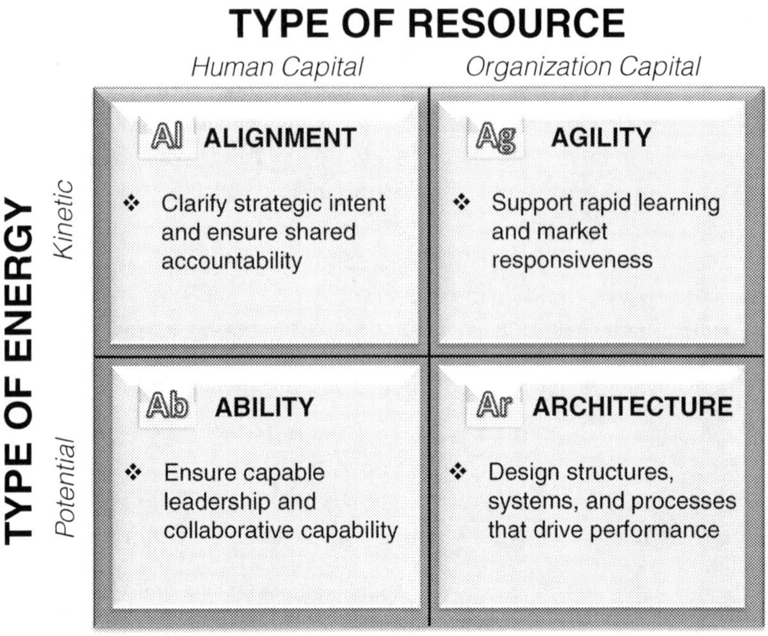

TYPE OF RESOURCE

Human Capital   *Organization Capital*

TYPE OF ENERGY
Kinetic — *Potential*

Al ALIGNMENT
❖ Clarify strategic intent and ensure shared accountability

Ag AGILITY
❖ Support rapid learning and market responsiveness

Ab ABILITY
❖ Ensure capable leadership and collaborative capability

Ar ARCHITECTURE
❖ Design structures, systems, and processes that drive performance

Figure 10.1 The 4A framework
From Carrig and Snell (2019). Used with permission of Stanford University Press; permission conveyed through Copyright Clearance Center, Inc.

- *Alignment*: Everyone is focused on the same goals, with a shared understanding of their roles, commitment, and accountability to deliver exceptional performance.
- *Architecture*: The organization's design creates clear authority structures, supports efficient workflow, and enables good decision-making to drive performance.
- *Ability*: The organization has the leadership and talent needed to perform at a high level as well as the ability to collaborate effectively across the enterprise.
- *Agility*: The organization has the capability to respond quickly to emerging opportunities, reallocate resources, and learn continuously.

Alignment

The concept of alignment conveys the deceptively simple notion that execution depends on everyone working together toward the same objective. Consider the premise that organizations exist only because people can accomplish more working together than they can on their own. When aligned, organizations bring different elements together into a unified whole. The rich diversity of talents, resources, experiences, and opportunities can combine with focused intensity to achieve greater performance. Alignment channels effort and resources toward desired outcomes. It provides clarity of purpose and direction, momentum to overcome inertia, a focus for decisions and actions, and resilience in the face of change or disruption.

Left unattended, a complex, multiunit organization can easily become misaligned (Leinwand & Mainardi, 2016). Managers often assert that their unit's activities are important, and typically they are, but in the aggregate the overall enterprise may lose its focus (Bossidy & Charan, 2002). Such dispersion of resources and priorities can lead to suboptimal performance. Organization size exacerbates this problem. If strategic priorities are not clearly communicated deep in the organization, managers and employees lose perspective on how their efforts work in service of the whole. Further complicating the alignment challenge is organizational change (Burgelman & Grove, 1996). Alignment is not a static state – it is an ongoing challenge. Better alignment generates more energy and momentum. In contrast, misalignment can become a vicious cycle. How can alignment be achieved? Three factors offer the most leverage: clear strategic intent, shared expectations of high performance, and mutual accountability for results (Carrig & Snell, 2019).

Clear strategic intent. Alignment requires senior executives to formulate a clear strategic intent, a process that energizes employees around an ambitious vision of the future (Hamel & Prahalad, 2005, 2010). When strategic intent is clearly articulated, it empowers organization members to realize their contributions to that vision by providing a shared logic for sensing, framing, and responding to the external environment (Bettis & Prahalad, 1995). Keller and Price (2011) found that a firm's financial performance was almost twice as likely to be above the industry median when its employees were clear about and excited by the company's direction. Achieving that level of clarity, of course, is difficult to attain. Over two decades ago, Treacy and Wiersema (1995) found the vast majority of executive teams they studied were unable to articulate their company's value proposition succinctly. In our experience, the same is true today. Without a clear strategic intent, it is difficult to establish a focal point for collective goal alignment and performance.

When formal processes for creating and communicating strategic intent are put in place, the organization benefits. Tools such as scenario analysis, strategy mapping, visioning, and the like are designed to obtain broader input and multiple perspectives to generate a shared strategic intent and facilitate the process of translating that intent across areas of the business (O'Shannassy, 2016; Schoemaker, 1992). The processes include both bottom-up and top-down engagement.

Shared performance expectations. To improve strategic execution, senior leaders may need to recalibrate performance standards – raise the bar of what's possible and what's expected. Individuals and entire organizations can become complacent, perhaps lulled by their routines and insulated from dramatic feedback about their performance. Leaders need to continually refresh their commitment to excellence and demonstrate that commitment to others (Tushman, Newman, & Romanelli, 1986). Raising shared expectations for performance does two things. First, it lifts the organization's collective ambitions, energizing a sense of what's possible in the future. Second, it grounds the organization by reflecting what's required or necessary – the normative behaviors, values, and standards of excellence to which all organization members must adhere.

There are concrete steps that leaders can take to raise and reinforce shared performance expectations. In an email in his first few days as CEO of Microsoft in 2014, Satya Nadella challenged his leadership team, and employees throughout the organization, to be "all in" regarding their commitment to excellence. He saw this symbolism as key to the culture change needed for Microsoft's transformation. To buttress those expectations, Nadella instituted weekly meetings with his direct reports to review enterprise-wide priorities, surface emerging issues, and reinforce cross-functional collaboration with the goal of creating "One Microsoft." Each of Nadella's executive team members implemented the same process with their own teams, thereby cascading the process vertically throughout the company.

Mutual accountability for results. Closing the loop from creating clear strategic intent and building shared expectations for high performance is the final step of establishing mutual accountability for performance results. A study of 12,000 teams by the Table Group found a whopping 65 percent scored in the lowest category of accountability for results (Lencioni, 2012). According to that study, accountability problems are prevalent in organizations that avoid confrontation, suppress conflict, or mistakenly believe that accountability is somehow antithetical to enlightened management. From a design standpoint, accountability can be improved by simply making consequences (both positive and negative) more explicit and building this into the performance management system and, more broadly, into other elements of human resource management such as training and rewards. But "consequence management" is only one aspect of mutual accountability. The other is the shared, reciprocal part. To achieve better alignment, leadership teams often build processes to engage employees, recognize interdependencies, raise performance issues, provide frank feedback, and resolve emerging conflicts. The overall effect of such processes is to acknowledge that context matters, that team members depend on one another to get work done and are accountable to one another, and that results are collectively owned (Levy & Williams, 2004).

Achieving collective accountability is difficult when performance metrics are vague or missing. Without the ability to clearly account for progress toward goals, it is difficult to maintain a focus for action or to energize commitment to it. Alignment can be improved by attaching well-conceived metrics to performance objectives and then nurturing progress along the way. This is good for both the organization and its members (Kaplan & Norton, 1996). A note of caution, however, is worth sounding in regard to performance management systems. In many organizations, performance management is a perfunctory, typically annual event. Research indicates that traditional performance management systems backfire if they lead to fear, unhealthy competition among employees or to a sense of being micromanaged (DeNisi & Murphy, 2017). Feeding back performance measurements also has indirect effects that need to be recognized and managed. Performance below expectations increases actors' risk tolerance, and performance above aspiration levels decreases their risk tolerance (Cyert & March, 1992). Therefore, effective performance management is a balancing act that involves developing (1) means of empowering and incentivizing actors to take appropriate risks and (2) controls that curb excessive risk taking. Shared accountability can result only from a continuous developmental process that encompasses shared goal setting, well-designed feedback systems, and rewards for high performance.

Architecture

The design of the organization, including infrastructure, processes, technologies, and controls can make a large difference in terms of reliability, scalability, and continuity of performance. The organization's architecture affects decision-making processes as well as flows of information and resources. Neilson, Martin, and Powers (2008) found that poor information flows and unclear decision rights were the largest causes of poor execution. Architecture that is misaligned with organizational purpose and strategy slows down decision-making in a morass of reporting relationships, required approvals, and other bureaucratic impediments. How does architecture become misaligned? First, in many cases, the current architecture was designed for yesterday's work. Over time, when companies want to pursue emerging opportunities, they adjust their strategic intent but not their organization. Organizational structures, processes, and systems are intractable, and they usually stay in place while the organization goes after new opportunities. Second, to cope with the mismatch between what the organization wants to do and having the means for going about it, managers devise workarounds or administrative add-ons that may reduce problems in the short-run but do not provide the fundamental fix that is needed.

Three key actions can be taken to improve the effectiveness of organizational architecture: validate the operating model, simplify organizational structures, and streamline information systems (Carrig & Snell, 2019).

Validate the operating model. The axiom in architecture that "form follows function" is the idea that the organization's design should fit its purpose. In theory, an architectural design incorporates everything it needs to support its purpose with no waste or extraneous elements to lessen its effectiveness. Improving the organizational architecture begins with an analysis of the business's operating model – the set of core capabilities that drive customer value as well as the processes, systems, and structures that support those capabilities. Clarifying and validating the operating model serves to highlight areas and priorities for improved execution. Companies that have a robust operating model tend to have better revenue growth and operating margins than those that do not (Blenko, Garton, & Mottura, 2014).

The process of validating the organization's operating model helps designers and executives determine which activities are most critical for value creation. Those activities become candidates for improvement, reconfiguration, and/or investment. The validation process also reveals those activities that impede performance and need to be modified or eliminated. The result is that a validated operating model helps to prioritize execution, establish a focus for allocating resources, and identify those initiatives that are needed to positively influence performance (Johnson, Christensen, & Kagermann, 2008).

Simplify organizational structures. Many execution problems stem from the fact that organizations are inherently complex systems. Some complexity is inevitable – even necessary – for organizations to operate in complex environments. Systems theorists refer to this as the "law of requisite variety" (Ashby, 1956). Every system needs to reflect the complexity of the environment in which it operates. Otherwise, it cannot respond to the diversity of problems and opportunities it faces. At the same time, organizations want to minimize the ambiguity and uncertainty associated with complexity so that they can perform well (Sull & Eisenhardt, 2015).

Extraneous layers of hierarchy and duplicated work make the organization slow and internally focused (Kates & Kesler, 2015). A bloated organization also increases costs. Overly elaborate structures, inefficient processes, and weak accountabilities are much more likely to increase power struggles, communication gaps, and fractionalized work than improve performance. Organizations make progress in managing complexity by identifying those intersections where decisions, resource flows, and accountabilities get held up (so-called choke points). Choke points tend to proliferate between organizational units where collaborative work needs to occur but does not. They can be eliminated by removing structural elements that hinder collaboration and by clarifying the roles individuals and units in the hierarchy are intended to perform.

Streamline information systems. Deming (1986) estimated that 94 percent of performance problems are *systems* problems, not people problems. A well-designed organizational architecture can improve execution by channeling relevant data and information to actors so that they can make informed decisions. Broken or inefficient information-processing systems leave gaps in information flows, resulting in one unit or actor having critical resources another needs but no easy way to connect with those resources. Often, information systems are designed for purposes of reporting rather than informing – they provide information that can be used to assess performance rather than guide execution (Carrig & Snell, 2019).

Information and communication technologies affect execution in three ways: operationally, relationally, and transformationally (Snell, Pedigo, & Krawiec, 1995). *Operationally*, information systems standardize data and automate transactional work, eliminating inefficiencies that inhibit decision-making. *Relationally*, communication technologies connect people in real time, providing them with shared access to data and information and, further, enabling synchronous collaboration and knowledge-sharing opportunities. At their best, information and communication technologies *transform* processes by reducing or eliminating the separation of time and distance, supporting decisions that are both better and faster. Digital transformation is accelerating and creating a paradigm shift for strategy execution. For example, Briggs et al. (2018) found that firms use digital technologies to automate processes, build enterprise platforms, improve customer engagement, and incorporate data analytics so that they can respond faster to changing demand and external disruptions.

Ability

An organization's ability to perform at a high level rests on the quality of its human resources – the knowledge and skills employees possess, their well-being, and the extent to which they are empowered to apply their talents. Unfortunately, many organizations suffer from the "talent syndrome," a debilitating pattern of recurring symptoms that lead to stagnant performance: (1) The organization is chronically short of talent, especially in key positions; (2) the company does not make talent management a high priority; (3) senior leaders scramble to fill key jobs instead of having a talent development plan; and (4) the company executes poorly against its business opportunities (Carrig & Snell, 2019). To realize its performance potential, an organization needs an integrated talent management system, defined as a senior-executive-led process of leadership development, succession planning, critical capability development, and continuous developmental performance reviews (O'Leonard & Harris, 2010). Well-designed leadership development and succession planning systems can make a performance difference, both by increasing the breadth and depth of the talent pool (so-called bench strength) and improving the pipeline of up-and-coming leaders over time (Shen & Cannella, 2003).

Differentiated talent. Like any asset, some people have a bigger impact on organizational performance than others, and that impact is not always associated with position in the hierarchy. The priority with regard to execution is generating more high performers, particularly in critical roles. A study by Lesser, Brousseau, and Ringo (2009) highlighted the importance of identifying "focal jobs" that make the most difference to firm performance and channeling more time, energy, and resources toward those jobs. Such a targeted approach is at the heart of a differentiated talent management system.

When executives identify critical talent pools, and invest heavily in their development, the impact on firm performance can be significant (Lepak & Snell, 1999, 2002; Lepak, Takeuchi, & Snell, 2003). Executives that take a differentiated approach to talent management tend to have a comprehensive and systemic view of the organization, and this helps them avoid the talent syndrome. Moreover, each organization has its own unique configuration of human resources that is most valuable. To ensure that firms have deep bench strength to manage key projects and pursue business opportunities, senior executives increasingly are combining talent reviews with business and strategy reviews. Those expanded reviews begin within business units, and as they roll up, they serve as preparation for a final set of reviews with the CEO and senior HR leaders, giving them a window to the organization's leadership capability and pipeline strength. The sessions also shine a light on diversity and inclusion as part of the talent pipeline and feed ongoing succession plans.

Collaboration as a talent multiplier. In an increasingly connected world, individual performance alone will not suffice in accomplishing collective goals. The time spent by managers and employees in collaborative activities has ballooned by more than 50 percent over the past two decades (Cross, Rebele, & Grant, 2016). In the context of execution, the ability to collaborate is a requirement for joint decision-making, coordinating resources, and sequencing actions to drive high performance. From a design standpoint, collaborative capability is a "talent multiplier" called human capital leverage (Hitt et al., 2002).

Professional service firms have long understood the power of collaboration as the basis of their business model. Senior professionals with extensive experience create teams with junior associates to distribute their knowledge over a broader set of projects, clients, and opportunities. Clients win because they get better counsel at a lower cost. The firm wins because it gets the most out of the consulting team. And employees win because they maximize their contribution while growing and learning from others across the firm. Collaboration as a talent multiplier, however, is more than teamwork. It goes beyond the willingness of individuals to cooperate and depends crucially on developing a system of shared understanding and collective knowledge. Collaborative relationships can be conduits for knowledge sharing and learning. This increases the knowledge base of individuals, effectively multiplying their talent. Such social capital may be as important as human capital in driving organizational performance (Youndt & Snell, 2004). In addition, continuing advancements in artificial intelligence are allowing organizations to augment the work of human actors with digital actors, often resulting in significant performance gains. Standardized tasks can be fully automated using algorithms and/or robots, and judgmental tasks frequently can be performed better and faster when humans and machines execute those tasks collaboratively. Increasingly, talent planning includes digital actors and the roles they will play in the performance of activities (Daugherty & Wilson, 2018; Major & Shah, 2020).

Agility

Because organizations exist in dynamic business ecosystems, high performance depends on being agile and adaptive in the face of change and discontinuity. An agile organization can respond quickly and adjust to unforeseen disruptions. Organizations seek to become agile so that they can better anticipate external shocks, respond faster than competitors, and continuously learn and innovate. The most common inhibitor of agility is how the organization currently carries out its activities and new initiatives. Sull, Homkes, and Sull (2015) describe the "execution paradox": When performance stalls, organizations respond by tightening existing alignments, tracking more metrics, scheduling more meetings to monitor progress, and so on. Such top-down scrutiny can devolve into micromanagement, stifling the autonomy, experimentation, and collaborative interactions that are associated with agility. The end result is that the organization can become trapped in a downward spiral of threat-rigidity that leads to even worse results (Staw, Sandelands, & Dutton, 1981).

To increase agility, an organization must first reinforce its stability; it must strengthen its internal and external alignments and stay focused on its mission, purpose, and strategic intent (Prange, 2021). Then it must invest in its capacity to respond to change by building flexible capabilities (Gibson & Birkinshaw, 2017). Three useful areas to target for investment are situation awareness, organizational learning, and dynamic resourcing.

Situation awareness. Situation awareness helps organizational actors make better decisions, a key feature of agile organizations. It is the perception of environmental conditions and events, comprehension of their meaning, and projection of their future status (Endsley & Jones, 2004). Simply put, situation awareness involves picking up cues from the environment, putting those cues together to understand what is going on, and using that understanding to predict what may happen next. Shared situation awareness – a state in which organization members have a common up-to-date mental portrait of their task environment – is a powerful means for localizing decision-making.

Sometimes situation awareness involves paying attention to faint signals, small cues that portend larger events. Situation awareness requires building a capability to interpret and understand the implications of those interconnected events. Day and Schoemaker (2006) found that less than 20 percent of firms have the capacity to be vigilant and constantly attuned. They argue that organizations can design effective early warning systems by attending to five factors: (1) scoping widely enough to ask the right questions, (2) scanning actively in the right places, (3) interpreting what signals mean, (4) probing carefully for more information, and (5) acting wisely on signals before others do. For example, large companies in high-velocity environments use corporate venture funds to take a small stake in promising entrepreneurial enterprises, in part to stay abreast of emerging opportunities and in part to learn how to take advantage of those opportunities.

Organizational learning. Cohen and Levinthal's (1990) concept of *absorptive capacity* refers to an organization's ability to recognize and evaluate task environment information, assimilate it, and apply it in ways that improve its adaptive capabilities. Organizations adapt better – and faster – by taking small steps, questioning and learning as they go, iterating with repeated tests of data, and validating their progress. This approach sits in contrast to strategy execution as a mega-launch, replete with fanfare and exhortations to join in. Agile companies place a premium on learning as quickly as possible and then translating that learning into action. Organizational learning is aided by (1) openness to the outside world, (2) employees that are empowered to own and solve problems, (3) experimentation and small bets, and (4) sharing knowledge throughout the organization (Leonard-Barton, 1992).

Principles of design thinking and lean start-up have much to offer in this regard. Instead of running pilot projects before launching big initiatives, companies are increasingly using design practices such as prototyping, minimum viable product, and proof of concept. There is a necessary change in mindset that accompanies this approach, getting the organization to let go of an impatience to scale and replacing it with an understanding of the value of iterating on a smaller scale – more experiments, more feedback, more adjustments, and more learning. Private equity firms, venture capital funds, biopharma companies, and other organizations often operate this way, where the expected return from any single investment may be lower but the expected return of the overall portfolio of investments is high. By collecting data, seeing what works and what does not, it is possible to test assumptions about the market and make adjustments more quickly. Experimentation and learning provide the organization with options. From those options it is possible to identify the solutions that work best. Sometimes that is a universal best practice that can be applied across the whole company, and sometimes it is finding different approaches that can be applied or adapted locally. One of the things that inhibits organizational learning is when knowledge gets bottled up, hoarded, or trapped in one location, unavailable to others around the company (O'Dell & Grayson, 1998). In turbulent environments where agility is paramount, no amount of knowledge or insight can keep a company moving ahead if it is not distributed where it is needed.

Dynamic resourcing. A third area to target for agility development is *dynamic capability*, the ability to reconfigure the organization's resources to orchestrate rapid change (Teece, Pisano, & Shuen 1997).

Dynamic capability is not separate from situation awareness and organizational learning; indeed, it depends on them. Without shared situation awareness and capacity for organizational learning, it is difficult to reshape the organization's assets in ways that improve responsiveness. In that regard, the capacity to bring about change is itself a capability.

A study by Hall, Lovallo, and Musters (2012) found that dynamic resource reallocation – shifting money, talent, and information to where they will deliver the most value – was significantly correlated with firm performance (measured as total returns to shareholders). Unfortunately, the evidence suggests that companies are not adept at dynamic resourcing, and this is due to their budgeting processes, talent management systems, and information systems. For example, in terms of capital budgeting, Hall et al. (2012) found that firms on average reallocate only 8 percent of capital from one year to the next, and a third only reallocated 1 percent. At the same time, 83 percent of senior executives identified it as the primary lever for spurring performance gains. Sull et al. (2015) found that less than one-third of managers believe their organizations reallocate funds to the right places quickly enough to be effective. Further, the reallocation of talent is even worse. Only 20 percent of managers say their organizations do a good job of shifting people across units to support strategic priorities (Sull et al., 2015). Organizations designed to support staff rotation and redeployment have a better chance of creating agile resourcing (Morris, Snell, & Bjorkman, 2015).

Summary

Execution is how organizational actors perform their activities, both in existing operations and in new initiatives. When execution is done well, organizational performance can be strong and sustainable. Table 10.1 summarizes key points about alignment, architecture, ability, and agility. The table summarizes questions that executives and designers should ask about each of the 4As, major barriers to effective execution, areas that can be designed or redesigned to improve execution, and practices and tools that can help in taking effective action. Each of the 4As supporting execution is important in its own right. The 4As also need to form an integrated system, reinforcing one another to increase their joint impact.

Table 10.1 *Four elements of execution*

	Key questions	Barriers	Focus areas
Alignment	How do you ensure that everyone is focused on the same strategic intent?	Distraction, diversion of attention away from goals	Strategic intent
	Have you built a high-performance culture with shared aspirations and expectations?	Dispersed resources that diminish impact	Shared performance expectations
	How do you instil a sense of mutual accountability for results?	Flagging engagement	Accountability for results
Ability	Do you have the right leadership team, working as a strong unit?	Chronic talent shortage	Strong leadership bench
	If talent is your most important asset, what does your investment portfolio look like?	Reactive approach and short-termism	Talent capacity
	Where is collaborative capability needed?	Insufficient talent needed to pursue growth goals	Collaborative capability
Architecture	How well understood is your organization's operating model?	Repeatedly letting the customer down	Clear operating model
	How do you ensure your infrastructure propels performance rather than impede it?	Working in silos or poor decision structures	Streamlined organization
	Do processes and systems enable or inhibit workflow and strategy execution?	Flying blind without required information	Intelligent systems support
Agility	Is your organization able to respond quickly, or are you blindsided by change?	Chin-down management	Situational awareness
	How do you support organizational learning to drive innovation and knowledge sharing?	Threat-rigidity	Organizational learning
	How well have you developed the ability to redeploy resources quickly?	Inertia and momentum	Dynamic capability

Source: Adapted from Carrig and Snell (2019)

Conclusion

To achieve high performance, an organization needs to know what to do and be able to do it. This is the essence of effective execution. Responding to complex, rapidly changing environments favors agile adaptation over detailed planning. Effective execution needs to be guided by feedback that corrects performance problems and by feed-forward that enables corrective actions to be taken anticipatorily.

References

Ashby, W. R. 1956. *An Introduction to Cybernetics.* Wiley, New York, NY.

Bettis, R. A. & Prahalad, C. K. 1995. The dominant logic: retrospective and extension. *Strategic Management Journal* 16(1): 5–14.

Blenko, M., Garton, E., & Mottura, L. 2014. Winning operating models that convert strategy to results. *Bain Brief.* www.bain.com/insights/winning-operating-models-that-convert-strategy-to-results/

Bossidy, L. & Charan, R. 2002. *Execution: The Discipline of Getting Things Done.* Crown Publishing, New York, NY.

Briggs, B., Kark, K., Shaikh, A., & Lamar, K. 2018. Manifesting legacy: looking beyond the digital era. *Deloitte Insights.* www2.deloitte.com/content/dam/insights/us/articles/4774_CIO-survey/DI_CIO-survey-2018.pdf

Burgelman, R. A. & Grove, A. S. 1996. Strategic dissonance. *California Management Review* 38(2): 8–28.

Carrıg, K. J. & Snell, S. A. 2019. *Strategic Execution: Driving Breakthrough Performance in Business.* Stanford University Press, Stanford, CA.

Cohen, W. M. & Levinthal, D. A. 1990. Absorptive capacity: a new perspective on learning and innovation. *Administrative Science Quarterly* 35: 128–152.

Cross, R., Rebele, R., & Grant, A. 2016. Collaborative overload. *Harvard Business Review* (January–February): 74–79. https://hbr.org/2016/01/collaborative-overload

Cyert, R. M & March, J. G. 1992. *A Behavioral Theory of the Firm* (2nd ed.). Wiley-Blackwell, Oxford.

Daugherty, P. R. & Wilson, H. J. 2018. *Human + Machine: Reimagining Work in the Age of AI.* Harvard Business Review Press, Boston, MA.

Day, G. S. & Schoemaker, P. J. H. 2006. *Peripheral Vision: Detecting the Weak Signals That Will Make or Break Your Company.* Harvard Business School Press, Boston, MA.

Deming, W. E. 1986. *Out of the Crisis.* MIT Press, Cambridge, MA.

DeNisi, A. S. & Murphy, K. R. 2017. Performance appraisal and performance management: 100 years of progress? *Journal of Applied Psychology* 102(3): 421–433.

Endsley, M. R. & Jones, D. G. 2004. *Designing for Situation Awareness: An Approach to User-Centered Design* (2nd ed.). CRC Press, Boca Raton, FL.

Gibson, C. B. & Birkinshaw, J. 2017. The antecedents, consequences, and mediating role of organizational ambidexterity. *Academy of Management Journal* 47(2): 209–226.

Hall, S., Lovallo, D., & Musters, R. 2012. How to put your money where your strategy is. *McKinsey Quarterly* (March): 1–11. www.mckinsey .com/business-functions/strategy-and-corporate-finance/our-insights/ how-to-put-your-money-where-your-strategy-is

Hamel, G. & Prahalad, C. K. 2005. Strategic intent. *Harvard Business Review* 83(7): 148–161.

Hamel, G. & Prahalad, C. K. 2010. *Strategic Intent*. Harvard Business Press, Boston, MA.

Hawkins, A. J. 2021. Tesla rewrote its own software to survive the chip shortage. www.theverge.com/2021/7/26/22595060/tesla-chip-shortage-software-rewriting-ev-processor

Hitt, M. A., Bierman, L., Shimizu, K., & Kochhar, R. 2002. Direct and moderating effects of human capital on strategy and performance in professional service firms: a resource-based perspective. *Academy of Management Journal* 44(1): 13–28.

Johnson, M. W., Christensen, C. M., & Kagermann, H. 2008. Reinventing your business model. *Harvard Business Review* (December): 1–11.

Kaplan, R. S. & Norton, D. P. 1996. *The Balanced Scorecard: Translating Strategy into Action*. Harvard Business Review Press, Boston, MA.

Kates, A. & Kesler, G. 2015. Activating global operating models: the bridge from organization design to performance. *Journal of Organization Design* 4(2): 38–47.

Keller, S. & Price, C. 2011. *Beyond Performance: How Great Organizations Build Ultimate Competitive Advantage*. Wiley, New York, NY.

Leinwand P. & Mainardi, C. 2016. *Strategy That Works: Closing the Gap between Strategy and Execution*. Harvard Business Review Press, Boston, MA.

Lencioni, P. 2012. *Advantage*. Jossey-Bass, San Francisco, CA.

Leonard-Barton, D. 1992. The factory as a learning laboratory. *MIT Sloan Management Review* 34(1): 23–38.

Lepak, D. P. & Snell, S. A. 1999. The human resource architecture: toward a theory of human capital development and allocation. *Academy of Management Review* 24(1): 31–48.

Lepak, D. P. & Snell, S. A. 2002. Examining the human resource architecture: the relationships among human capital, employment, and human resource configurations. *Journal of Management* 28(4): 517–543.

Lepak, D. P., Takeuchi, R., & Snell, S. A. 2003. Employment flexibility and firm performance: examining the moderating effects of employment mode, environmental dynamism, and technological intensity. *Journal of Management* 29(5): 681–705.

Lesser, E., Brousseau, D., & Ringo, T. 2009. Focal jobs: viewing talent through a different lens. *IBM Institute for Business Value.* www.ibm.com/downloads/cas/DQM6ERJA

Levy, P. E. & Williams, J. R. 2004. The social context of performance appraisal: a review and framework for the future. *Journal of Management* 30(6): 881–905.

Major, L. & Shah, J. 2020. *What to Expect When You're Expecting Robots: The Future of Human-Robot Collaboration.* Basic Books, New York, NY.

March, J. G. & Simon, H. A. 1958. *Organizations.* Wiley, New York, NY.

Morris, S. M, Snell, S. A., & Bjorkman, I. 2015. An architectural framework for global talent management. *Journal of International Business Studies* 47(6): 723–747.

Neilson, G. L., Martin, K. L., & Powers, E. 2008. The secrets to successful strategy execution. *Harvard Business Review* 86(6): 60–138.

O'Dell, C. & Grayson, C. 1998. If only we knew what we know: the transfer of internal knowledge and best practice. *California Management Review* 40: 154–174.

O'Leonard, K. & Harris, S. 2010. *Talent Management Factbook 2010: Best Practices and Benchmarks in U.S. Talent Management.* Bersin/Deloitte, Oakland, CA.

O'Shannassy, T. F. 2016. Strategic intent: the literature, the construct and its role in predicting organizational performance. *Journal of Management and Organization* 22(5): 583–598.

Prange, C. 2021. Agility as the discovery of slowness. *California Management Review* 63(4): 27–51.

Schoemaker, P. J. H. 1992. How to link strategic vision to core capabilities. *MIT Sloan Management Review* 34(1): 67–81.

Shen, W. & Cannella, A. A. 2003. Will succession planning increase shareholder wealth? Evidence from investor reactions to relay CEO successions. *Strategic Management Journal* 24(3): 191–198.

Snell, S. A., Pedigo, P., & Krawiec, G. M. 1995. Managing the impact of information technology on human resource management. In G. R. Ferris (ed.), *Handbook of Human Resources*: 159–174. Blackwell, Oxford, UK.

Staw, B. M., Sandelands, L. E., & Dutton, J. E. 1981. Threat rigidity effects in organizational behavior: a multilevel analysis. *Administrative Science Quarterly* 26(4): 501–524.

Sull, D. & Eisenhardt, K. M. 2015. *Simple Rules: How to Thrive in a Complex World*. Houghton Mifflin Harcourt, New York, NY.

Sull, D., Homkes, R., & Sull, C. 2015. Why strategy execution unravels – and what to do about it. *Harvard Business Review* 93(3): 57–66.

Teece, D., Pisano, G., & Shuen, A. 1997. Dynamic capabilities and strategic management. *Strategic Management Journal* 18(7): 509–533.

Treacy, M. & Wiersema, F. D. 1995. *The Discipline of Market Leaders: Choose Your Customers, Narrow Your Focus, and Dominate Your Market*. Addison-Wesley, Reading, MA.

Tushman, M. L., Newman, W. H., & Romanelli, E. 1986. Convergence and upheaval: managing the unsteady pace of organizational evolution. *California Management Review* 29(1): 29–44.

Weiner, N. 1948. *Cybernetics: Or Control and Communication in the Animal and the Machine*. Hermann & Cie and MIT Press, Paris and Cambridge, MA.

Youndt, M. A. & Snell, S. A. 2004. Human resource configurations, intellectual capital, and organizational performance. *Journal of Managerial Issues* 16(3): 337–361.

11 | *The Healthy Organization*

IAN HESKETH AND CARY L. COOPER

The nature of work has changed dramatically in recent years, as have the expectations of the modern workforce. An individual's well-being – feeling happy, healthy, socially connected, and purposeful – is a critical feature of these expectations. Potential employees expect that work will be challenging and fulfilling, they will have opportunities for development, they will be looked after, and when they struggle there will be help available. To attract talented individuals, organizations need to ensure that such expectations can be met in the workplace.

Developing and sustaining a healthy organization is an increasingly important design consideration (Hesketh & Cooper, 2018; Lowe, 2020; Pfeffer, 2018a). An organization that strongly supports employee well-being can reap large benefits including a productive workforce, vibrant employee engagement, strong organizational performance, and lower overall costs. Achieving an organization's potential rests heavily on its employees' knowledge, health, and security. A commitment to employee well-being includes not only the reduction of negative factors such as psychosocial stress and substance abuse, it also includes promotion of employees' physical and mental health.

Although there are numerous positive outcomes for good employee well-being, we focus here on the benefits for organizations in terms of business outcomes. The argument for productivity and performance benefits from good employee well-being has been, until recently, largely prospective. However, recent research has established that investments in employee well-being can produce large returns. Weinberg et al. (2018) reported, in response to a call for organizations in the United Kingdom to follow National Institute of Clinical Excellence (NICE) guidelines, that the cost to organizations of mental ill health in the United Kingdom was estimated to be between £33 billion and £42 billion annually. In the United States, expenditures due to poor mental health reach $187 billion annually (Goh, Pfeffer, & Zenios, 2016).

In a recent Australian study, Milligan-Saville et al. (2017) reported that for every £1 investment made in workplace mental health training, organizations could expect a return of approximately £10 in reduced sickness absence alone.

This chapter examines employee well-being and its implications for organization design. First, we trace the concept of well-being to early concerns for employees' physical health and safety. Over time, the concept of well-being has expanded to include mental as well as physical health, and the scope of employee well-being has been extended from the work domain into the nonwork domain. Next, we discuss four current topics that reflect the physiological, psychological, and social-psychological aspects of well-being: employee engagement, sleep deprivation, work-related technologies, and the multigenerational workforce. Lastly, we present the key tenets of a healthy organization as well as general guidelines for designing and implementing wellness initiatives.

Evolution of the Healthy Organization Concept

A concern for occupational health can be traced to Bernardino Ramazzini, a professor of medicine at the University of Padua, in seventeenth-century Italy. Ramazzini recommended that physicians inquire about the occupation of their patients to establish what they were exposed to, and he wrote what is thought to be the first book on occupational medicine, *De Morbis Artificum Diatriba* (Diseases of Workers). The study of healthy organizations most likely began with Turner Thackrah's wonderfully titled book of 1832, *The Effects of the Principal Arts, Trades and Professions, and of Civic States and Habits of Living, on Health and Longevity: With a Particular Reference to the Trades and Manufacturers of Leeds, and Suggestions for the Removal of Many of the Agents, Which Produce Diseases, and Shorten the Duration of Life*. In that book, we find chapters on "men of active habits, whose employments are chiefly in the open air" and "operatives, whose skin is exposed to injurious agents." A particularly interesting section in Thackrah's book is entitled "Persons who live in a bad atmosphere, maintain one position most of the day, take little exercise, and are frequently under the excitement of ambition." Almost 200 years later, Thackrah's focus on occupational health is still relevant!

The UK Factories Act of 1833, which mandated the appointment of factory inspectors, began to address occupational welfare needs legislatively. In 1878, further ground-breaking legislation came into being that stipulated women and children could not work more than sixty hours per week. In 1913, a conference for welfare workers was organized by Seebohm Rowntree, and this movement eventually became the Chartered Institute of Personnel and Development (UK). The advent of unions and the outbreak of World War I increased the emphasis on workforce welfare, in large part to reduce the number of accidents caused by poor work practices, faulty equipment, and worker fatigue. It was not until clear gains in performance and productivity were realized, however, that employees' physical health and safety were established as a business essential.

In the past decade, there has been a steady stream of scholarly research and proven workplace practices that look beyond the physical health and safety of individuals to get at the underlying organizational factors that contribute to overall employee well-being (Lowe, 2020). Research has shown a connection between employee well-being and desirable business outcomes. Important outcomes include greater corporate social responsibility, environmental protection, charitable outlooks, extensive stakeholder relationships, and organizational credibility, many of which enjoy far more public respect and support than mere corporate profitability. Good organization design considers such outcomes up front. In many organizations, employee well-being is the responsibility of a unit called Occupational Health; in some organizations, it may sit under Learning and Development or Human Resources. We posit that employee well-being should be everyone's business. Wellness has become a central narrative in leading organizations, and in many cases, it has become a major business heading to attract new talent and develop existing talent within the organization.

Current Topics in Healthy Organizations

In this section, we discuss four topics that reflect the range of wellness issues facing modern organizations. The first topic is *employee engagement*. Employees who are engaged with their work are more likely to be motivated and committed to their employer, so engagement is critical to retaining valuable talent. The second topic is *sleep deprivation.* Not getting enough sleep, whether caused by a sleep disorder or a person's lifestyle choices, can affect mood, memory, and health in ways that reduce productivity and otherwise harm the organization. The third topic is *work-related technologies.* In modern, highly digitized organizations, an individual's facility with various work-related technologies strongly affects their ability to make a contribution to the organization. The final topic is the *multigenerational workforce.* In many organizations today, leaders must design work for employees of different generations. Each generation has its own ideas as to what constitutes a meaningful and healthy workplace, creating a significant managerial challenge in deciphering what is important and how to respond.

Employee Engagement

Employee engagement is the extent to which employees feel good about their jobs, are committed to the organization, and put discretionary effort into their work. According to a recent Gallup poll, 32 percent of US employees say that they are engaged with their work. That means over two-thirds of American employees feel disengaged from their work to some extent. Although sickness absenteeism is an oft-cited metric, it does not tell the full story. *Presenteeism*, as described by Johns (2010), posits that many people come to work even though they are not well. The costs of presenteeism, where people are less productive and may negatively affect their coworkers, have been estimated to be roughly double the costs of traditional sickness absence. A large research study called the American Productivity Audit calculated the cost of presenteeism in the United States to be more than $150 billion a year (Stewart et al., 2003). In the United Kingdom, the cost of presenteeism to the economy may be as high as £15 billion annually. Moreover, employees may resort to *leaveism* (Hesketh & Cooper, 2014). Leaveism occurs when workers are unwell but do not want to report as sick, often out of fear of being treated unfairly or being overlooked for development or advancement. Here, workers prefer to take days off their allocation of annual leave or flex-time rather than report being sick. A large study of UK police officers reported that 59 percent had practiced this form of leaveism (Houdmont, Elliott-Davies, & Donnelly, 2018). Another form of leaveism is when employees take work home with them or even on holiday, in order to make up for time lost at work. Leaveism is found in both the public and private sectors (Hesketh, Cooper, & Ivy, 2014, 2015). A combined study from the Chartered Institute of Personnel and Development (CIPD, 2018) and Simply Health in the United Kingdom asked over 1,000 human resource professionals, representing 4.6 million employees, to estimate the extent to which leaveism was practiced in a wide variety of occupations. This study found that 69 percent of employees had practiced leaveism during the previous twelve months. Not surprisingly, those who perceived presenteeism also noticed leaveism (72 percent), and they further indicated that technology affects people's ability to "switch off" work, taking work-related phone calls and answering emails being prime examples. Table 11.1 helps to clarify distinctions across absenteeism, presenteeism, and leaveism.

If strong employee engagement leads to increased productivity, then absenteeism is not the only factor that hinders productivity. The largely invisible processes of presenteeism and leaveism harm productivity as well.

Sleep Deprivation

Sleep affects both physical and mental health and is as important for our survival as food and water. We spend about a third of our lives sleeping. Sleep research has increased in recent years, and it shows that sleep deprivation is linked to a range of diseases including neurodegenerative diseases, obesity, Type 2 diabetes, cardiovascular disease, cancer, impaired immune functioning, and some chronic pain conditions. The role sleep plays in the body's biological processes is not yet fully understood but is known to involve neural processing, inflammation, metabolism, gene regulation, toxins, and hormones (Walker, 2018). The US Centers for Disease Control and Prevention declared sleep to be a "public health problem," reporting over a third of American adults as not getting enough sleep on a regular basis (Hafner et al., 2017). A similar picture is seen in the United Kingdom, detailed in a study that noted women reporting more sleep problems than men. The research also associated lack of sleep with poor work performance and quality of life (Groeger, Zijlstra, & Dijk, 2004).

Our bodies carry out a host of functions while we sleep. Specifically, our brain is hard at work regulating growth and repairs and removing waste products. The brain also carries out emotional processing,

Table 11.1 Classifications of absenteeism, presenteeism, and leaveism

Health	Employee unwell			Employee well			
Status	Not working		Working	Not working		Working	Working (outside hours)
Employee location	Not at work		At work	Not at work		At work	Not at work
Employee option	Sick leave	Annual leave	Present	Sick leave	Annual leave	Present	Working
Definition	Absenteeism	Leaveism	Presenteeism	Absenteeism	On leave	Working	Leaveism

Source: Hesketh et al. (2014)

replaces energy reserves, develops memories, and processes information. As such, sleep disruption can have significant negative consequences – on both employee well-being and organizational productivity. In the short term, individual consequences can include loss of attention, loss of empathy, reduced cognition, and impulsivity. Long-term consequences can include the serious conditions mentioned earlier (cardiovascular disease, impaired immune functioning, etc.). In terms of healthy organizations, one of the serious issues with suboptimal sleep is fatigue. In addition to employees not performing at their best in the workplace, there have been many reports of accidents on the way to and from the workplace. The 2009 Massachusetts Special Commission on Drowsy Driving (Moore, Kaprielian, & Auerbach, 2009) estimated that there could be as many as 1.2 million automobile accidents, 8,000 lives lost, and 500,000 injuries due to drowsy driving each year. The effects of sleep deprivation can lead to difficulties in coping with everyday life such as increased frustration, lower self-esteem, and increased stress (Walker, 2018). Furthermore, negative consequences similar to those of sleep deprivation can also occur from poor nutrition and lack of exercise.

Both workplace properties and employee behavior can be the cause of sleep deprivation. The employee–employer relationship should not be one-way. As part of the *psychological contract* (Rousseau, 1995) at work, employees should be rightly expected to keep themselves in good health, and they should be able to expect working conditions that do not negatively affect their health and well-being. Managers must have an understanding with their employees that together they will create – and continually improve – a healthy work culture. In return, employees should keep themselves healthy by taking reasonable steps to avoid unhealthy behaviors. They should be expected, as part of their work, to have regular health checks and act on medical advice. Employers should facilitate and promote a healthy workplace. They should develop leaders that consider the well-being of employees and engage with employees about health-related issues, create cultures free of stigma around health issues, and continually search for ways to improve.

Work-Related Technologies

When it comes to workplace support, the paradox of technology comes squarely into play. On the one hand, it is the largest enabler of home, flex-time, remote, and virtual working, with up to 74 percent of respondents agreeing this was a positive outcome, according to a UK study (CIPD, 2018). In the same survey, 87 percent of respondents noted the negative effects of work-related technology, most notably the inability to switch off from work outside of contracted working hours (one of the elements of leaveism behavior discussed earlier). A good example of this is the debate around responding to emails outside working hours and what is reasonable. Some organizations have experimented with turning off their servers outside of working hours to regulate the practice. For other organizations, it is an expectation of employees in certain roles. Nevertheless, the advent of email and remote email access has meant an extension of the working day for many employees. We submit this cannot be good for any individual, no matter how much meaning, purpose, or connectivity they feel toward an organization or occupation. We all need downtime to recover and exercise, enjoy our relationships beyond work, and experience new things.

Wearable technologies (activity-tracking devices) also present opportunities and challenges for both employers and employees (Howarth et al., 2018). A balance between improving services and efficiency, highlighted in delivery services, for example, and employee rights to privacy and autonomy is difficult to specify. "Wearables" such as Fitbits are available to monitor a plethora of human behaviors and functions, but does that necessarily mean that organizations should utilize them? If they do, how is the relationship with the employee handled? Do employees believe the organization is making their work easier and helping them to achieve their goals, or do they feel that the organization is interfering with or spying on them? Work-related technologies increasingly pervade the modern workplace, but certain aspects of their use may not be healthy for employees.

Artificial intelligence (AI) has even greater potential to transform workplaces. AI applications already are enabling real-time tracking of health status, sleep, stress, happiness, and potential health and safety risks and hazards. However, AI also enables employers to engage in excessive surveillance of their employees (Pfeffer, 2018b), which may affect their psychological well-being. Striking a desirable balance between useful and harmful with respect to the use of AI in employee well-being programs is an important design consideration.

Multigenerational Workforce

Organizations are increasingly grappling with generational differences in their workforces (Betz, 2019; Meister & Willyerd, 2010). Problems can arise from differing mindsets, communication and learning styles, and other personal characteristics of employees born in different eras. Those problems may be exacerbated by new technology and work practices that mix employees of different ages in teams and decision-making processes. Baby Boomers, born between 1946 and 1964, are competitive and think younger employees should pay their dues in an organization before advancing. Generation X, individuals born between 1965 and 1979, are more likely to be skeptical of authority and independent-minded. Gen Ys, also known as Millennials, were born between 1980 and 1994, and they like teamwork, purpose in work, feedback, and technology. The most recent generation, Gen Z, are individuals born between 1995 and 2015, and they are the most diverse generation and the first to grow up in the Internet era. Gen Zers are just now entering the labor force, and it is as yet unclear what those individuals want from work and what will attract them to organizations.

In 2015, Millennials became the largest generation in the US workforce, and by 2025 they will constitute 75 percent of that workforce (Meister & Willyerd, 2010). By contrast, the UK working population is aging, and the retirement age continues on an upward trajectory (Centre for Ageing Better, 2017). These vastly different workforces present their respective organizations with large challenges in training, mentoring, telecommuting and offsite working, reward systems, and other management processes.

Hybrid Work Models

One of the challenges for organizations moving forward from the COVID-19 pandemic is what the new work paradigm will be. With most of the workforce having adapted to remote working, will the new workplace be the home? Alternatively, will people be expected to return to the workplace they used prior to the direction to work from home? We hear different views of what is desirable among employers and employees (see, e.g., Hesketh & Cooper, 2021). Moreover, the challenges of remote working appear to be greater for younger employees. This may be due to the fact that younger workers may not have their own homes, so they cannot create a suitable space for conducting their work. Older workers with their own homes may have converted some rooms into an office and are now set up to work effectively from home post-pandemic. We suspect that what will emerge is a hybrid model – a combination of remote and office-based work. This will save employers real estate and other costs, and it will save employees travel time and costs. During the period when many employees worked from home, instances of both presenteeism and leaveism increased slightly. In the most recent Wellbeing Survey (CIPD, 2021), the majority of respondents (84 percent) had observed "presenteeism," both in the workplace (75 percent) and while working at home (77 percent), over the past twelve months. Further, seven in ten respondents (70 percent) had observed some form of "leaveism," such as working outside contracted hours or using holiday entitlement to work, over the past twelve months. Although more organizations are taking steps to address "presenteeism" and "leaveism," more than two-fifths of those experiencing these issues reported that no actions are being taken to remedy the situation (43 percent for those experiencing presenteeism, 47 percent for leaveism). Presenteeism, leaveism, and work–life balance in hybrid work models will have to be addressed by managers. Emerging from the pandemic, managers must develop healthy hybrid work models that benefit both employees and employers.

Designing Healthy Organizations

In order to obtain desirable business outcomes, creating a healthy work environment is clearly a worthwhile goal. Work is fundamental to an individual's feelings of achievement and self-esteem, and jobs and workplaces can be designed to enhance those feelings. Job design, workload, work–life balance, feelings of control, fairness, and autonomy – all are factors affected by organization design. Good work practices should also be supported by good policies. Clear and supportive policies signal what an organization believes is valuable and important, and they indicate areas where the organization will make lasting commitments. In Figure 11.1, we provide a broad conceptual framework for the design of healthy organizations.

Healthy Organizations – Key Tenets

Environment	Leadership	Resilience	Employee Well-being
Creating an environment in which all employees can lead a meaningful and purposeful life.	Knowing enough about your staff to be able to recognize when things are not right, and to have the skills to intervene both quickly and effectively.	The ability to cope with adversity, and to be able to "bounce back." Being able to deal with the stressors of everyday life.	• Psychological • Physiological • Sociological • Financial

Figure 11.1 Key tenets of healthy organizations

Leadership

Leading a healthy organization is challenging, and knowing enough about the people you lead in order to spot when things are going astray is a good start. Further, having noticed a problem, good leaders also have the skills to intervene quickly and effectively. How do you come to know what the "health baseline" is for your people and the current state of the situation in which you are leading? What level of intrusiveness is appropriate for this situation? To what extent should work be redesigned so that employees can control and coordinate themselves? The situation is further complicated by the multigenerational employee issues discussed earlier and the organization's management philosophy. Modern leaders have largely dispensed with the autocratic and paternalistic approaches of the past and embrace empathy, compassion, and authenticity as skills better suited to today's workforces.

In the United Kingdom, the National Forum for Health and Wellbeing at Work consists of over thirty top companies from the public, private, and third-party sectors. Meeting quarterly, and currently chaired by Professor Sir Cary Cooper, the forum discusses the challenges that healthy organizations face, both day-to-day and strategically. Based on the ongoing discussions, a recent project generated a Compassion at Work Toolkit (Meechan, 2017). This toolkit details the business benefits that arise from compassionate work practices. Having empathy, sympathy, and benevolence toward another person's circumstances gives rise to workplace harmony, trust, and a feeling of belonging. This results in employees going the extra mile, freely giving discretionary job effort (Hesketh, Cooper, & Ivy, 2017). Moreover, it appears that empathy can be taught to leaders (Riess, Kelley, & Bailey, 2012) and deployed as a collaborative tool to drive profitability (Parmer, 2014). In organizations where empathy and compassion are not present, it seems the opposite occurs, with what Holt and Marques (2012) describe as the potential for "ethical disasters."

Resilience

Another key tenet of a healthy organization is personal resilience. What makes a person resilient, and why do two people who experience the same exposure respond in different ways? As neuroscience advances, our understanding of resilience is becoming clearer. What is particularly encouraging is that personal resilience can be improved through training programs and stress management techniques (Hesketh & Cooper, 2019). Southwick and Charney (2012) defined resilience as the science of mastering life's challenges, and their Resilience Prescription consists of the following elements:

1. Positive attitude
2. Cognitive flexibility
3. Moral compass
4. Role models
5. Facing fears
6. Coping skills
7. Supportive networks
8. Physical well-being
9. Regular training
10. Signature strengths

   Healthy organizations recognize, promote, and support initiatives to improve personal resilience in the workplace. They also recognize when employees are at their limits of coping – whether it is because of external or internal stressors (or both) and whether it is due to a build-up of stressors or a specific negative life event (e.g., loss of a loved one or other serious occurrence). An organization committed to a healthy workplace expects its leaders to spot warning signs and intervene appropriately, and it provides the resources necessary to support personal resilience.

Employee Well-Being

Employee well-being is what results from leaders working with employees to cocreate individual resilience through comprehensive wellness initiatives in their organizations. Every organization is at its own unique place on a healthy organization trajectory, and every organization must design programs that are appropriate for its particular needs and goals. One template that can be used to frame a wellness approach is the Healthy Organization Assessment tool (Lowe, 2020). This tool focuses on four building blocks of a healthy organization: vibrant workplaces, inspired employees, inclusive leadership, and positive culture. Using this or a similar tool, organizations can collect data on their wellness initiatives, measure progress, and learn from the data about how to improve employee well-being programs.

Measurement and Implementation of Well-Being Approaches

It is not always possible to carry out robust research within a work environment. This is particularly true for employee wellness programs since, as indicated in Figure 11.1, well-being has multiple dimensions. What may appear to be negative on the one hand actually can be an indicator of the right trajectory on the other. For example, when health checks take place within the workplace it is not uncommon for there to be a short-term rise in sickness absence, as some of the health checks expose medical or clinical worries in participants. However, those checks may have the overall impact of destigmatizing seeking medical help and promoting the practice of regular health checks, both of which are good for long-term health. As such, employers are advised to hold steady during the implementation of wellness programs, especially if they are adopting practices related to workplace health for the first time. Measures of both progress and outcomes should be considered as experimental and evolving, with final measures selected only after obtaining considerable experience with an established program.

It is important to look at the effectiveness of any well-being approach or intervention, asking *if* it will work and *how* does it work? What will be the process, and does this matter, to both employee and employer? Organizations should also consider implementation issues – for example, if changes can be introduced all at once or if they need to be introduced incrementally. Although health-oriented interventions may be well received, they also need to be affordable. There are many sources of help available. For example, many higher education institutions are willing and able to carry out workplace research and reporting. There are many specialized consultancy firms that are involved with organizational health, and they have a wide array of customized tools and reports that can be helpful. Lastly, there is the Internet of Things that can provide a range of options, case studies, and academic literature to assist in decision-making and offer a variety of approaches for consideration.

Conclusion

Organizational health is affected by organization design – the work environment, roles and tasks, and leadership and managerial practices. Both workforce generational changes and technological progression affect employee health and well-being and thereby organizational performance. Managing the multigenerational workforce requires a deep understanding of human thinking and behavior. Digital technologies are changing the nature of work in many organizations. Technology may alleviate workers of harmful tasks, but it may also lead to loss of job control and excessive monitoring. Advancements in neuroscience enable us to monitor, predict, screen, diagnose, and treat at a level and rate unheard of only a few years ago. The introduction and acceptability of wearable technologies and collaborative work tools have added a new dynamic to the workplace, and we now have the capability, for small financial outlays, to monitor productivity and work performance. In addition to monitoring and control, other digital technologies support employee collaboration and well-being.

   While the scenario we are describing is optimistic, it comes with a big caution. For example, "new public management" (Hood, 1991) introduced many new work ideas and practices in the United Kingdom, but so too did it result in many unintended consequences. Managing rotely by the numbers, leaders who focus only on performance, and work practices that stretch human resources to their limits are no longer acceptable in the modern workplace. The consequences of such work schemes are the failing health and rising morbidity of the labor force. We have an opportunity, on the brink of the Fourth

Industrial Revolution, to right this wrong and make workplaces part of our meaning and purpose in life. The challenge for organizations is to promote and reward healthy work practices and foster a culture of commitment and continuous improvement. It is also incumbent that organizations engage with their workforces in efforts to achieve a healthy workplace.

The benefits a healthy organization can bring are numerous. Employee well-being is good for business and society. Work is good for us – it provides meaning and purpose in life. We spend approximately a third of our time at work, so it is important that work provides us with fulfilment. Healthy organizations attract the best people. Long-term sustainability, sound work practices, ethical behavior, and productivity are optimized in organizations that have the well-being of their workforce at the core of what they do.

References

Betz, C. L. 2019. Generations X, Y, and Z. *Journal of Pediatric Nursing* 44: A7–A8.

Centre for Ageing Better. 2017. People are living longer. Report. www .ageing-better.org.uk/living-longer.

CIPD. 2018. Health and well-being at work. www.cipd.co.uk/knowledge/ culture/well-being/health-well-being-work.

CIPD. 2021. Health and wellbeing at work survey 2021. Chartered Institute of Personnel and Development, London. www.cipd.co.uk/Images/health-wellbeing-work-report-2021_tcm18-93541.pdf.

Goh, J., Pfeffer, J., & Zenios, S. A. 2016. The relationship between workplace stressors and mortality and health costs in the United States. *Management Science* 62(2): 608–628.

Groeger, J. A., Zijlstra, F., & Dijk, D. 2004. Sleep quantity, sleep difficulties and their perceived consequences in a representative sample of some 2000 British adults. *Journal of Sleep Research* 13(4): 359–371.

Hafner, M., Stepanek, M., Taylor, J., Troxel, W., & Stolk, C. 2017. Why sleep matters: the economic costs of insufficient sleep: a cross-country comparative analysis. *Rand Health Quarterly* 6(4): 11.

Hesketh, I. & Cooper, C. 2014. Leaveism at work. *Occupational Medicine* 64(3): 146–147.

Hesketh, I. & Cooper, C. 2018. *Managing Health and Well-Being in the Public Sector: A Guide to Best Practice*. Routledge Psychology Press, New York, NY.

Hesketh, I. & Cooper, C. 2019. *Wellbeing at Work: How to Design, Implement and Evaluate an Effective Strategy.* Kogan Page, London, UK.

Hesketh, I. & Cooper, C. 2021. *Managing Workplace Health and Wellbeing during a Crisis: How to Support Your Staff in Difficult Times.* Kogan Page, London, UK.

Hesketh, I., Cooper, C., & Ivy, J. 2014. Leaveism and public-sector reform: will the practice continue? *Journal of Organizational Effectiveness: People and Performance* 1(2): 205–212.

Hesketh, I., Cooper, C., & Ivy, J. 2015. Leaveism and work–life integration: the thinning blue line? *Policing* 9(2): 183–194.

Hesketh, I., Cooper, C., & Ivy, J. 2017. Well-being and engagement: the key to unlocking discretionary effort? *Policing* 11(1): 62–73.

Holt, S. & Marques, J. 2012. Empathy in leadership: appropriate or misplaced? An empirical study on a topic that is asking for attention. *Journal of Business Ethics* 105(1): 95–105.

Hood, C. 1991. A public management for all seasons? *Public Administration* 69(1): 3–19.

Houdmont, J., Elliott-Davies, M., & Donnelly, J. 2018. Leaveism in English and Welsh police forces: baseline reference values. *Occupational Medicine* 68(9): 593–599.

Howarth, A., Quesada, J., Silva, J., Judycki, S., & Mills, P. R. 2018. The impact of digital health interventions on health-related outcomes in the workplace: a systematic review. *Digital Health* 4. DOI:10.1177/205 5207618770861.

Johns, G. 2010. Presenteeism in the workplace: a review and research agenda. *Journal of Organizational Behavior* 31(4): 519–542.

Lowe, G. 2020. *Creating Healthy Organizations: Taking Action to Improve Employee Well-Being.* University of Toronto Press, Toronto, Canada.

Meechan, F. 2017. *Compassion Toolkit.* www.alliancembs.manchester .ac.uk/media/ambs/content-assets/documents/health-and-wellbeing-forum/compassion-at-work-toolkit.pdf.

Meister, J. C. & Willyerd, K. 2010. *The 2020 Workplace: How Innovative Companies Attract, Develop, and Keep Tomorrow's Employees Today.* HarperCollins, New York, NY.

Milligan-Saville, J. S., Tan, L., Gayed, A. et al. 2017. Workplace mental health training for managers and its effect on sick leave in employees: a cluster randomised controlled trial. *The Lancet Psychiatry* 4(11): 850–858.

Moore, R. T., Kaprielian, R., & Auerbach, J. 2009. "Asleep at the wheel": report of the Special Commission on Drowsy Driving. Massachusetts General Court, Boston, MA. https://sleep.med.harvard.edu/ file_download/103

Parmer, B. 2014. *The Empathy Era: Women, Business and the New Pathway to Profit*. Lady Geek Ltd., London, UK.

Pfeffer, J. 2018a. *Dying for a Paycheck: How Modern Management Harms Employee Health and Company Performance – and What We Can Do about It*. HarperBusiness, New York, NY.

Pfeffer, J. 2018b. Warning: AI may be hazardous to employee health. Forbes, December 4. www.forbes.com/sites/insightsteam/2018/12/04/warning-ai-may-be-hazardous-to-employee-health/#4f1c810acbc9

Ramazzini, B. 2001. De Morbis artificum diatriba [Diseases of workers]. *American Journal of Public Health* 91(9): 1380–1382.

Riess, H., Kelley, J. M., & Bailey, R. W. 2012. Empathy training for resident physicians: a randomized controlled trial of a neuroscience-informed curriculum. *Journal of General Internal Medicine* 27(10): 1280–1286.

Rousseau, D. M. 1995. *Psychological Contract in Organizations: Understanding Written and Unwritten Agreements*. SAGE Publications, Thousand Oaks, CA.

Southwick, S. M. & Charney, D. S. 2012. *Resilience: The Science of Mastering Life's Greatest Challenges*. Cambridge University Press, Cambridge, UK.

Stewart, W. F., Ricci, J. A., Chee, E., Morganstein, D., & Lipton, R. 2003. Lost productive time and cost due to common pain conditions in the US workforce. *Journal of the American Medical Association* 290(18): 2443–2454.

Thackrah, C. T. 1832. *The Effects of the Principal Arts, Trades and Professions, and of Civic States and Habits of Living, on Health and Longevity: With a Particular Reference to the Trades and Manufacturers of Leeds, and Suggestions for the Removal of Many of the Agents, Which Produce Diseases, and Shorten the Duration of Life*. From the London ed., with improvements. Porter, London, UK.

Walker, M. 2018. *Why We Sleep: The New Science of Sleep and Dreams*. Penguin, London, UK.

Weinberg, A., Hudson, J. H., Pearson, A., & Chowdhury, S. B. 2018. Organizational uptake of NICE guidance in promoting employees' psychological health. *Occupational Medicine* 69(1): 47–53.

12 | *Modern Organizing*

CHARLES C. SNOW AND ØYSTEIN
D. FJELDSTAD

Organizing is the basis for any goal-directed activity involving more than one actor. It is arguably our most valuable social technology, as the ability to organize has produced much of what constitutes modern society. Organizing affects an enterprise's efficiency, effectiveness, and ability to adapt. Modern organizing puts a premium on rapid adaptation – the gains afforded by modern approaches to organizing are the result of a combination of more knowledgeable organizational actors, improved tools and practices, and the widespread use of digital technologies. Compared to traditional organizations, modern organizations are flatter and more open to their environment. Their processes are more generative and interactive – actors continuously generate and coordinate solutions rather than follow hierarchically devised plans and directives. This evolution toward self-organizing enables organizations to adapt quicker and more effectively to a changing, uncertain environment. In this final chapter, we bring together the concepts, means, and principles of modern organizing discussed in the book. Going forward, we believe that anyone who needs to organize goal-directed activities will benefit from incorporating these ideas into their designs. Indeed, embracing the new design paradigm may become a requirement for sustaining organizational viability.

In the quest for organizational adaptability, actors must develop the ability to comprehend emerging situations and act appropriately (Ashby, 1956; Endsley, 1995; Simon, 1993). When an organization encounters novel circumstances, effective responses generate the variety of capabilities needed to again comprehend and act appropriately. Typically, organizations increase variety by experimentation, new hires, acquisitions, alliances, and so on (March, 1991). In order to truly benefit from new resources, they must be effectively organized (Barney, 1995). What the modern approaches to organizing laid out in this book have in common is that they enable self-organization of both intra- and interorganizational relationships, thereby improving actors' ability to combine diverse resources needed for rapid adaptation in dynamic environments (Brown & Eisenhardt, 1997; Eisenhardt & Martin, 2000; Yoo et al., 2012).

Leaders and designers of organizations have an abundance of useful ideas and tools that allow them to organize collective efforts at any scale – from a cross-functional team to a global corporation. The focus of the new design paradigm is on the *means* that enable and empower organizational actors to form collaborative structures, align goals and resolve conflicts, and coordinate their activities in response to emerging opportunities and challenges. This focus on means reflects the importance of fluidity in modern organizations – in a complex, dynamic environment, actors must be able to change repeatedly and unexpectedly. The new design paradigm is manifested in actors – entities capable of acting with intent – that self-organize based on a shared understanding of goals and an awareness of the current situation at the team, firm, and ecosystem levels.

At the *team* level, the new means of organizing allow individuals to freely form and dissolve relationships around shared goals. Increasingly, digital agents serve as team members. Modern development approaches, such as Design Thinking and Agile, iteratively enable mutual adaptation among physically or virtually co-located team members around a shared understanding of user needs and solutions. At the *firm* level, platforms and hierarchical structures are used to aggregate team activities. When platforms are used for aggregation, software supports the self-assembly of networks of teams and digital task environment representations that facilitate stigmergic coordination and control. When hierarchy is used to aggregate team efforts, alignment of goals and integration of activities are achieved through incentives, exhortations, and directives. In an *ecosystem*, actors that complement and compete with each other to meet user needs in a particular space fluidly contribute to and draw upon common tangible and intangible resources (Moore, 1993, 1996). Entrepreneurial activity in social ecosystems goes on continuously as actors search for new resources and form new relationships for new purposes (Chesbrough, Kim, & Agogino, 2014; Furr, Ozcan, & Eisenhardt, 2022; Jacobides, Cennamo, & Gawer, 2018; Ostrom, 2009). In ecosystems, the primary means of organizing tend to be generative – they enable actors to form new goal-directed relationships. The role of leaders and designers is to create and proliferate concepts and values, infrastructures (platforms, physical spaces, etc.), and interaction protocols and practices.

To conclude, we would like to emphasize three aspects of designing modern, adaptive organizations. First, designers must *collaborate* with organizational actors in the design process because they are the users of the designs. Second, organizers and designers must adopt a *dynamic view* of organizing that focuses on generativity and adaptation. Effective organization designs are those that fit the complexity and pace of change in the environment. Third, designers should devise *actor-oriented architectures* that allow self-organizing of resources and activities at the team, firm, and ecosystem levels. The focus of modern organizational architecture is on principles that foster coherence and health and enable growth and rapid adaptation (Fjeldstad et al., 2012). We believe that the chapters in the book, written by leading voices in the field of organization design, collectively offer a comprehensive and authoritative account of the theory and practice of modern organizing.

References

Ashby, W. R. 1956. *An Introduction to Cybernetics*. Wiley, New York, NY.

Barney, J. B. 1995. Looking inside for competitive advantage. *Academy of Management Perspectives* 9(4): 49–61.

Brown, S. L. & Eisenhardt, K. M. 1997. The art of continuous change: linking complexity theory and time-paced evolution in relentlessly shifting organizations. *Administrative Science Quarterly* 42(1): 1–34.

Chesbrough, H., Kim, S., & Agogino, A. 2014. Chez Panisse: building an open innovation ecosystem. *California Management Review* 56(4): 144–171.

Eisenhardt, K. M. & Martin, J. A. 2000. Dynamic capabilities: what are they? *Strategic Management Journal* 21(10–11): 1105–1121.

Endsley, M. R. 1995. Toward a theory of situation awareness in dynamic systems. *Human Factors* 37(1): 32–64.

Fjeldstad, Ø. D., Snow, C. C., Miles, R. E., & Lettl, C. 2012. The architecture of collaboration. *Strategic Management Journal* 33(6): 734–750.

Furr, N., Ozcan, P., & Eisenhardt, K. M. 2022. What is digital transformation? Core tensions facing established companies on the global stage. *Global Strategy Journal* 12(4): 595–618.

Jacobides, M. G., Cennamo, C., & Gawer, A. 2018. Towards a theory of ecosystems. *Strategic Management Journal* 39(8): 2255–2276.

March, J. G. 1991. Exploration and exploitation in organizational learning. *Organization Science* 2(1): 71–87.

Moore, J. F. 1993. Predators and prey: a new ecology of competition. *Harvard Business Review* 71(3): 75–86.

Moore, J. F. 1996. *The Death of Competition: Leadership and Strategy in the Age of Business Ecosystems.* Wiley and HarperBusiness, New York, NY.

Ostrom, E. 2009. A general framework for analyzing sustainability of social-ecological systems. *Science* 325(5939): 419–422.

Simon, H. A. 1993. Strategy and organizational evolution. *Strategic Management Journal* 14(S2): 131–142.

Yoo, Y., Boland Jr, R. J., Lyytinen, K., and Majchrzak, A. 2012. Organizing for innovation in the digitized world. *Organization Science* 23(5): 1398–1408.

Index

216

Printed in the United States
by Baker & Taylor Publisher Services